"Tom Carey and Don Schmitt have taken the investigation of Roswell from New Mexico to Wright-Patterson Air Force Base, adding valuable and documented evidence about what is now the history of the UFO field. Their important research will significantly aid in uncovering what is becoming the greatest mystery of our time."

—Kevin D. Randle, Lt. Col. USAR (Ret.), author of *Crash: When UFOs Fall from the Sky*

"Tom Carey and Don Schmitt have once again dug deeply to uncover credible witness testimony, documentation, and other evidence that our military recovered ET technology many decades ago. Their latest work is highly suggestive that Wright-Patterson's role in the exploitation of that discovery was—and may still be—substantial."

—Anthony Bragalia, author and UFO researcher

"What if the truth we seek from UFO disclosure has been hidden in plain sight? Alien bodies and technology were recovered more than once by our military. Who orchestrated the cover-up and where would that invaluable wreckage be held? Two of the most dedicated investigators in the field, Don Schmitt and Tom Carey, have turned from the Roswell, N.M. UFO Crash of 1947 to where the Air Force policies of cover-up and secrecy were first implemented—Wright-Patterson AFB. There are more reasons for high security than classified airplanes. If you want to know why the disclosure of UFO secrets has not occurred in the USA, this is a must-read."

—James E. Clarkson, Washington State Director of the Mutual UFO Network

"In their previous book, *Witness To Roswell: Unmasking the Government's Biggest Cover-Up*, researchers Tom Carey and Don Schmitt presented riveting, ground-breaking information that provided new insight into the case. Their cautious, well-documented approach to the subject of crashed UFOs steers the proper course between debunkery and blind acceptance. *Inside the Real Area 51* will undoubtedly enhance their well-deserved reputations as credible sources of information on the topic."

—Robert Hastings, author of *UFOs and Nukes: Extraordinary Encounters at Nuclear Weapons Sites*

"Where others rely on a reanalysis of secondary data, Carey and Schmitt demonstrate their ability to keenly analyze and critically evaluate the reliability of new primary data, as well as to identify, bring forward, and objectively interview new firsthand witnesses. As a result they are able to publish not only the most interesting, but also what will prove to be among the most historically valuable and accurate information available."

—Joseph G. Buchman, PhD, moderator for the Citizen Hearing on Disclosure

INSIDE THE REAL
AREA 51

Thomas J. Carey and Donald R. Schmitt

Best-selling authors of *WITNESS TO ROSWELL*

INSIDE THE REAL
AREA 51

The Secret History of Wright-Patterson

STARTLING NEW EYEWITNESS ACCOUNTS

New Page Books
A division of The Career Press, Inc.
Pompton Plains, N.J.

INSIDE THE REAL AREA 51
EDITED AND TYPESET BY KARA KUMPEL
Cover design by Wes Youssi
Printed in the U.S.A.

Images on pages 26, 41, 44, and 101 are courtesy of the Library of Congress. Images on pages 76, 84, 92, 107, 133, 136, 141, 154, and 219 are courtesy of the U.S. Air Force. Image on page 38 is courtesy of Legacy Entertainment, Inc. Image on page 47 is courtesy of Ben Hansen. Image on page 85 is courtesy of Anthony Bragalia. Image on page 87 is courtesy of the U.S. Senate Historical Office. Image on page 97 is taken from the RAAF Yearbook. Image on page 110 is courtesy of James Clarkson. Images on pages 120 and 124 are courtesy of Mark Magruder. Image on page 68 is taken from Wikimedia Commons. Image on page 71 is courtesy of the Department of Defense Technical Information Center. Images on pages 130–132 are courtesy of the National Archives. Images on pages 147, 188, and 206–213 are courtesy of CUFOS. Image on page 158 is taken from CIA photo archives. Images on pages 167 and 216 are courtesy of Tom Carey. Image on page 168 is courtesy of Whitley Strieber and Timothy Greenfield-Sanders. Image on page 178 is courtesy of the Washington University Special Collections Archive. Image on page 182 is courtesy of Betsy McDonald. Image on page 190 is courtesy of the Department of Defense. Images on pages 100, 226, and 236 are courtesy of Mrs. Dell Stringfield.

To order this title, please call toll-free 1-800-CAREER-1 (NJ and Canada: 201-848-0310) to order using VISA or MasterCard, or for further information on books from Career Press.

The Career Press, Inc.
220 West Parkway, Unit 12
Pompton Plains, NJ 07444
www.careerpress.com
www.newpagebooks.com

Library of Congress Cataloging-in-Publication Data

Carey, Thomas J., 1940-

Inside the real Area 51 : the secret history of Wright-Patterson
/ by Thomas J. Carey and Donald R. Schmitt.

pages cm

Includes bibliographical references and index.

ISBN 978-1-60163-236-4 (paperback) -- ISBN 978-1-60163-563-1 (ebook) 1. Unidentified flying objects--Sightings and encounters--United States--History. 2. Wright-Patterson Air Force Base (Ohio)--History. 3. Official secrets--United States--History. I. Schmitt, Donald R. II. Title.

TL789.4.C37 2013

001.94209771'73--dc23

2013021664

Dedicated to the fond memories of

Dr. J. Allen Hynek, *who was enough of a scientist to admit he was wrong, and*

Carlton William "Carl" Day, *who was enough of a journalist to discover why.*

ACKNOWLEDGMENTS

This work is intended to inform those among you who desire—no, dare—to know the truth behind an extraordinary event that occurred 66 years ago (as of this writing). It begins where our previous works regarding the Roswell "incident" of July 1947, left off: with the arrival of the UFO-crash wreckage and little bodies at Wright Field (now Wright-Patterson Air Force Base) in Dayton, Ohio. What happened next is what this book is about.

Although we have a combined 45 years of focused research dedicated to the Roswell case and its aftermath, any investigation of this magnitude, covering so many years and time zones, is not accomplished in a vacuum. Many others have contributed in so many, many ways to our ongoing research that this book could not have been written without their help and support. For that, we hereby acknowledge them.

We would first like to thank all of the witnesses and others with source-information who have come forward, often with great reluctance out of fear for their own well-being, and agreed to talk to us "on the record" about long-ago events. Regrettably, Father Time waits for no one, and many of these witnesses have since passed away. But without their courage and cooperation our investigation and this publication would not have been possible.

Special thanks must go to:

Del Stringfield, not only for her wonderful support of our work, but also her ongoing loyalty to her late husband and our dear friend, Len.

The International UFO Museum and Research Center, for their extensive research facility, which is second to none. One could spend a year there and not touch all of the accessible data. What a treasure.

Julie Shuster, the Museum's former director, for her deep and abiding friendship, strength, and inspiration to us all.

Jerome Clark, for his long friendship and the deep respect and admiration we have for his presence. If we had a team of Jerry Clarks, this riddle would have been solved 25 years ago.

Nathan Twining, Jr., who made us part of the Twining family, treated us like brothers, and often told us his late father would have encouraged us more than anyone else.

Anthony Bragalia, whose tenacity in ferreting out witnesses and getting them to talk is beyond belief, for his peerless ability to locate people, documents, and photos online, and for his Nitinol research, which formed the basis for Chapter 4.

Grant Cameron, Lee Graham, and Brian Parks, for providing pertinent documents to help us learn what was behind the door to the "Blue Room" at Wright-Patterson.

Kevin Randle, for his counsel on a number of historical issues.

Bill Kilbourne, for all of his kind technical assistance.

Christopher Carson, for all of his legal counsel.

Colonel Jeffrey Thau, for all of his military counsel.

John Mosgrove, for his bravery in times of sadness, and his devotion to the truth.

Tracy Torme, for his 25-year friendship and continuing support. His work continues to shine out from his Hollywood contemporaries.

Finally, we must thank the late Carl Day. It was Carl's idea to write this book. In fact, we were honored that an award-winning journalist with a stellar reputation would have asked us to write it with him. Sadly, he passed just months before we started. Carl...we know you were with us all along.

Very special thanks must go to those closest to us who share our daily ups and downs and highs and lows. Without them, we would still be back at the starting gate:

To my loving wife of 45 years, Doreen, for believing in me and encouraging me to persevere even on rainy days; and to our son, Don, and our daughter, Erin, who have lighted up our lives more than they can ever know.

—TJC

To my dearest loving wife, Marie, for all of the patience and back rubs, and allowing me to come to bed night after night hours after her; and to my dear mother and father, for constantly reminding me that my journey to the stars always begins with loved ones right here.

—DRS

…just the facts, Ma'am.
—Sgt. Joe Friday, Detective Division, L.A.P.D.

Record enough facts, and the answer will fall to you like a ripe fruit.
—Franz Boaz, American anthropologist

CONTENTS

FOREWORD

By Tracy Torme

I was working on *Star Trek: The Next Generation* when the disconcerting word came down that Gene wanted to see me. This was Gene Roddenberry, the creator of the *Star Trek* franchise, famously nicknamed "The Great Bird of the Galaxy."

As I entered his office I could instantly tell he wasn't pleased about something. Uh-oh. It was never a good idea to upset Gene. I had a unique and wonderful father-son relationship with him, but I had also witnessed his temper on certain occasions, and it's fair to say I always wanted to remain in his good graces.

Gene looked up at me with a tense hint of a smile. "I understand you're thinking about working on a movie about Travis Walton," he said. I was surprised, as I would never have expected he even knew who Travis Walton was. I cautiously told him it was true. I was in the early stages of working on the project that would eventually become the Paramount feature film, *Fire in the Sky*.

Roddenberry practically leapt to his feet, his face turning crimson with rage. **"Don't you know this UFO stuff is bullshit?"** he bellowed. **"It's all nothing but crap! They are never seen by astronomers. Never seen by pilots. Just drunken farmers at three in the morning. There's not a shred of physical evidence. No real photographs. Tracy, how on Earth could you do anything to promote this myth?"**

Gene's anger and indignation were truly surprising and a bit intimidating. Throughout the years when I've told *Star Trek* fans his position on UFOs, many refused to believe me. This is the world of scorn that my friends and colleagues Don Schmitt and Tom Carey must cope with as they pursue their excellent work in the badly misunderstood field of ufology.

I was to have similar confrontations throughout the years with Ray Bradbury, Seth Shostak, and Carl Sagan. They each treated my fundamental belief in the existence of UFOs as if it equated with believing in Santa Claus or the Easter Bunny. It is in this difficult arena that Don and Tom have done their groundbreaking and vitally important work—the latest being this seminal book on Wright-Patterson Air Force Base.

Don and Tom have excelled at separating the wheat from the chaff in all their books. Their wonderful and thorough work about the Roswell incident has exposed several truisms about the field in general. The Sagans and Roddenberrys of the world are dead wrong. Schmitt and Carey are the ones who see the light. UFOs are a serious and endlessly compelling mystery that demands the kind of first-class examination that only top-notch investigators like Tom and Don can bring to the table.

When they sunk their teeth into the Roswell story, it was fascinating and illuminating to see how they approached the challenge of exposing a now 66-year-old event. The fact that firsthand witnesses are getting old and dying was the least of their problems. Both authors banked on their impeccable reputations and personal integrity to form a layer of trust with those who are brave enough to come forward with their recollections. The fact that Don and Tom are intelligent, personable, and trustworthy to the extreme has been a key factor in convincing vital witnesses to come forward. Don and Tom have relied on these same qualities to help unearth the fascinating history of Wright-Patt.

So how do they manage to produce such vital and compelling work? Well, there is certainly a method to their madness. It all begins with their disciplined and comprehensive approach to whatever they are tackling. The two men are outstanding researchers who leave no stone unturned in their quest to get to the truth. Wright-Patterson is a key player in the UFO story—we all owe Don and Tom major kudos for taking on such a difficult and important task.

Don and I are old friends; although Tom and I don't know each other as well, I hope that changes in the future. Don is a baseball fan (and so is Tom)—a big plus in my book—and we share a common belief in American exceptionalism, which got me thinking...

After the critical Battle of Yorktown during the American Revolution, when the defeated British army marched out to lay down their arms to the upstart rebels, their band played a song called "The World Turned Upside Down." This could be the theme song for first-class UFO researchers like Tom and Don. For them, the world is in many ways upside down. The UFO quandary is misunderstood, misreported, and routinely distorted. We should all be truly grateful that we have men like Don Schmitt and Tom Carey who have the persistence and fortitude to expose the truth to a world that is largely asleep at the wheel.

Tracy Torme
Los Angeles, California
March 2013

INTRODUCTION

Psychologist Dr. Thomas Gilovich has succinctly defined our objective in writing the book you are about to read. He portrays the condition known as "healthy skepticism" this way: "An awareness of how and when to question, and recognition of what it takes to truly know something, are among the most important elements of what constitutes an educated person." With that supposition, the authors of this tome question the official version of what we will demonstrate to be the biggest secret in the history of this country.

Within the past 20 years, the Roswell incident has become an international household phrase, synonymous with cover-ups and government deception. The true nature of what actually crashed in New Mexico in 1947 remains classified, even above the Oval Office, as evidenced by the failed disclosure efforts of Presidents Gerald Ford, Jimmy Carter, and Bill Clinton. As earth-shaking as that event was to humankind, only a select few have ever had access to the truth.

Initially, the media was essentially banned from reporting all pro-UFO research that would contradict the more mundane official explanations—surely a blow to the egos of journalists seasoned from their coverage of WWII. Moreover, to preempt any future curiosity about the true nature of UFO events, the press has been systematically indoctrinated in outright dismissal of the subject. Derisiveness and debunking of such tales became the rule of the day, and public deception has risen to an astronomical level. Never in the course of American history have elected officials tasted more cynicism and rejection from the doubting Thomases of society, whose efforts planted the seeds of suppression. Yet, the story is too big, too important to relegate to the cold, abandoned warehouse of forgotten history.

President John F. Kennedy had this to say about such secrets:

> **The very word *secrecy* is repugnant in a free and open society. And we are as a people, inherently and historically opposed to secret societies, to secret oaths and to secret proceedings. For we are opposed around the world by a monolithic and ruthless conspiracy that relies primarily on covert means for expanding its sphere of influence. On infiltration instead of invasion...on subversion instead of elections...on intimidation instead of free choice. It is a system which has conscripted vast human and materialistic resources into the building of a tightly knit, highly efficient machine that combines military and diplomatic intelligence, economic, scientific and political operations. Its preparations are concealed, not published. Its mistakes are buried, not headlined. Its dissenters are silenced, not praised. No expenditure is questioned, no secret is revealed.**

As investigative authors, we are confident that we have provided enough circumstantial evidence sufficient for victory in any courtroom—evidence that a craft and crew of unknown origin crashed outside of Roswell, New Mexico, in 1947. It is this premise from which we will work throughout this book, probing the depths of Wright-Patterson Air Force Base—the *real* Area 51. Among the many questions we ask is this: If an event of such significance as this—the crash of an extraterrestrial craft—took place, what should we expect from the government and those placed in charge of the aftermath? How would they react? History has documented very specific actions on the part of officialdom that clearly suggest they were responding to an event of an extraordinary nature. For example, the Roswell incident did not just fade into the background with the explanation of a mere weather-balloon device; to the contrary, the military's action gave every indication that something far beyond their control had taken place. What transpired in the shadows after all the physical evidence was retrieved and transferred up the intelligence channels left our government totally in the dark.

For one brief moment on July 8, 1947, the public's worldview was totally altered with the Army's announcement: **"RAAF [Roswell Army Air Field] captures flying saucer on ranch in Roswell Region."** Within the next five hours, the substituted balloon explanation provided reprieve— but not for those assigned to defend and protect us. To them, the world would never be the same. From their perspective, our sovereign shores had just been obliterated. Eyes were fixated on the skies. That which was once relegated to the domain of science fiction was now a reality as stark as death itself. And just as with death, no living creature on planet Earth knew what was on the other side.

As the chapters unfold, you, the reader, will see countless attempts by our leaders and our military to wrestle with not only the notion of being threatened by a power beyond our own, but also the complete impotence they felt when dealing with such a phenomenon. What began in the most remote desert region of New Mexico continued at the ultra–top secret military facility named Wright-Patterson Air Force Base in Dayton, Ohio. Truly, it was only the end of the beginning. The futile attempts at reverse engineering, the dissection of biological remains— all would find this Top Secret facility as deep and black as space itself. Our visitors from the stars were swallowed into the underground morass known as Wright-Pat.

If the National Museum of American History is America's attic, Wright-Patterson AFB is definitely its basement. It was there, with all the accumulated physical proof and documentation that we were being observed from outside our planet, that this nuclear-equipped United States Air Force stronghold earned a stellar reputation for secrets going in but seldom coming out. How tragic that the needs of a few have decided for all of humankind that such seismic news should be kept from us forever—pieces of history now quickly dwindling into oblivion as the last of the secret-keepers pass away. In spite of its rich and historic military service to our nation, Wright-Patterson stands as a tombstone over one of the greatest discoveries in all of recorded history. For more than 30 years, it was ground zero in the government cover-up of UFOs.

Be prepared. The UFO vault is about to be opened....

CHAPTER 1

Wright-Patterson AFB: Even Secret Locations Have a History

Military installations are similar to government buildings, schools, post offices, and the like: They are typically named after a famous person with no other connection to the facility than that they happened to be next on the honors list. Wright-Patterson was clearly the exception. Its namesake could not be more appropriate or more deserving of such a distinction.

The land on which the base is located to\day has much more history than ever taught in any schoolbook outside of Dayton, Ohio. However, anyone with any knowledge of aviation fully knows where it all began: when man first tried to put an engine in a crude skeleton of a machine and get it off the ground. Wright-Patterson has the distinction of being founded on a dream—a dream that man could fly. It's where Orville and Wilbur Wright risked life and limb on an 84-acre stretch of land known then as the Hoffman Prairie Flying Field back in 1904. They kept hoping their new flying contraption would stay in the air for just a few seconds more, but gravity relentlessly prevailed. Like the biblical Noah and the construction of the ark, the brothers Wright stood on their personal conviction that destiny was just beyond the next cloud.

A flat, open field was the best they could manage, and they could not make the device any lighter. Then, on December 17, 1903, in another vacant patch of grass at Kitty Hawk, North Carolina, the first successful powered flight took place. While Orville watched from the ground, Wilbur wrestled with the makeshift cable controls and managed to keep their Wright Flyer in the air for a whole 12 seconds, flying just 120 feet. Through pure perseverance and a good tailwind, the modern age of aviation was etched in all the history books on that monumental day. Man could fly, albeit for just a dozen heartbeats. Could the moon be that far away?[1]

In the next five years, the famous brothers started their own instruction facility and named it the Wright Company Training School of Aviation. Manned engine flight was about to gain the watchful attention of Uncle Sam. Ironic that this invention was not mothered by war, but it was about to be drafted by its presidium.

As the Kaiser spread his aggression throughout Europe, the United States was obligated to assist its allies and entered WWI in 1917. In short order, three government-funded military installations were built in Dayton, each to provide for the accelerating war effort. In addition, as fate would have it, two of these would eventually become part of what today is Wright-Patterson Air Force Base. One site was Wilbur Wright Field and the adjoining installation Fairfield Aviation General Supply

Orville and Wilbur Wright.

Depot that was operated by the army and provided logistical support to its neighbor along with other military needs throughout the Midwest.

After about a year, in 1918, the two airfields successfully staged a number of joint exercises. Both used McCook Field in downtown Dayton for the storage, service, and assemblage of aircraft and their engines. Aviation was quickly becoming a corporate enterprise, and the Wright brothers were still in the forefront, as no one could match their know-how. With the ending of the war, the Wright training school was eventually shut down, and the two merged to become the Fairfield Air Depot. But, as destiny would have it, the military was not finished with the brothers. In 1924 Wright Field was established as a new appurtenance in the continuing effort of the Pentagon to build on the successes of the previous air war. The Army Air Corps was a proven war machine and Wright Field would lead the way in protecting the United States from the sky. It was only fitting that the newly formed base would be dedicated to both Wilbur and Orville Wright. To this day, their name and legacy remain synonymous with all things aeronautical.

Soon thereafter, Wright Field became the headquarters of the Materiel Division, which was a main branch of the Army Air Corps, and in 1920, the Technical Data Section (TDS) was created. Together, it was their main responsibility to develop and design advanced aircraft, equipment, and accessories. Engineering laboratories were constructed, and all concepts of flight were studied and perfected at the growing facility.

Lieutenant Frank Stuart Patterson had long championed the mission of the base and worked diligently to keep Wright in the heart of Dayton. It was only fitting that the city rewarded him by designating Patterson Field as an adjoining base on the east side. Even though Wright and Patterson were two separate installations, their projects often augmented and strategically complemented one another, each providing areas of technical support or facilities and technicians the other did not have. For example, in 1942, Patterson re-designated TDS the Technical Data Laboratory (TDL) and then T-2 Intelligence on July 1, 1945, which specialized in metallurgy and reverse engineering.[2] Whenever a more advanced foreign design was recovered for analysis and study, Patterson Field was the most likely destination. It was also at that time that T-2 became especially learned in the physical aspects of the newly arrived phenomenon of "flying saucers." If such flight characteristics as commonly described by witnesses were accurate, visionary minds must have reeled with all the possibilities.

Is it then any wonder that during and after WWII both facilities saw a dramatic expansion? From 3,700 employees in 1939 to more than 50,000 by the end of the war, they played an important role in the allied victory. The Materiel Division at Wright handled the procurement of aircraft and their parts on production lines around the country, which resulted in increased testing and development, whereas the Air Service Commission at Patterson maintained the hardware's logistical assimilation into the war. By 1944, the Pentagon realized that this was a duplication of effort and dropped the separate commands at each base. In August, both were then placed under the newly established Air Technical Service Command.[3]

It was during the war years and immediately thereafter that major project funding and facility improvements were done—all deemed necessary by Washington. Extended concrete runways were poured—the first at any American base—along with larger labs and test sites, and an increasing number of office buildings for the growing number of civilian employees on the base. During the war, more than 300 new buildings were constructed to house such headquarters as the Air Materiel Command, the USAF Medical Center, the Air Force Institute of Technology, and the Air Force Research Laboratory.[4]

After the surrender of Germany in 1945, both airfields gained major military advancements from the Luftwaffe. Patterson focused on the hardware and what advancements, if any, made it superior to our own, while Wright conducted all the testing. On the Pacific front, the Technical Air Intelligence Unit (TAIU) took possession of all captured Japanese aircraft and equipment after the final surrender. In December of that year, TAIU was transferred to the operation of T-2 at Wright Field under the directorship of Lt. Colonel Howard McCoy.[5]

It was one thing to recover the enemy hardware; it was another thing to learn how to use it. Fortunately, we were able to capture their inventors. "Show us how it works" was the principal objective of Operation Paperclip, which provided the United States with more than 200 German scientists of the highest regard. Though most of them were former Nazi Party members, they worked in close collaboration with their American counterparts on all aspects of military technology. This would cause an explosion of aerial technological advancement—of which most of the data ended up at Wright Field for testing. Many of the German scientists worked closely with T-2 tacticians who specialized in engines, aerodynamics, and new material construction. It was their mandate to:

1. Ensure the prevention of strategic, tactical, or technological surprise from any source.

2. Provide intelligence required for command decisions and counsel upon air preparedness and air operations.

3. Enact appropriate counterintelligence measures.

Both logistically and in matters of national security, T-2 was the single most proficient agency to handle the recovery, containment, and disinformation of anything recovered from the air. General Douglas MacArthur had previously instructed Air Technical Intelligence, a predecessor to T-2, at the end of the War in the Pacific, to "take complete charge of all enemy crashed or captured aircraft or personnel as early as possible after the crash."[6]

With the ever-expanding role of the Air Corps, the decision was finally signed into law that the Air Force would officially become a separate branch of the military in September 1947. "Army Air Fields" simply became "Air Fields," and in 1948 the term "Air Field" was dropped in favor of "Air Force Base," concomitant with the merger of Wright and Patterson "Air Fields" into a single, unified base: Wright-Patterson Air Force Base.

Now that the air was conquered, could space be far behind? The facility would create one of the first labs experimenting with monkeys and apes for upper atmospheric testing. During the 1960s, sonic booms rattled nearby windows as B-52 Bombers roared over Dayton from dawn until dusk. Clearly harbingers of things to come, former Wright-Patt test pilots were astronauts: Neil Armstrong, the first man to set foot on the moon, and Edward White, the first American to walk in space. Hangars were now housing wind tunnels and tests concerned super-sonic and sub-orbit aircraft—and Wright-Patterson led the way.

Ever the center of high-technology war strategy, the base became headquarters of the USAF Logistics Command. Wright-Patterson leads the way into the future of America's defense with the National Air and Space Intelligence Center. This is the DOD's primary source for both foreign and space threats. As a fitting tribute to the base's dedication to our national security, the personal files of Nikola Tesla are preserved there.

Outside of the UFO community, few are aware of Wright-Patterson's distinction of maintaining the U.S. government's official investigation of the UFO phenomenon from 1947 until 1969. With its vital experience of testing and reverse-engineering all materials both foreign and "from space," it is a historic fact that whatever crashed outside of Roswell fell under their purview. It is also a documented fact that the "debris" from New Mexico was sent to Wright Field, clearly demonstrating that it qualified for one of those two distinctions. Our investigation will demonstrate which of the two has the most supporting evidence.

Again we ask, if it was only a weather balloon device manufactured with the most common materials, why was it sent to Wright Field for identification and analysis in the first place? By the time you read the final pages of this book there will remain little doubt what the true answer to that perplexing question is. The event in 1947 required the most sensitive and secret facility our military could provide, and Wright-Patterson AFB wrote the very book on the question, "What makes something fly?" Today, it arguably is the most important Air Force base in the world. Respectfully called "The Field" by residents of Dayton, Ohio, it has become a state-of-the-art military installation covering nearly 13 square miles of secured buildings, labs, hangars, and runways. Likewise, from all accounts, a good portion of it is underground. It employs more personnel, both military and civilian, than the Pentagon, with a payroll of more than a billion dollars a year. Nuclear-armed aircraft from the 906th, the 2750th, and the 4950th stand ready to answer the call to all corners of the globe. Air Force logistic systems developed there, including most of the engineering of future aeronautical breakthroughs, will soon take us to the stars—and Orville and Wilbur will be waiting.

CHAPTER 2

The Mystery of Hangar 18—*Solved!*

"No, Sir. There is no Hangar 18 here on the base, and there never has been." So says the perfunctory voice on the other end of the line that has been trained for more than 30 years by the Office of Public Information at Wright-Patterson Air Force Base to respond that way to people inquiring about Hangar 18. When visitors come to Wright-Patterson for tours of the base, the main question they all seem to still want the answer to is "Where is Hangar 18—you know, where the aliens are stored?" So are the public relations representatives of Wright-Patterson AFB shamelessly lying to the public when this question is asked? Well, yes and no. As a certain U.S. president once told us, "It all depends on what the meaning of 'is' is."

A statement in a recent issue of *Air Force Magazine* concerning the Air Force's unfortunate mishandling of the UFO phenomenon throughout the years echoed this theme: **"...there is no Hangar 18 at [Wright-Patterson Air force Base]."**[1]

If there is no "Hangar 18" on the base, as the pronouncements from Air Force officials clearly indicate, why do we continue to receive letters and e-mails from ordinary citizens that say the opposite? For example, the International UFO Museum & Research Center in Roswell received an e-mail from Janis Yoder of Dayton, Ohio, some years ago stating, **"I have lived by the [Wright-Patterson] base all my life and have heard** about the bodies and 'Hangar 18.'"[2] Lance Winkler, also of Dayton, more recently told us that he had worked for a contractor at Wright-Patterson for about 12 years. **"You can imagine the scuttlebutt that went on about the subject. Talking with the motor pool guys, they told me that almost every time some group of people new to the base got on the bus, they always asked where 'Hangar 18' was, and if they could drive them to it."**[3] Winkler wasn't finished:

> One time years ago, I was at a social function with a family friend who was a retired Air Force officer formerly based at Wright-Patt. In the course of our conversation, I broached whether there were really UFOs and Little Men at the base. He guffawed and looked at me like I was a little crazy to ask such a thing. I apologized and said that I had heard this stuff all of my life and figured that if anybody knew, he would [he was an aeronautical engineer]. He then became rather serious and told me that only upon three conditions would he say anything about the matter: (1) I would never mention his name or rank, (2) it was strictly off the record, and (3) if anyone ever got back to him for confirmation, he would deny he ever said it. I agreed to those terms.
>
> *"They're there,"* he said.[4]

Dr. Allen P. Kovacs is an engineer with a PhD in computational multi-body dynamics, which is about the physics of moving things. In the 1980s and '90s, Dr. Kovacs worked for an engineering software developer in Ann Arbor, Michigan, that developed software for use in the automotive industry. It was in that timeframe that he led a group of employees to attend a seminar on topics concerning "the numerical integration of the differential equations of motion" at the Air Force Institute of Technology (AFIT) located on the Wright-Patterson Air Force Base in Dayton.[5]

The group drove down to Wright-Patterson in one car and arrived at the main gate for security clearance and directions to the AFIT Building where the seminar was being held. Dr. Kovacs got out of the car and walked over to the lady who passed out maps and provided information to base visitors. Dr. Kovacs was already aware of the Roswell incident and the fact that the bodies and debris had allegedly been delivered to the base years before. He gave us this account of his conversation with her:

> **I went up to the directions lady and asked for a map. Then I looked at her and said, "By the way, can you tell me where they keep the UFO aliens here at Wright-Patterson?" She looks up at me and in a straight face, no emotion or smile, and says, "They're here, but I can't tell you exactly where." Then I laugh and say, "Oh really? You're kidding me. Right?" And she replies, "No, they are here, but I can't tell you where they are."**[6]

Taken aback and somewhat startled by this response, Dr. Kovacs immediately thought to himself that the woman might be trying to play him for a fool, probably because so many visitors must be asking her the same question. Upon reflection, however, it seemed appropriate at the time, according to Dr. Kovacs, because the Freedom of Information Act had recently been enacted, and he thought she might have had a duty to respond truthfully to such questions, but without giving details.[7]

After the conference, Dr. Kovacs relayed his encounter with the security woman to his friends, none of whom had any idea about the Roswell incident and its alleged connection to Wright-Patterson. The map given to him showed the layout of the base campus with all the buildings numbered. He remembered that there was a certain "hangar" where the alien bodies were supposed to be stored, but he had forgotten the exact number of it. He thought it might have been 52. He then drove the group around the campus looking for it and noticed that most of the buildings were low-storied structures. He thought to himself that most of Wright-Patterson must lie below ground. At the end of his quest, according to Dr. Kovacs, **"We found Building 52, and it wasn't a hangar for planes. It was a storage building, and again it was a small, one-story structure. Much of its storage, therefore, must have been *below ground*"**[8] (authors' emphasis). We shall see from testimony later on that Dr. Kovacs's surmise was not too far off target.

So, what gives? Which is it? Are the statements that there is no Hangar 18—meaning no alien presence on the Wright-Patterson base—true, or just clever word games meant to disguise that presence? The answer is that the people of the Office of Public Information at Wright-Patterson are correct when they tell callers on the telephone or visitors to the base that there is no "Hangar 18"—and never was one. What they do know but do not tell questioners, however, is that there is a "*Building 18*" on the base, and that they know this is the building that is being inquired about. Not only is there a Building 18, but there is also a Building 18A, 18B, 18C, 18D, 18E, 18F, and 18G, all of which is known as the "Building 18 Complex." And standing right next door to Building 18, ominously connected to it above and below ground level, is a *hangar*. "Hangar 23" to be exact. Word games? You bet, designed to send inquisitive people merrily on their way, scratching their heads and feeling stupid about themselves for asking The Question. And what about the security woman who told Dr. Kovacs that there really were alien bodies on the base, but that she couldn't tell him where they were? Was that just a momentary slip-up on her part, a partial telling of the truth to conform to a new law, or a new twist on word games to get rid of somebody who might know more about it than the average visitor? Dr. Kovacs, who was face to face with her, judged that she was telling the truth within the narrow confines of her instructions to be responsive to such questions.

The roots of the Hangar 18 legend can be traced back to the 1947 Roswell incident that allegedly involved the crash and recovery of a craft and crew from another world. The original press release regarding the crash spoke of the wreckage as being sent from the Roswell Army Air Field to "higher headquarters" for further analysis.[9] When the next press release came from the commanding officer at 8th Air Force Headquarters at Fort Worth Army Air Field—to which the 509th Bomb Group at Roswell AAF was attached—it was assumed that this was the "higher headquarters," the end of the line for the wreckage mentioned in the first press release. As students of the Roswell incident are aware, it was at a July 8, 1947, press conference that General Roger Ramey killed the burgeoning Roswell story by offering up the infamous "weather balloon" explanation for the crash.[10] To the press and to the public at large, the Roswell story died at that point and remained so for the next 30 years.

Lost on the press and the public in all of the excitement, posturing, and histrionics attending General Ramey's balloon press conference was the fact that Fort Worth AAF in Texas was *not* the ultimate destination of the alleged flying saucer wreckage flown in there from Roswell. The second leg of the original flight plan was to have the wreckage continue on from Fort Worth by air to an airbase in Dayton, Ohio: Wright Field. But, perhaps to emphasize to the press that he was driving the stake into the heart of the Roswell story, General Ramey publicly "cancelled" the second flight (to Wright Field) with a loud, verbal command accompanied by a wave of his arm for effect.[11] But did he really cancel it?

Anyone who has ever been in the military service is familiar with the term "scuttlebutt," which is Navy jargon for "rumors" making the rounds of one's duty station. Just as the townsfolk of the city of Roswell had learned of the flying saucer crash and "little bodies" found just north of town via the rumor mill within 20 minutes of its being reported to the local sheriff's office and fire station,[12] so too did the boots on the ground involved in the Roswell retrieval operation learn where most of the wreckage and bodies recovered from the crash were destined: Wright Field in Dayton, Ohio. This included Major Jesse Marcel, the 509th Bomb Group's intelligence officer at the RAAF, who was the first military person to visit the crash site to see the wreckage, and who also accompanied the flight to Fort Worth to show General Ramey some of the wreckage. Marcel thought that his flight was ultimately headed for Wright Field.[13] He was blindsided, however, by General Ramey when he was permanently pulled from his flight and made to pose like a stage prop with a weather balloon for Ramey's press conference. Marcel returned to Roswell the following day registering a deep bitterness at what had happened to him in Fort Worth.[14] Other officers, both in Roswell and in Fort Worth, knew that most everything associated with the crash would wind up at Wright Field. Among the enlisted ranks we have interviewed throughout the years, those who did most of the physical labor involved in the site cleanup, the moving of the materials and bodies to the Roswell base, and the boxing-up of the wreckage and bodies for shipment, most "understood" that most everything had been sent to Wright-Patt.[15] The FBI also knew that, contrary to General Ramey's antics, the "instrument" (in other words, the crash wreckage as well as the balloon) was in the air and on its way to Wright Field by special transport aircraft.[16]

Again we ask, why Wright-Patterson in Ohio? Why not send the crash remains to a base closer to Roswell—say, another base with the necessary facilities for analysis in New Mexico, Texas, or California? The answer is that, since its inception in 1917 as a military facility, Wright Field had gradually become the most secret and most important base in the U.S. military establishment. It was the place where foreign technology from the air was brought to be taken apart, analyzed, and back-engineered to understand its operating features better for combat advantage. During World War II, captured German Messerschmitts and Japanese Mitsubishis were brought to Wright-Patt for back-engineering. During the Korean "Police Action," the Vietnam War, and the Cold War, it was Russian MiGs, Yaks, and Sukhois. The Roswell wreckage was first thought to be something of Russian origin. When the strange "little bodies" were found, however, the "Russian theory" of origin was tossed in favor an interplanetary origin—all the more reason to bring the physical wreckage to a place where it could be best analyzed, a place that already had the equipment and the experienced personnel to do the job—in secret. That place was Wright Field in Dayton, Ohio. The base also was equipped with a sophisticated AeroMedical Squadron, the best in the Army Air Forces of the time, which could call upon the latest equipment and techniques available to tackle the toughest or newest medical procedures. The decision of where to send the Roswell crash material was, therefore, an easy one. To Wright-Patt without passing "Go," it was.

To present to you a detailed history of Wright-Patterson AFB, from its inception in 1917 to the present, with all of its mergers, acquisitions, subtractions, iterations, and name changes, would cause your eyes to glaze over, your head to start spinning, and your sinuses to start throbbing. For the purposes of this book, it is not necessary. Suffice it to say that Wright-Patterson AFB is located on a prairie just northeast of the city of Dayton, Ohio. The original airstrip was established by the Wright brothers, Orville and Wilbur, sometime after their first "heavier than air" flight in 1903 in order to improve and continue the development of their new invention. Since its absorption into Wilbur Wright Field in 1917 as the United States was entering World War I, it has become arguably the Air Force's most important base in its inventory. If the Pentagon in

Washington, D.C., represents the brains of the Air Force, then certainly Wright-Patterson AFB is its heart, pumping life's blood into its facilities and organizations in the country and around the world to keep them operating at the highest level. In 1931, the eastern part of the base was renamed Patterson Field to honor Lt. Frank Patterson, who was killed in 1918 during a test flight at the base. The western part of the base retained the name Wright Field. In January of 1948, four months after the Air Force distinguished itself from the Army by becoming a separate branch of the U.S. armed services, Wright Field and Patterson Field were merged together to become Wright-Patterson Air Force Base.

Prior to the 1948 merger, Patterson Field (identified today as Areas "A" and "C" on a current map of the base) became a center for aviation logistics, maintenance, and supply, whereas Wright Field (identified as Area "B" on today's map of the base) became synonymous with R&D (Research and Development) in the field of aeronautical engineering for developing advanced aircraft and all of the equipment necessary to maintain them. As a result, Wright Field became saturated with office and laboratory buildings and test facilities in the form of hangars. In addition to the engineering function, the Air Force's technical intelligence function was also located at the Wright Field side of the equation, with the latter function becoming the Foreign Technology Division (FTD) in the Air Materiel Command (AMC).[17] In 1947, the Foreign Technology Division was known as "T-2 Intelligence," and it is because of its presence at Wright Field, coupled with its experience during World War II in analyzing and back-engineering foreign aerial technology, that the Roswell wreckage was brought there. It should also be pointed out that the aforementioned Building 18 Complex is located on the Wright side of the base as well.

If the Roswell UFO crash event was only a two-day story that was killed in its tracks in July of 1947 with nary a mention for the next 30 years, and if there truly was never a "Hangar 18" on the Wright-Patterson airbase (which appears to be the case), how did the mythology regarding a hangar bearing that name originate, and how has it persisted for so long? Our first thought was that it probably originated with the publication of *The Roswell Incident* by Charles Berlitz and William L.

Moore in 1980. After all, what has become the most famous UFO case of all time takes its very name from the title of that book. But, whereas the book states that the crash wreckage went to Wright-Patterson, it does not mention a Hangar 18.

Our next thought was that maybe it came from the movie *Hangar 18*, starring Darren McGavin and Robert Vaughn, which by coincidence also appeared in 1980. The plot involved an alien craft that crashes in the Arizona desert. The craft, along with its deceased crew (who more resembled Curly of the Three Stooges comedy team than visitors from outer space), are removed to a "Hangar 18" on an abandoned Air Force base in Big Spring, Texas, by the government to examine it and to keep it secret from everybody else. In the end, the government cover-up literally

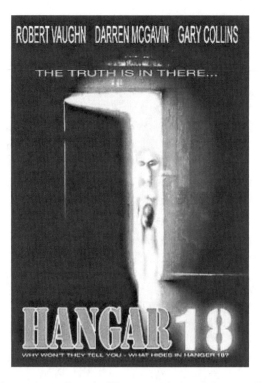

The 1980 motion picture *Hangar 18* served to codify in the public's mind the notion of crashed UFOs and alien bodies with a storage "hangar" at Wright-Patterson AFB in Dayton, Ohio.

blows up in everyone's face as the forces of goodness and light take over. *Hangar 18* also bombed at the box office, but its appearance in theaters around the county, as well as the publicity on television, on the radio, and in the print media surrounding its release, served to cement "Hangar 18"—real or not—in the public's mind with UFOs, alien bodies, and sinister government cover-ups. But was that where it all started?

Did the producers of the movie *Hangar 18* simply make the title up out of whole cloth, or had they heard the phrase used previously somewhere? It was one or the other. If it was the former, our search would end there; if it was the latter case, we would have to look farther back in time. With the help of fellow researcher Anthony Bragalia, we located the movie's writer/director, James Conway. As we suspected, Conway said that he had heard the term a lot, mostly in the early 1970s, but he couldn't remember where he had heard it first. **"Rumor had it that Hangar 18 was where the spaceship and aliens were [stored]."**[18] Rumors heard in the 1970s? What rumors? From whom?

The only pre-1980 book about an alleged crash of a UFO and crew was the discredited "nonfiction" novel *Behind the Flying Saucers* written in 1950 by a *Variety* features columnist named Frank Scully.[19] It told the story of a flying saucer that had allegedly crashed near the town of Aztec, New Mexico in 1948. Found inside the ship were the corpses of a dozen or more diminutive aliens who had apparently perished from decompression when a porthole on their ship had cracked and sprung a leak. The book did not mention "Hangar 18," but it *did* allege that the wreckage and bodies were sent to Wright-Patterson. It became an instant best-seller, but by 1952 the honeymoon was over. In an article in *True Magazine* that year, a reporter for the *San Francisco Chronicle* by the name of J.P. Cahn exposed the sources of Scully's book as two oil con-men with a history of trying to fool the public. So discredited was Scully's book that UFO proponents of the 1950s and '60s such as Donald Keyhoe refused to go near crashed-saucer or saucer-occupant stories for fear, by extension, of discrediting themselves. The "contactee" phenomenon of the 1950s, whereby self-styled messianic types claimed to have been taken aboard flying saucers and whisked around the solar system by their personal "space brothers" also served to chill research into "close encounters" and dampen discussion of UFOs in general.

During this period, a Cincinnati, Ohio, businessman named Leonard Stringfield with an interest in UFOs and a special interest in crashed UFO stories was quietly collecting first- and secondhand accounts regarding the latter. Living in proximity to Wright-Patterson AFB, he also had many friends and contacts who either worked on the base or who lived in Dayton. Most of them had one thing in common: They knew or had heard about some of the secret goings-on at the base, which they then passed along to Stringfield. By 1978, Stringfield had accumulated enough stories to publish. Starting that year and up to his death in 1994, Stringfield self-published a series of seven monographs concerning what he called the "Crash/Retrieval Syndrome" (crashed saucer stories). In his *Status Report II*, published in January of 1980, one of the accounts mentioned for the first time a certain "Building 18F" at Wright-Patterson AFB as a possible "holding tank" for the alien bodies allegedly being stored there.[20] Unlike the *Hangar 18* movie and *The Roswell Incident* book, both of which came out that same year of 1980, the "Building 18F" story was just one small story out of many stories in an obscure, low-circulation monograph that most people had never heard of. Consequently, its import did not register in the rumor mill for future reference.

One thing we have learned in our 20-plus years of investigating the Roswell case is that success often comes unexpectedly or by plain old luck, and the best laid plans often disappoint. In researching this book we had finally reached a dead end in figuring out where the "Hangar 18" business at Wright-Patterson AFB got started. We knew that it had to have been prior to 1980 when the movie came out that propelled it into the public consciensness. We reluctantly concluded, therefore, that the original reference must have been written in a book or an article in one of the magazines of the day, such as *Argosy, Saga,* or *True,* that we just could no longer remember.

Being an Air Force veteran, Tom Carey has been a subscriber to *Air Force Magazine* for a number of years. It is an excellent source of information about Air Force command structure throughout the years, along with the names of who commanded what, when, and where. A few years ago, it published an *apologia* for the Air Force's mishandling of the UFO

Building 18 at Wright-Patterson, where recovered UFO wreckage
was stored for many years. Because of its close proximity to
Hangar 23, it mistakenly became known as "Hangar 18."

phenomenon in the public arena. As expected, but nevertheless disappointing, the author of the article parroted the Air Force's long-standing position regarding UFOs: that they don't exist, and that the USAF has been as truthful as it could be in its statements regarding them. As for Roswell, the article supported the thoroughly discredited Project Mogul "explanation": that what crashed was a top-secret, high-altitude balloon built to detect sound waves from Soviet atomic bomb tests—currently espoused by the Air Force and subscribed to by Roswell debunkers across the land.[21] No surprise there. In researching another matter for this chapter, Carey again read the article in *Air Force Magazine* and, although he disagreed with its author on just about everything he had written, especially about Roswell, all of a sudden there it was, staring him in the face—THE ANSWER to our "Hangar 18" conundrum!

In discussing the problems encountered by the Air Force after Project Blue Book shut down its operations in 1969, the author of the *Air Force Magazine* article continued, **"Nevertheless, the Air Force continued to draw sporadic fire on the UFO issue. In 1974, a UFOlogist accused** the Air Force of keeping two saucers and 12 alien bodies from a saucer crash in New Mexico *in Hangar 18 at Wright-Patterson Air Force Base"* (authors' emphasis).[22]

Of course! How could we have forgotten? Not the article, which Carey had already forgotten without regrets, but the ufologist— "Professor" Robert Spencer Carr, who, in the fall of 1974 had received national and international attention with his charges against the United States Air Force. It was Carr's 15 minutes of fame on the national stage, to be sure, but his claims that the Air Force was engaged in a massive cover-up regarding UFOs and that they had saucers and alien bodies secretly stored away at a base in Ohio lasted much longer. And he even knew the exact location: "Hangar 18" at Wright-Patterson Air Force Base! Carr claimed to have half a dozen firsthand sources for his claims but refused to name them. One of these ironically was allegedly a nurse who had claimed to have been present during an autopsy of one of the alien bodies.[23] The rest of his sources were claimed to have been members of the saucer crash-recovery team at the crash site near Aztec, New Mexico.

"Professor" Carr turned out not to have been a professor at all. According to his son, Carr was only a high school graduate who was in the habit of signing his UFO articles with the appellation "Dr.," which apparently was enough for him to be conferred his doctorate in the minds of an unsuspecting public.[24] But where did Carr come up with the phrase "Hangar 18" if, as we now know, there was never such a place at Wright-Patt? Most likely, one of his sources might have mentioned a "Building 18" at Wright-Patt to him, or he had heard rumors of such a building somewhere along the way, but when he told his tale for public consumption, it had morphed into *"Hangar 18."*

When Carr continued to resist disclosing the names of his sources, and when it was realized that he was actually just resuscitating a warmed-up version of Frank Scully's discredited Aztec crash story from *Behind the Flying Saucers*, it spelled the end of "Professor" Carr's moment, and he became a curious footnote in UFO history—but his claim of a "Hangar 18" at Wright-Patterson sustains. Carr's son, Timothy Spencer Carr, perhaps best summed up the lasting influence his misguided father's tale had on subsequent UFO debate in a 1997 interview: **"I am so very sorry that my father's pathological prevarication has** turned out to be the foundation on which such a monstrous mountain of falsehoods has been heaped."[25]

We are now certain that James Conway, the writer/director of the movie *Hangar 18*, received the inspiration for it, as well as its memorable title, from the Robert Spencer Carr *affaire* of the early 1970s. Appearing fortuitously in the same year as the publication of *The Roswell Incident* (1980) served to weld "Hangar 18" to *The Roswell Incident* and, by extension, to all alleged UFO crash and alien-body stories.

Everything needed to prove that Roswell represented the crash of an extraterrestrial spacecraft and crew was, at one time at least, housed at Wright-Patterson AFB. The base remains shrouded in mystery after more than 60 years of rumors and whispers. Like all former Strategic Air Command bases (those bases with nuclear strike forces), Wright-Patt is an underground maze of secret vaults, tunnels, and multi-level hangars. At ground level, newly poured concrete has sealed off entrances and resurfaced hanger floors long suspected of securing the base's biggest secrets. Former base commanders have told us that there were specific areas that were off-limits even to them. Robert Collins, a retired former Air Force intelligence officer who worked at Wright-Patterson's Foreign Technology Division, has described the extensive subterranean maze of tunnels and vaults hidden there, many of them now sealed up for posterity, in great detail.[26]

In a 1996 signed and notarized affidavit, Robert L. Marshall Jr., a now-deceased Navy veteran who had held a Top Secret Crypto security clearance, stated that both his father and grandfather had worked at Wright-Patterson Air Force Base in the 1940s and '50s.[27] According to Marshall, his father had worked as an iron worker under the supervision of his grandfather, who was himself in charge of erecting a four-level underground facility that included a hangar at ground level, which corresponded with the other hangars in that area. **"There were secret doors, vents, and various secret compartments all [located] under the hangar,"** he said. The work was apparently completed just in time: **"Wright-Patterson Air Force Base received the craft from the Roswell Incident in 1947, and it was placed in one of the lower levels. My** father was called into the complex to adjust one of the doors. At that particular time, he saw—he stated to me on his deathbed—what appeared to him to be the wreckage of a comparatively small, circular craft. He couldn't make it out in great detail, because it was behind some kind of plastic cover that was hanging from the ceiling."[28]

That's not all Robert Marshall's father got a glimpse of during his below-decks maintenance call. **"While my father was in this portion of the underground facility, he also saw one of the small beings involved in the [Roswell] event as he was passing down one of the corridors. Quoting him, 'It wasn't green or purple. [It was] just a small being.'"**[29] Based upon the statements of his father and grandfather to him over the years, Robert Marshall believed **"It is obvious that this underground facility was in existence prior to the Roswell incident and used for Top Secret, test-center operations [which were] ideal for the Roswell cover-up."** From his deathbed, sounding like the late

Hangar 23 at Wright-Patterson. Connected to Building 18's underground levels, it was where the Roswell wreckage was first deposited prior to permanetn storage in Building 18.

Walter Cronkite signing off at the end of one of his newscasts, Robert Marshall's father added a final exclamation point for his son's benefit regarding his observations of things otherworldly at Wright-Patt: **"This is the way it is, and that's it!"**[30] We now believe that Robert Marshall's father and grandfather were working in Hangar 23 where the Roswell wreckage was initially dropped off prior to its transfer to Building 18 for permanent storage.

In the fall of 2010, we received an e-mail from Mark Magruder, Marion "Black Mac" Magruder's son, who had been so helpful to us in recounting his late father's "close encounter" at Wright-Patterson Air Force Base (see Chapter 8). Mark had recently had several conversations with David and Ben Hansen, a father and son who had some interesting information about Wright-Patterson Air Force Base, and Mark wanted to put us in touch with them, if we were interested. The Hansens had seen Mark discussing his father's career in an appearance on a SyFy Channel documentary about Wright-Patterson AFB called *Inside Government Warehouses: Shocking Revelations*, which had aired on July 9, 2010. Both were "astounded" by what Mark had said about his father's experiences, as they paralleled some of the events that had occurred in their own family. They were subsequently able to track down Mark Magruder through the producers of the show.

Ben Hansen, a former FBI agent, hosted and starred in a series on the SyFy Channel for three years called *Fact or Faked? Paranormal Files*. His father, Dr. M. David Hansen, is retired and resides in northern Utah; his grandfather, Merlin Hansen, is now deceased. In late December 2010, after several misfires, we were finally able to get Tom Carey, Ben Hansen, and David Hansen together at the same time for a conference call.

After the introductions and exchange of pleasantries, Ben started the ball rolling: **"My grandfather, Merlin Hansen, worked as a civil engineer at Wright-Patterson Air force Base on a 'TDY' [temporary duty] basis during several summers in the mid-1960s. His specialty was designing and maintaining *underground hangar elevator systems*"** (authors' emphasis).[31]

At this point, Ben's father, David, took over most of the ensuing conversation. **"My father [Merlin Hansen] was in the Army infantry serving on Iwo Jima in World War II. After he came back, he became a civil engineer working at Hill Air Force Base in northern Utah from 1955 through 1985. Beginning in 1964, he agreed to do some TDY assignments at Wright-Patterson AFB in Dayton, Ohio."**[32] According to Dr. Hansen, these assignments could come up at any time, on a moment's notice, and his father would be gone for weeks at a time without any direct contact with his family. Unlike his other trips, however, the trips to Wright-Patterson were always conducted in the utmost secrecy. These irregular, unscheduled trips continued through 1968, at which point they stopped without explanation. **"He was a 'specialist,'"** David said. **"He designed lift systems for hangars down four to six levels at the base. This facility was considered to be nuclear-proof and, as he relayed to us at the time, able to store four to six fighter planes below ground."**[33]

As Merlin Hansen lay on his deathbed after cancer had taken its toll, his son Dr. David Hansen finally asked his father a question that had been on his mind for some time: **"Are we alone in the universe, Dad?"** After a few moments of silence, Merlin replied to his son, **"You are going to take care of your mother."**[34] This non-answer seemed to end the conversation—for the moment at least. Then, according to Dr. Hansen, **"Not long thereafter, with just a few minutes remaining in his life, my father looked up at me and, making firm eye contact with me, he said softly and matter-of-factly, 'Son, we're not alone....' He passed away minutes later."**[35] For the record, Dr. Hansen states the following about his father: **"My father *never* lied to me. Not once in our 46-year friendship and life together did I find that he fabricated anything... even to save my feelings. He was a man of total integrity...he was a man who lived the quiet life of a dedicated American. I try to live by the same standard."**[36]

Ben Hansen clarified for us the exact location where his grandfather had worked on the Wright-Patterson base: **"I asked my father... if he is positive that my grandfather Merlin worked in Hangar 18. He states that he is 'absolutely sure' and that my grandmother can confirm this was the building number where they were instructed to call the operator to speak with Merlin. My father tells me that Merlin**

Ben Hansen's grandfather Merlin (left) and father, David (right).

never referred to a 'Hangar 18' though. Although he said that he was working in hangars, he said it was called *'Building 18'"*[37] (authors' emphasis).

According to a review of the facilities located in "Area B" on the Wright-Patterson base conducted by the Department of the Interior in the early 1990s, Building 18 was one of eight buildings (18–18G) comprising the Power Plant Laboratory Complex. The original function of the complex was conducting aircraft engine research, but during World War II additional structures were added as its role expanded. Constructed in 1928, Building 18 was the main research laboratory in the complex, while Building 18A was the laboratory office. Of particular interest to us here is Building 18F, constructed in 1945, which was described in the report as containing "four cold rooms" for the testing of engines at low temperatures. The cold rooms vented to the outside via the west side of the building.[38] (See Chapter 6 for testimony regarding the strange smells "wafting" out of Building 18F.) Also of interest was the notation that the eastern half of this building contained "refrigeration equipment, a transformer vault, offices, and storage areas."[39]

From these descriptions and testimonies, we are persuaded that most of the Roswell crash wreckage as well as at least four alien cadavers from that crash were initially delivered to Hangar 23 at Wright-Patterson AFB (then known as Wright Field) and remained there until a suitable underground passage connecting it to Building 18 for permanent storage could be constructed. Autopsies of the bodies were most likely carried out at the AeroMedical Facility also located in Area B (Building 29) on the base, after which the bodies were returned to Building 18F (due to its cold storage capability). The physical wreckage would have remained in storage at Building 18 except when it was being analyzed and tested in Hangar 23. This hangar was located for all intents and purposes in the Building 18 Complex, as it was situated between Building 18A and Building 18F.[40] Easy access to it from Building 18 was a given, and its historical function of back-engineering foreign technology of earthly origin was crucial to trying to figure out the nature of the Roswell wreckage.

Originally built in 1934 to be the Static Test Facility for aircraft and parts thereof, Building 23 has recently been restored in the Wright Field Historic District as a lab used for research and development, more specifically the new state-of-the-art Advanced Thermal Research Lab.[41] Established in 1927 as the experimental engineering arm of the U.S. Army Signal Corps, the historic district was the "site of some of the most advanced aeronautical engineering work in the history of aviation.... [Building 23] provides a working environment to serve vital functions in the ever changing research missions at Wright-Patterson."[42] Pertinent to our discussion today is the fact the restoration project also included the construction of a "skywalk" connecting Building 23 to Building 18!

Throughout the years, stories have surfaced of "body sightings" in other locations on and off the Wright-Patterson base. For instance, in 1982 a lieutenant colonel reported being escorted down long passageways past several checkpoints to a large underground vault beneath Building 45 in Area B of the Wright-Patterson base. There he witnessed a series of four or five horizontal tubes that looked like "caskets" or "lung-breathers." Two of these were opened for him. The first body, according to the colonel, was so badly cut up from all the autopsy work done on it that he got sick to his stomach, but the second one was in much better shape and conformed to the general description of Roswell aliens depicted in Chapter 6.[43] If true, this suggests that the bodies were at some point relocated to another building on the base, perhaps to one with more sophisticated preservation technology. It is interesting to note that both Building 45 and Building 18F are part of the Air Force Research Laboratory at Wright-Patterson AFB today.[44]

Senator Barry Goldwater, although he didn't know exactly where it was located, unsuccessfully tried to gain entrance to Wright-Patt's infamous "Blue Room" in the early 1960s to see the UFO "artifacts" (see Chapter 5). And Leonard Stringfield, the "father of UFO crash stories," was a business consultant on a project for the Air Force in the 1960s that required him to utilize the library services at the Foreign Technology Division building on the base for an extended period of time. According to the publisher of Stringfield's early books, he came away convinced that UFO artifacts as well as alien bodies were being stored in the FTD building, which was also known as the "Pink Building" because of its exterior Pepto-Bismol-pink paint job.[45]

Moving off base and later in time, the Chief of FTD for seven years in the 1960s and '70s, Colonel George Weinbrenner, told a trusted friend shortly before he passed away in 2010, **"We have five aliens [stored] in Utah."**[46] Presumably he was referring to a facility at the Dugway Proving Grounds in western Utah where whatever extraterrestrial artifacts and biology that were being stored at "Area 51" in Nevada have allegedly been moved. According to Robert Collins, the UFO material left Wright-Patterson in the 1982–83 time frame when the underground vaults were sealed, and then perhaps forwarded to Area 51.[47] If correct, this would seem to bring us full circle to the present in tracking a journey that began 66 years ago in 1947 in a remote desert region north and west of a dusty New Mexico town called Roswell.

One additional prescient testimony will underscore the conclusions we have drawn as to where the Roswell wreckage and alien bodies—and perhaps other alleged UFO "artifacts"—were stored for several years. It concerns a discussion that our source had with someone in 1977 about aliens at the Wright-Patterson base. Our source's friend was a captain at the base and a supervisor in charge of base security who had the highest security clearance. He told our source that he could go anywhere except one installation, and that the security detail for it was totally separate from the rest of the base and was comprised of all captains. He also said that no one but the most powerful people came and went from it, and what went on inside was totally unknown. He leaned forward and whispered to our source, **"If the bodies exist, they are in that [Building 18] complex."**[48]

CHAPTER 3

The Summer of the UFO: Panic at the Pentagon

"Yet across an immense ethereal gulf, minds that are to our minds as ours are to the beasts in the jungle, intellects vast, cool and unsympathetic, regarded this earth with envious eyes and slowly and surely drew their plans against us."

So begins the classic H.G. Wells's novel *War of the Worlds*. After Orson Welles's famous radio dramatization of the novel in 1938, there's no doubt that the idea of an invasion scenario remained quite vivid in the minds of Americans in 1947. The late Dr. Carl Sagan often warned that we earthlings should refrain from announcing our existence by transmitting radio signals into space "because we do not know the intentions of a superior galactic society."[1] Though science fiction writers such as Wells and Sagan had been imagining extraterrestrial invasions for many years, the people of our world remained unprepared for the intrusion of a phenomenon that heretofore existed solely on the pages of their novels.

The summer of 1947 was the season of the flying saucers, when it became clear that someone else's hardware was invading our sovereign airspace and that its presence demonstrated an immediate threat to United States national security. The unknown aircraft seemed to outperform, outmaneuver, and out-speed anything in our own arsenal at that time. The Pentagon found itself at a complete loss as to who or what was violating our airspace. Leading officials in Washington denied any knowledge of the origin of the flying disks, but a growing number of experts realized that the world could very well be facing a threat from off the planet.[2]

It seemed that the world's first atomic bomb detonation, in Alamagordo, New Mexico, on July 16, 1945, had drawn the attention of more than the inhabitants of our own planet: Afterward, there were more UFO sightings in New Mexico than anywhere else in the world. Our visitors were definitely curious about our military potential at that time.

The following is a time line of how events unfolded that fateful summer.

July 3, 1947. The Army Air Force states, **"If some foreign power is sending flying disks over the United States, it is our responsibility to know about it and take proper action."**

July 4. The press reports that military facilities along the West Coast of the United States have fighters on standby in case the "disks" returned.

July 5. Pentagon Army Air Force Captain Tom Brown tells Major Donald Keyhoe, USMC, **"We just can't ignore it. There are too many reliable pilots telling the same story—flat, round objects able to outmaneuver ordinary planes, and faster than anything we have."** Brown confirms that military facilities were on alert to investigate the appearance of the flying disks. Another source tells Keyhoe that some commanders had been given orders to "shoot the unknowns down" if possible.

July 6. An Army Air Force representative states, **"We still haven't the slightest idea what they could be. However, we don't believe anyone in this country, or outside of this country, has developed a guided missile...."**

Rancher W.W. Brazel, outside of Roswell, New Mexico, reports a crash of a flying saucer. Army intelligence officers are sent to investigate. Major General Clements McMullen, deputy commander/chief of Staff of the Strategic Air Command, orders some of the wreckage to be flown immediately to Washington.

July 7. New Mexico Senior Senator Carl Hatche requests an emergency meeting with President Truman.

General Hoyt F. Vandenberg, chief of staff of the Army Air Force, has his entire day occupied by phone calls and meetings about the arrival of the disks.

Lt. General Nathan Twining, commander of the Air Materiel Command (AMC) headquartered at Wright Field in Dayton, Ohio, unexpectedly flies to New Mexico. He remains there for the next five days. Wright Field admits to investigating reports of disks seen in the Pacific Northwest and in Texas.

July 8. Army Air Force intelligence is a flurry of activity because of military sightings in California. The chief of the Requirements Intelligence Branch of Army Air Force Intelligence, Brigadier General George F. Schulgen, brings one of the F-51 pilots from Muroc who saw a "flat, light-reflecting object" at high altitude near Mount Baldy to the Pentagon for interrogation.

A special meeting is called at the Pentagon by Vandenberg of the Office of Scientific Research and Development (OSRD), chaired by electrical engineer and initiator of the Manhattan Project, Dr. Vannevar Bush. Immediately after the meeting, the Pentagon issues a press release stating that the "flying saucers definitely were not spaceships."

The Army publicly announces, in a press release by RAAF Public Information Officer Walter Huat, their recovery of an actual "flying disk" on a ranch outside of Roswell, New Mexico.[3] The Air Force also reveals it was checking out a report from C.T. Zohm, a Navy rocket engineer who, in the company of three other scientists, was on a secret mission in New Mexico when they observed a silvery, bright disk at low altitude moving northward across open desert.[4] Later that afternoon, the FBI is informed that the disk brought to Fort Worth AAF from Roswell was suspended by a balloon and was sent, after transfer to the Eighth Air Force in Fort Worth, Texas, to Wright Field for analysis.

The FBI states, **"Disc and balloon being transported to Wright Field by special plane for examination. Information provided this office because of national interest in case and fact that National Broadcasting Company, Associated Press, and others attempting to break story of location of disc today. Major Kirton [Headquarters, 8th**

Air Force] advised would request Wright Field to advise Cincinnati Office results of examination."[5]

From Washington, the intelligence division of the War Department sends out the order that all of their field agents should **"suggest saucers are radar targets for weather observation purposes."**

Meanwhile, back in Roswell, rumors escalate that aliens were invading their community and were out in the street. Rancher Brazel, who first discovered the strange debris, is abducted by the military and kept in custody for the next five days.[6]

July 9. General Schulgen calls the FBI and urgently requests their cooperation in solving the problem of the flying disks.

At 10:30 a.m., Lt. General James Doolittle, former Commander of the Eighth Air Force, and General Vandenberg meet with Secretary of War for Air, Stuart Symington. Major General Leslie Groves, head of the Armed Forces Special (Atomic) Weapons Project, and General Robert Montague, commander, Army Guided Missile School, meet with Lt. General Curtis LeMay, deputy chief of Air Staff for Research and Development at the Pentagon. Doolittle had investigated the 1946 ghost rocket phenomenon for Vandenberg and allegedly informed President Harry S. Truman that the objects were "most likely of unknown origin." Vandenberg will join the meeting in progress.

At 10:50, Doolittle, Vandenberg, and Symington meet in the office of General Dwight D. Eisenhower, the chief of staff of the Army. Major General Lauris Norstad, director of the Plans and Operations Division of the War Department, is also present.

At 11:58, Vandenberg calls President Truman.

At 12:15 p.m., Doolittle and Vandenberg meet with the president.

At 12:50, Vandenberg and Symington meet with the Joint Chiefs.

At 2:20, Vandenberg and Symington meet again.

At 2:40, Secretary of War Robert Patterson meets with Groves and Montague.

New Mexico Senator Carl Hatche has an unscheduled private meeting with President Truman that same afternoon.

At 4:15, Vandenberg meets with Major General Emmett O'Donnell, director of information, Army Air Force Public Relations. The year before, O'Donnell was the deputy chief of engineering of the Army Technical Services Command, which would become the AMC.[7]

Elsewhere around the nation, banner headlines fill the morning and afternoon edition newspapers explaining away all the excitement in the sleepy southwestern town of Roswell. The country breathes a sigh of relief; it is merely a weather balloon device. However, some are not buying it.

The *Las Vegas Review-Journal*, along with dozens of other newspapers, carries a United Press story: **"Reports of flying saucers whizzing through the sky fell off sharply today as the Army and the Navy began a concentrated campaign to stop the rumors."** The story went on to describe that AAF headquarters in Washington "delivered a blistering rebuke to officers at Roswell." In reality, the latter never occurred. The *Washington Post* reported, **"At first they gave the bare details of the finding of the object, then they clamped down a security lid on any further information on the grounds that it was high-level stuff."** The *Roswell Daily Record* added, **"The Army isn't telling its secrets yet, from all appearances when this was written."**[8]

During the next week, however, an inconsistent reaction on the part of the government began to develop. Something had happened to send officials into cover-up mode, and every effort was being made to play down the situation. On its face, this was totally inconsistent with the responsibility of the U.S. military to defend the country from the air in the case of unknown objects reported in the sky. The Pentagon was forced to admit that they did not have full radar coverage of the continental United States. All the more reason for pilots throughout the nation to be on 24-hour alert during this alarming situation. Unofficially, numerous pilots confirmed that they were ordered to bring down the disks if humanly possible.

July 10. U.S. government intelligence feigns disinterest in the phenomena. President Truman holds a news conference, during which he is asked about the flying disks. He says they reminded him of the notorious Moon Hoax of 1835, when a writer for the *New York Sun* published a series of articles about the discovery of people on the moon by astronomer Sir John Hershel. The articles were written as a satire.[9]

Brigadier General Roger Ramey, commander of the Eighth Air Force, who had just identified the Roswell disk at a press conference in Fort Worth, gives a radio interview in El Paso, Texas. When the radio announcer asks about all of the other flying disk reports throughout the country, Ramey jokes that that was true, except for Kansas, "which is a dry state."

In the next few days, the Pentagon instructed the Army to demonstrate launches of the radar weather balloon devices to the press, in an attempt to show how they accounted for many of the flying disk reports. Contrary to the public's perception that the government couldn't care less, military and FBI agents were hard at work downplaying events and ridiculing witnesses even as the number of reports dropped. Sightings continued, but fear of public embarrassment was a great deterrent to reporting them.

As the days of July marched on, both military and civilian intelligence agencies became aware of a bewildering silence from the Pentagon. Where there had first been extreme urgency and pressure from the highest levels of authority for answers, suddenly there was silence. Finally, after getting all of their field operatives in place and data under control... nothing. This might lead one to believe that someone at the top had discovered what was behind the mystery. The wall of silence had shut out even the highest office of intelligence in the Air Force. Lt. Colonel G.D. Garret, who served directly under Schulgen, agreed with FBI Special agent S.W. Reynolds that the disks were probably **"a very highly classified experiment of the Army or Navy."** A scientist attached to Air Force intelligence had reached a similar conclusion. **"Colonel Garret stated that we have reported sightings of unknown objects over the United States and the 'high brass' appeared to be totally unconcerned. He indicated this led him to believe that they knew enough about these objects to express no concern."**[10] After vouching for the reliability of the reporters of these unknowns, Garret concluded, **"there are objects seen which somebody in the government knows all about."**

However, if Air Force intelligence was not being told what the disks were, who was? Reynolds followed up this conversation with a visit to his contact at the War Department, Colonel L.R. Forney. Forney assured Reynolds that he had inquired about secret Army projects to his superiors, and the Army had no idea what the objects were.[11] Garrett subsequently addressed his boss, Schulgen, about Air Force projects and got the same response—but perhaps Schulgen did not know everything that Air Force Research and Development was doing. The FBI and the Air Force agreed that Schulgen should send a query further up the corridors of secrecy to General Curtis LeMay, head of R&D. The response, given to the FBI on September 5, 1947, was that **"a complete survey of research activities discloses that the Army Air Force has no project with the characteristics similar to those which have been associated with the Flying Discs."**[12] Navy Admiral Calvin Bolster, chief of aeronautics research on experimental craft, expressed the same ignorance for the Navy's part in the ongoing puzzle.

Nevertheless, the FBI remained concerned that this was like chasing ghosts: no answers, just questions. Schulgen's staff, tired of being out of the loop, decided to make a direct request of General Twining, the commanding general at Wright Field. Twining, along with the base's secret project testing labs, was asked for an official statement on the new phenomenon and whether further intelligence activity was warranted. Along with this request, he received the intelligence community's very first study of the nature of UFOs, supposedly a **"detailed study of reports selected for their impression of veracity and reliability"** called **"Analysis of Flying Disc Reports."**[13]

Schulgen's Air Intelligence Requirements Division (AIRD) put out its own call to arms. On October 28, 1947, a secret five-page AIRD "Draft of Collection Memorandum" listed the **"current intelligence requirements in the field of Flying Saucer–type aircraft."**[14]

Especially noteworthy is Requirement No. 3: Items of construction:

(a) Type of material, whether metal, ferrous, non-ferrous, or non-metallic.

(b) Composite or sandwich construction utilizing various combinations of metals, metallic foils, plastics, and perhaps balsa wood or similar material.

(c) Unusual fabrication methods to achieve extreme light weight and structural stability.[15]

Under "Power plant" the draft request states: "Information is needed regarding the propulsion system of the aircraft.... The presence of an unconventional or unusual type of propulsion system cannot be ruled out and should be considered of great interest."[16]

What is quite telling is the degree of detail that could hardly have advanced from merely observing distant objects in the sky. Is there any doubt that these particular descriptions closely resemble the eyewitness accounts from Roswell?

Unfortunately, the UFO investigations conducted by Army Air Force Intelligence in July 1947 were disorganized, unprofessional, and confused. The report also showed that the Army Air Field was not sharing all of its data with the Air Materiel Command. Whatever was going on at Wright Field behind closed doors may have been an entirely different—and thorough—matter, but the public investigation was inept. It was incomplete, even though the investigators were willing to let people like Schulgen, FBI Director J. Edgar Hoover, and, ultimately, Twining examine it. The investigators showed total inefficiency in interviewing principal witnesses. A number of incident dates were wrong, suggesting that such cases were never even looked into. What remains most suspicious is the strange omission of some of the most important incidents that had drawn all of the concern in the first place.[17]

Captain Edward Ruppelt, a decorated and highly experienced WWII pilot with a degree in aeronautics, who served as director of Project Grudge in 1951 and Project Blue Book in 1952, summed up the situation at that time based on the premise that the military needed answers, not mysteries: "Before, if an interesting report came in and they **wanted an answer, all they'd get was an 'it could be real, but we can't prove it.'"** Ruppelt would also refer to this developing period as the "Dark Ages" based on the eventual Air Force theorem: "It can't be; therefore, it isn't." He added, **"Everything was being evaluated on the premise that UFOs couldn't exist."**[18]

This low level of alertness also allowed American research projects to move forward under a cloak of secrecy. The Cold War between the two superpowers was placing all field agents on standard alert, and the arrival of the flying disks only raised the level of suspicion at a time when "national security" was becoming a code phrase for lack of public disclosure. The apparent invasion of UFOs over America was akin to someone launching a first assault. We just did not know whom to counter-attack.

It was due to this clandestine reaction to the arrival of the flying saucer phenomenon in the summer of 1947 that many early records of the Air Force's investigation were destroyed or remain secret. We are forever grateful to Ruppelt, who had access to this unknown history. For example, he was the first to disclose the Twining letter that confirmed the existence of the UFO phenomenon in the first place, and he even coined the term "Unidentified Flying Object" to replace such distasteful (to the military) terms as "flying saucer." But more importantly, the officer painted the true picture of exactly what was going on at all the smoke-filled meetings in Washington and at Wright Field back in 1947. In his book, *The Report on Unidentified Flying Objects*, he stated, **"By the end of July [1947] the UFO security lid was down tight. The few members of the press who did inquire about what the Air Force was doing got the same treatment that you would get today if you inquired about the number of thermonuclear weapons stockpiled in the U.S. atomic arsenal.... At ATIC [Air Technical Intelligence Center] there was confusion to the point of panic."**

What has truly become comical is the notion that the Pentagon's alarm was over something as trivial as a weather balloon. (On the other hand, maybe it was the time-traveling wooden crash dummies. For an added threat, let us throw in 13-year-old mutant German children, as maintained by another author.) Just a couple of weeks after the balloon explanation was accepted by the national media, the National Security Act was passed, and the CIA, the National Security Council, and the Department of Defense were all officially established. And yet, an International News Service article quoted the public relations officer at Wright Field as stating, **"So far we haven't found anything to confirm that saucers exist. We don't think they are guided missiles.... As things are now, they appear to be either a phenomenon or a figment of somebody's imagination."**[19]

Something that journalists and researchers tend to forget when appraising U.S. military intelligence activities is that, basically, the only thing these agencies are concerned with is national security. Every action taken by military offices and projects must be viewed primarily in that context. We must continually ask ourselves, "Is there any potential threat to U.S. security in this scenario?"

For discussion purposes, we will assume the craft in the skies that summer were manufactured off the planet. Then we ask the national security question again. On the one hand, we could feel relief that the Soviets were not responsible. However, the alien nature of the craft would not remove the Russians from the national security equation. Pentagon and Wright Field authorities needed to shut this discovery down to absolute secrecy so that the Soviets would find out nothing—which immediately created the need-to-know situation within the U.S. government. None of the personnel in intelligence below the very top were to be informed. If any information was disclosed at all, it typically was disinformation. The fewer people who knew the facts, the less chance that the information could be leaked, stolen, or compromised. The potential for new military advances and breakthroughs was at stake, which, when added to our atomic superiority, could place the United States as the lone superpower in the world.

Almost all of this—except the extraterrestrial reality of the Roswell incident—is documented in uncontroversial sources. However, allow us to pull back the curtain and speculate what would have transpired under the veil of U.S. national security. If Roswell did happen, was alien, and was recovered for study, what would the procedure be?

National security concerns would now coincide with scientific concerns up to a certain point. Any knowledge harnessed from the crash debris could open the door through reverse engineering. Materials beyond our comprehension and the manner in which specific alloys were arranged at the molecular level could provide a quantum leap in technology unprecedented in the history of humankind. Nevertheless, terrestrial science of 1947 might not be able to comprehend the advanced technology of materials just as alien as the crew that piloted the ship. It would be a fair conclusion that little if any headway was made in this category—if you can't plug it in, you can't get it to work.

Today, after more than 60 years, it appears likely that the U.S. Air Force got nowhere on what they really wanted to know about the craft and how the materials were structured. They were unable to determine how the device functions, what the intentions of the visitors were, and where they originated. Is it any wonder that by the fall of 1947, nothing was trickling down from the highest levels of the military? There was nothing to disclose. They were forced to concede that they were likely years from any answers.

It was during the post-Roswell period that pressure was applied again for the intelligence community to go underground and then come up with UFO information that would help the Pentagon comprehend their enigma. Its focus was at Wright Field: UFO investigations would be conducted from there. Dayton was out in the suburbs and the military elite still needed breathing room to get a handle on the situation.[20]

Therefore, the intelligence community found itself taking the subject seriously again, not by chasing flying disks in the sky, but rather by collecting both domestic and foreign information from lookout posts throughout the free world with the intent of solving the UFO mystery in prosaic terms.[21] The projects associated with the Roswell crash knew what they had, but they could not acknowledge what they could not comprehend.

CHAPTER 4

Reverse-Engineering the "Memory Metal"

From the moment a craft of unknown origin descended from the summer skies and crashed into the high desert of east-central New Mexico in July of 1947, high-level officials outside of Roswell clamored to get the craft's materials into their hands as soon as possible for analysis and possible exploitation. World War II had been over for two years, and a new global adversary had risen to the top of the leaderboard—Soviet Russia—to fill the void once occupied by the defeated Axis Powers.

At that time, and certainly as a consequence of World War II, there were a large number of national laboratories in the United States that specialized in a wide variety of military technologies. But there was only one organization that included the science of "reverse engineering" foreign technology in its repertoire of expertise. That was the Air Materiel Command (AMC) headquartered at Wright Field under the command of General Nathan F. Twining. It was composed of two separate but related functional units: "T-2 Intelligence" and "T-3 Engineering." In 1961, T-2 would be recast as the Foreign Technology Division (FTD), which became throughout the years the designation most commonly applied to the unit dealing with "foreign technology" at Wright-Patterson regardless of the year or iteration for it at any given time. For continuity and simplicity, "FTD" will be the referent used throughout this chapter. "Area 51" was at this time still just a spot on a map of the state of Nevada that had been used as a gunnery range during World War II. It would not be developed as a super-secret test facility of the same name for spy planes and stealth technology until the mid-1950s, and its reputation as the repository of choice for extraterrestrial "hardware" would not be made until the late 1980s.

Essentially, the Foreign Technology Division at Wright Field in Dayton, Ohio, is responsible for the breakdown and analysis of all weapons and equipment of foreign design captured or recovered from a crash from the air. During World War II, these were aircraft of German, Japanese, or Italian design. During the Cold War, these were almost exclusively aircraft of Russian design. With the coming of the saucers in the summer of 1947, any recovered wreckage, remains, or physical evidence from them would certainly have been deemed to be "foreign technology" and sent to FTD for dissection.[1] During times of war, of course, such analyses were done for the purpose of understanding the salient features of enemy technology in order to defeat or better combat it by negating or exceeding its inherent capabilities. In some instances, a complete reverse engineering of a captured or wrecked aircraft is undertaken to better understand its workings. Perhaps the best known example of this was ironically done by the Russians during World War II when they fortuitously came into possession of two United States B-29 bombers that had been forced to emergency-land in the USSR after a bombing run over Japan in 1944. After a protracted negotiation, the Russians eventually released the American flight crews but kept the B-29s, which they proceeded to painstakingly disassemble, part by part. At the time, the Russians had no heavy bombers and were still making fighter planes out of wood. After the war, foreign military experts who had been invited to watch Russia's first post-war May Day Parade, which always ended with a show of the Soviet's latest military hardware, were stunned when they saw a squadron of what they thought were American B-29 bombers fly by overhead. How could that be? In point of fact, they were not American-made bombers at all. They were Russian-made Tupolev TU-4 heavy bombers—*exact copies* of the American B-29!

When the Roswell wreckage arrived at Wright Field during the second week of July 1947, it quickly found its way into Hangar 23. As we learned in Chapter 2, Hangar 23 was where the breakdown, analysis, and back-engineering of enemy aircraft (in other words, "foreign technology") during World War II had taken place; and so it would be for the Roswell wreckage. As described in this book and elsewhere, the Roswell wreckage was mostly all in small pieces, having apparently exploded in the air before falling to the desert floor. It would be several months before the only intact part of the ship, the inner cabin or escape pod, was flown out of Roswell to Wright Field.[2] The wreckage consisted of four major types:

1. Pieces of thin, light, stiff, aluminum-colored metal, which were unbendable and impervious to the application of external forces.

2. Thin "I-Beam" structures with strange symbols or "writing" embossed on them.

3. Small wires that remind us of today's monofilament wires.

4. Pieces of a thin, light, aluminum-colored, cloth-like "metal" that could be wadded up in the hand and then, upon letting go, would quickly assume its original shape. It too was indestructible and impervious to external forces. For several years now, we have referred to #4 as the *"Holy Grail* of Roswell" because of its unique qualities—qualities that, by themselves, would serve as unequivocal, demonstrable proof, in our opinion, of the extraterrestrial nature of the 1947 Roswell events.

Once it was realized that the wreckage was extraterrestrial and not Russian as initially thought, the decision was made in Washington to keep this knowledge secret from not only the Russians (for obvious reasons), but also from the American people. Employing the World War II slogan that "loose lips sink ships," it was felt that the fewer people who knew about it the better. This strategy worked almost flawlessly for the next 30 years until the former intelligence officer at Roswell Army Air Field at the time of the incident broke his silence in 1978 and talked about having participated in the recovery of a bona fide UFO back in 1947. With the publication of Berlitz and Moore's *The Roswell Incident* in 1980 and Randle and Schmitt's *UFO Crash at Roswell* in 1991, "Roswell" was on its way to becoming a household name around the world. Although Robert Lazar's claims of being employed to help back-engineer alien technology at a super-secret facility in the state of Nevada called "Area 51" were discredited,[3] the notion of back-engineering captured or downed alien technology gained traction and popularity because of the renewed interest in the Roswell crash. Some believe that much of our current technology—everything from transistors, fiber optics, and night-vision goggles to computer chips, integrated circuits, and Velcro—has resulted from the reverse engineering of extraterrestrial spacecraft or parts thereof. Subscribers to this notion argue that these and a long list of other advanced technologies could not have been developed by us so rapidly after 1947 without an alien "assist."[4]

In 1997, this notion became the theme of the *New York Times* bestseller *The Day After Roswell*, by the late U.S. Army colonel Philip J. Corso along with future "UFO Hunter" William J. Birnes. In the book, published one year before he passed away, Corso claimed to have coordinated a re-engineering project of the Roswell material while working under the Army's head of Research and Development, Lieutenant General Arthur Trudeau. According to Corso, the project fostered new commercial technology in a number of areas such as fiber optics and computer chips that were developed from the back-engineering of artifacts retrieved from the Roswell wreckage. Although we have always felt that there is something to the notion of a Roswell derivation for present-day fiber optics technology, there were too many factual mistakes in Corso's tale for us to sign on to his thesis. And his bizarre claim that the world had fought and won an interplanetary war against extraterrestrials (unknown to the citizens of the real world, as far as we can tell) by employing the "S.D.I." (Strategic Defense Initiative) was a "bridge too far" for reasonable minds to accept. The stake in the heart of the book's credibility for many readers was administered by the late U.S. Senator Strom Thurmond, who had written the foreword for *The Day After Roswell*. Senator Thurmond, for whom Corso had once served as an aide, was apparently misled or was mistaken when Corso asked him to write the Foreword for his book. After penning a normal, positive recollection of his former aide that had nothing to do with UFOs, Thurmond requested a retraction of his Foreword when he learned of the book's contents. When a *New York Times* columnist quoted Senator Thurmond as saying he knew of no such cover-up and doubted that one ever existed,[5] not only was the credibility of Colonel Corso himself dealt a severe blow, but so too were his claims regarding the re-engineering of recovered alien technology. It would be another 10 years before the subject, like the *Flight of the Phoenix*, arose once again.

Life can surprise you. Sometimes, when one door closes, another door may open. And so it has been with our Roswell investigation in the person of Anthony Bragalia. A self-employed businessman, Bragalia has been conducting his own private investigation of the Roswell crash/retrieval for a number of years, including one phase of the Roswell story that has received scant attention from researchers: What happened to the crash wreckage *after* it was delivered to Wright Army Air Field in Dayton, Ohio? His research into this area of inquiry has been outstanding, and the results achieved so far have been astounding: He has unearthed scientific and document evidence nothing short of *proving* the extraterrestrial nature of the Roswell wreckage! Newly discovered documents from highly classified government reports written in the late 1940s regarding "**memory metal**" show that the Air Force—through the Battelle Memorial Institute in Columbus, Ohio, and other laboratories, such as at New York University (of Project Mogul infamy), Oak Ridge National Laboratory in Tennessee, and the Lawrence Livermore Labs in California—were attempting to replicate the "shape recovery" properties of the Roswell crash debris.

The impetus behind Bragalia's investigation was hearing us, Tom Carey and Don Schmitt, discuss our continuing (and largely unsuccessful) search for physical evidence from Roswell on a radio program some years back, and especially our reference to a special type of debris wreckage we dubbed the *Holy Grail of Roswell*—a piece of so-called "memory metal." Bragalia decided then and there to try to find out what became of the Roswell wreckage after it was reportedly sent to Wright Field.[6] His report regarding the early phase of this investigation was written up in the 2009 edition of our book *Witness to Roswell*. It and his follow-up investigation into what became of at least one element the Roswell wreckage—the memory metal—read like a scientific "Whodunit?" mystery novel, but with one difference: It's all true!

Bragalia's investigation began with an account of a former Battelle employee who had confessed to a family friend in 1960 that he had been tasked with analyzing crashed flying saucer debris when he worked

Front entrance to Battelle Memorial Institute in Columbus, Ohio. Wright-Patterson has been a "client" of Battelle's on technical engineering projects for decades.

there years earlier. The scientist, Elroy John Center, stated that he analyzed metal from a crashed UFO when he was employed at the institute. A graduate in chemical engineering from the University of Michigan, Center was a senior research chemist at Battelle for nearly two decades, from 1939 to 1957, specializing in the analysis and testing of metals and unique materials.[7] Center certainly possessed the qualifications and necessary skills to have been involved in the early analysis of the Roswell debris.

Bragalia then located and interviewed Dr. Irena Scott of Columbus, Ohio, a former biology professor and Battelle scientist. According to Dr. Scott, in 1992 she interviewed a close professional associate of Elroy Center. He told her that Center had privately related to him in 1960 that while he (Center) was employed at Battelle (he didn't give a specific year), he had been involved in a very strange laboratory project—a highly classified study his employer had been contracted to perform by the government (more specifically, by Wright-Patterson AFB). The project involved work on a very unusual material. Center came to understand that the strange "piece of debris," as he described it, had been retrieved by the U.S. government from the earlier crash of a UFO. He explained that this "piece" was not something with which anyone was familiar. As reported by a number of firsthand Roswell witnesses, Center also said that the debris he handled was inscribed with strange symbols that he termed "glyphics."[8] No further details were provided by Center throughout the course of his life. He passed away in 1991.[9]

Being the intrepid investigator that he is, in 2010 Bragalia located and interviewed by telephone a still-living Center family friend (name on file but withheld by request) mentioned by Irina Scott. This man confirmed meeting with Center as a young man in 1957 at Center's home. In a discussion about UFOs, Center allowed that he had analyzed a strange metal "piece" that he did not believe to be from Earth, and that he had understood was from a downed UFO. The informant distinctly remembered that Center said that the "piece" had hieroglyphic-like markings on it and that the chemical element boron was important in some way in the composition of the UFO material that was being studied. Center also revealed that the UFO material was kept in a secure safe when he was at Battelle.[10] Bragalia then quickly located and interviewed Elroy John Center's daughter (name also withheld by request), in her mid-70s, who lives in a western state. She said that her late father went by his middle name, John, rather than by his first name. She said that she was unaware of her father's story regarding the strange "piece" of metal, but she recalled that he had had visits at home from an FBI investigator, during which lengthy discussions regarding UFOs occurred. She distinctly remembered overhearing her mother and father in a discussion one day about UFOs when her father was heard to say, **"I don't know if we should tell [daughter's name] about this. She won't be able to leave it alone."**[11]

We had always suspected that the Battelle Memorial Institute of Columbus, Ohio, because of the nature of what it does, and where it does it—close to Wright-Patterson AFB, where the Roswell wreckage was taken—would have most likely been called upon by the Air Force to conduct studies of the wreckage there. But, due to the press of other investigative initiatives and general time constraints, we never got around to doing anything beyond speculating about it.

Now we had a story about a deceased former employee of Battelle Memorial Institute who claimed to have worked on a strange piece of metal he believed had come from a crashed UFO. Where to go from there? Concentrating on the memory-metal aspect of the case, Bragalia then plugged in the phrases *memory metal, morphing metal,* and *shape-recovery metal* into his Internet browser and let fly. Up popped a number of articles and Websites on something called "Nitinol," an amalgam of the elements nickel (Ni) and Titanium (Ti), which together possess properties similar to Roswellian memory metal. The "-nol" part of the Nitinol name stood for the Naval Ordnance Lab, where this memory alloy was "discovered" back in 1962. Because of its shape-recovery and bendability properties, Nitinol is used commercially today in many products, from eyeglass frames to medical instruments and much more. It can also be purchased as wire, coil, or by the sheet, if you so choose. But the Naval Ordnance Lab located in White Oak, Maryland, was *not* Wright-Patterson AFB, where the Roswell wreckage had allegedly been taken. What then was the connection between the two, if any, or was Nitinol simply developed at the NOL in the normal course of prosaic metallurgical research without a cosmic assist? To find the answer, Bragalia undertook a historical backtracking of the eyestrain- and headache-inducing technical literature regarding the development of shape-recovery metals, a journey that would take several years and lead back to the doors of Battelle Memorial Institute and Wright-Patterson AFB.

Recalling General Arthur Exon's comments regarding the physical make-up of the Roswell material as being **"titanium and some other metal...[but] the processing was different,"** as well as a secret memo from General George Schulgen (assistant chief of staff for Air Intelligence in 1947) stating that the wreckage in their possession was apparently constructed "by unusual fabrication methods," Bragalia focused on technical articles that dealt with the processing of titanium with another metal, such as nickel or zirconium. He found a number of such articles written in the 1960s, and in the footnotes of a few of these he found references citing Air Force contract numbers originating from Wright-Patterson AFB in Dayton, Ohio. Also cited were references to a "Second Progress Report" written in 1949 by scientists from

Battelle for the Air Force at Wright-Patterson AFB regarding Battelle's research into and development of titanium alloys. Bragalia's research also revealed that there had been no history of such research by the military, or by anyone else for that matter, regarding the element titanium prior to 1947. The fact that interest and studies pertaining to titanium seemed to take off after the Roswell crash is most interesting. Also, a "Second Progress Report" from Battelle to Wright-Patt presupposes a "First Progress Report," most likely written in 1948, which was not cited in any of these articles, suggesting that it was not provided to the researchers for their studies. Was it not provided because it might have mentioned certain background information regarding the origins and/or true nature of the project?

Bragalia then placed calls to the historians at both Battelle and Wright-Patterson to try to retrieve the two Battelle progress reports, if they still existed. Although the historians at both locations were able to locate these reports in their computer databases, the actual hard-copy reports were "missing," suggesting, according to the historians, that they had either been destroyed or were stored somewhere under a

SECOND PROGRESS REPORT

COVERING THE PERIOD SEPTEMBER 1 TO OCTOBER 31, 1949

on

RESEARCH AND DEVELOPMENT ON TITANIUM ALLOYS
Contract No. 33(038)-3736

to

WRIGHT-PATTERSON AIR FORCE BASE
DAYTON, OHIO

Battelle's "Second Progress Report" (1949) to Wright-Patterson detailing the initial results of experiments involving Titanium in attempting to replicate "memory metal" rcovered at Roswell.

very high security classification. Not giving up, Bragalia in 2009 enlisted his close friend, Sarasota *Herald Tribune* reporter Billy Cox, to file formal Freedom of Information (FOIA) requests for these reports with the proper authorities at both Battelle and Wright-Patterson AFB. As UFO researchers are fully aware, the FOIA process is usually one of frustration and long waits with an all-too-frequent "No Records" response, and not much different was expected by Cox and Bragalia here. But, again, life is full of surprises. Both progress reports, after many months and reminder inquiries, were located in the archives of the Defense Technical Information Center (DTIC) at the Department of Defense (DOD). After official reviews by the Office of the Secretary of the Air Force, both "DOD Restricted" reports were released to Billy Cox—the "Second Progress Report" in 2009, and the First Progress Report" in 2010.[12] Many pages were missing from each report, but there was enough information in them for researchers like Bragalia and Cox to develop a time line for the derivation of Nitinol—the best shape-recovery alloy currently in existence—from its progenitor, Roswell's *Holy Grail*, aka "memory metal." And just as stunning as the reports themselves, which were titled "Research and Development on Titanium Alloys," was one of the names of the reports' co-authors: Elroy John Center!

After studying the Roswell wreckage for a number of months after it had been delivered to them from Roswell, the intelligence and engineering departments at the Air Materiel Command (AMC) at Wright-Patterson were no doubt puzzled but also impressed by the properties of so-called memory metal. Having determined that Titanium was one of the constituent elements of memory metal, AMC contracted with Battelle to analyze and experiment with the strange material further in the hope of replicating it. Nickel was found by the scientists at Battelle to be the most promising element when combined with titanium to mimic memory metal, but it was the *processing* of this potential alloy that was most important. *Pure* titanium and nickel plus extreme heat were required to effect shape recovery. In the 1950s, AMC secretly seeded portions of the "Second Progress Report" from Battelle to various other laboratories around the country, including the Naval Ordnance Lab, to continue researching for the right titanium alloy to make memory metal. In 1962, the Naval Ordnance Lab announced the creation of the shape-recovery alloy Nitinol! It was composed of nickel and titanium—not as good as the real thing, but still the best "morphing metal" in our inventory.

In 2010, Bragalia interviewed by telephone one of the co-inventors of Nitinol, Dr. Fred Wang, formerly of the Naval Ordnance Lab. Wang confirmed his participation in the project and had no problem answering general questions about it, but, according to Bragalia, Wang became "cagey" when asked about several matters relating to the development of Nitinol. For instance, in the early 1970s, Dr. Wang was involved in bizarre "mind over matter" tests in which psychic Uri Geller was recruited to try to bend or "morph" Nitinol with his mind. Apparently, Geller was successful to some degree, but Wang was not all that happy to confirm his presence at the test. He agreed that he had been given a copy of Battelle's 1949 "Second Progress Report" for use in the study of Nitinol but would not reveal who had clandestinely given it to him. Then, when asked about his work's possible Roswell impetus, Bragalia heard Wang gasp and then fall silent. With the crickets chirping in the background for some moments, Wang finally said, **"I have no comment on that. I am not going to discuss it."**[13]

The other co-inventor of Nitinol was a fellow by the name of William Buehler. Years later, in an authorized Oral History, Buehler complained that after his "discovery," Battelle took back the project from the NOL and kept it when the National Aeronautical and Space Administration (NASA) retained Battelle to "conduct further characterization studies" on Nitinol.[14] No doubt NASA scientists were aware of Battelle's original involvement in the study of morphing metals and had also probably seen their two "Progress Reports" to Wright-Patterson that had been written in the late 1940s in the wake of the Roswell crash. Nitinol had come full circle.

And this makes sense. "Memory metal" was inspired by the materials of construction from a spacecraft found at Roswell, suggesting that the material must have application in aerospace. Today, NASA plans to apply the material in its most revolutionary and technologically advanced craft ever developed. Research is continuing, and one day such material may form the basis for a "self-healing spacecraft skin." And most incredibly, Nitinol or other "morphing metals" may hold the key to cosmic propulsion and infinitely "free energy" using "Nitinol Heat

Engines"—something NASA has been working on for more than 20 years![15] **"Morphing is the key to cosmic transport,"** Bragalia concludes. **"What material could be better for an interstellar vehicle than one that could provide its own energy source, disguise itself at will, work in all environments, and be able to heal itself when compromised?"** He continued, **"Perhaps there is 'intelligent material' of which UFOs are made that is so malleable that they are able to change state, allowing for interstellar travel."**[16]

The results of the Battelle studies of the Roswell wreckage bore fruit in the form of our own memory metal known today as Nitinol, an amalgam of nickel and titanium that displays shape-recovery properties similar to those described by Roswell witnesses. Nitinol "remembers" its original shape by returning to it after being crumpled. It possesses a high fatigue strength, is lightweight, is aluminum-like in color, and can

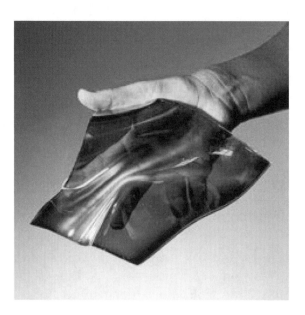

A piece of Nitinol: today's answer to "memory metal."

withstand a blowtorch. Perhaps covering its tracks, the Air Force let the U.S. Naval Ordnance Lab officially introduce Nitinol to the scientific community in the early 1960s. Today, Nitinol is used commercially in many products that require bendable properties. Variants of it are also currently being developed by NASA for potential aerospace travel. From Bragalia's reporting, it can be seen that Nitinol is not itself the Roswell debris. Rather, it is the result of attempts by Wright-Patterson, through Battelle, to simulate the properties of the Roswell debris, and exploit the obvious defense and technology value of "morphing" or "living" metals. This is perhaps why some UFOs are seen to morph! ET has mastered the "special process" that Generals Exon and Schulgen alluded to. Their craft is composed of manipulated material that has remarkable shape-recovery, memory, and other properties—properties that the Air Force recognized in 1947 and tried to duplicate through Battelle! It also could explain why so much of the Roswell wreckage debris, as described by the witnesses, was composed of memory metal.

In February 2005 renowned TV news anchorman and producer Peter Jennings stated on his ABC primetime special on UFOs, "The UFO Phenomenon: Seeing Is Believing," **"There were no credible Roswell witnesses."** To the contrary, we offered to provide more than a dozen credible witnesses to be interviewed, and one of them included *Apollo 14* astronaut Dr. Edgar Mitchell. Predictably, they had a pococurante attitude toward anyone who would dare state anything pro-UFO regarding Roswell. This merely confirmed to us that the press does not have the slightest inclination to report to the public the truth about UFOs. Their anti-UFO schooling has been more than thorough.

Another shining example of an exemplary eyewitness is retired Air Force Lt. Colonel Sydney Johnston. Through the kind efforts of Nathan Twining, Jr., the son of the famous general, we were introduced to Johnston, who had been a close friend to General Twining.[17] Among his impressive list of accomplishments, Johnston was an aeronautical engineer and pilot serving in the Army Air Corps during WWII starting in 1944. He flew 44 combat missions in a B-17 Flying Fortress Bomber originating from the United Kingdom into strategic German target areas.[18] He clearly impressed his superior officers, because he was called again for special flights providing close air support for U.S. fighters and bombers during the Korean War.[19] After retiring from the Air Force, he eventually found himself working at Northrop Aviation in Alamogordo, New Mexico at Holloman Air Force Base as a test engineer.[20] Wright-Patterson worked in close alignment with this desert ground zero (literally: Just to the north, the first atomic bomb was detonated). Moreover, whatever T-2 Intelligence was fortunate enough to take apart and put back together, rest assured most of the time it was additionally tested at Holloman.

One of their human guinea pigs with whom Sydney Johnson worked was John P. Stapp, who became famous as the "Rocket Man." Many of us have seen the old film footage of the man strapped into a rocket sled as it rifled across a barren desert, his face twisted and contorted like rubber as sudden G-forces were monitored and observed for their physiological effects. Few of us know that John Paul Stapp was an MD, PhD, and Air Force Flight Surgeon who earned the rank of colonel and pioneered the study of rapid acceleration and deceleration on the human body. The AeroMedical Laboratory and the Air Development Center at Wright Field originally conducted such tests in 1947 to test human tolerances in simulated aerial crashes.[21]

John "Rocket Man" Stapp.

Johnston also served as a pilot and aide-de-camp for Holloman base commanders General L.I. Davis, General Daniel E. Hooks, and General Douglas Branch. He also wrote the treatise on the Northrop SM-62 "Snark" cruise missile, which was the only surface-to-surface long-range guided missile from 1959 through 1961. Later, he was assigned to Kirtland AFB in Albuquerque to assist in a project to ascertain the effect of the Van Allen Radiation Belt on high-altitude rocket launches.[22]

Dr. Knox Missaps was a famous mathematician specializing in thermodynamics who had previously worked in metallurgy at Wright Field in 1947. It was there that he worked with T-3 branch, which was Research and Development under General LeMay at the Pentagon. During the 1950s, Missaps worked directly with base commander Hooks and Dr. Werner von Braun in Systems Command. Von Braun, the legendary German scientist, was almost single-handedly responsible for launching man into space.[23] The defeat of Germany after WWII led to the beginning of our space program, and these men were in the trenches whenever a rocket ascended out of sight or exploded on the launch pad. The Pentagon's dream was their conviction.

Now that we have set up the cast of players, we ask you now to envision this intriguing story....

It was in the late 1950s that Johnston, Missaps, and Hooks shared an office at Holloman. Missaps worked his desk between the other two. On one particular morning, Dr. Stapp made his daily stop for a cup of java and idle chat as Dr. Missaps joined them at Johnston's desk. However, this time he had more to offer than some extra sugar. All at once, Dr. Missaps removed something from his jacket pocket. It was roughly a foot square of **"aluminum-like metal, about 3/16 of an inch thick. The edge of it was not cut but separated like it had a rough edge, but straight."**

"What do you think this is?" queried Missaps with a touch of ebullience. Johnston described the object to us: **"The more you squeezed it, the more tension you could feel. It was flexible, but the four corners were straight, which suggested that it was stretched to its limit and broke. We couldn't break it or even scratch it in any way...yet it was flexible. We put a cigarette lighter to one end of it, and it immediately became the same temperature all over."**

"I had no idea what it was so I asked Missaps if he knew," added the befuddled Johnston. Missaps answered, "I'd like to know too."

Johnston asked, "Where'd you get this?"

"Go talk to the people over at Roswell," suggested Missaps.

"What are you going to do?" either Stapp or Johnston asked him. He rather shrugged his shoulders, and then Missaps said, **"I've got to talk to somebody up at Wright-Patterson about it."**

With that, Missaps grabbed the piece of metal and then went over to see General Hooks. After about 15 minutes, Missaps returned, and Johnston asked him again about the origin of the amorphous material and the prestidigitation he had just witnessed.

This is what Missaps related to him: **"A cowboy over at Roswell, who came over to Alamogordo to visit a friend or relative, presented him with this strange piece. The other man brought it to the base where his brother worked and brought it to my attention at Headquarters. He wanted to know what it was but I couldn't identify it myself. Wright-Patterson has a materials lab, which is where I am taking it."** Johnston added, **"As far as I know, Missaps took it to Wright-Patterson and left it there. That was the last I ever heard about it."**[24]

Like Missaps, Dr. Robert I. Sarbacher also worked for Research and Development under General LeMay in 1947. He was an expert in missile guidance systems and served on the R&D Board. Up until his death in 1986, he had described on a number of occasions the following: He was assigned to numerous classified projects and was in Washington, DC at the time of the Roswell incident.[25] He had heard about the recovery of the "ship and bodies" from New Mexico. Just before he died, he described a missed opportunity to observe the actual remains at Wright-Patterson. Unfortunately, he was committed to one of those classified assignments and could not leave Washington. Instead, he had to rely on a number of his colleagues for their firsthand observations. Sarbacher would keep silent as to what he was told for 30 years before relating their confidential testimony. Among other details, he revealed, **"Certain materials...were extremely light and tough...sufficient to withstand the tremendous deceleration and acceleration associated with their machinery."** Sarbacher would only add, **"The 'people'...were built different than we...."**[26]

As seems to be happening at an ever-increasing rate in our Roswell investigation, last year we lost another member of the 509th Bomb Group who was present on the Roswell base at the time of the 1947 incident: Sergeant William C. Ennis was a flight engineer with the 393rd Bomb Squadron at the RAAF. Hangar P-3 was the primary facility of the 393rd as well as the primary receiving facility for the wreckage and bodies recovered from the crash. It stood to reason that anyone who had worked in that hangar might know something, so we first interviewed Bill Ennis in 1992, and he just laughed everything off. After years of denial, we reconnected with him in 2008, and things were different. No longer laughing, Ennis confessed to not being truthful with us years before. He said that, yes, he was there when the wreckage came into the hangar and got a good look at it. **"It was a spaceship,"** he told us. **"And after all these years, I still don't know how that ship flew. *There was no engine!* Before I go, I want you fellas to promise me that you will find out for me [how it flew]. I'd like to know."**[27] Well, Bill, if you are up there listening or reading, we can now answer your question. The "engine" was all around you on the floor of the hangar in little pieces that you could wad up in your hand, and when you let it go, it would go back to its original shape! We're sorry that we just missed you.

CHAPTER 5

The Senator and the "Blue Room"

"I think at Wright-Patterson, if you could get into certain places, you'd find out what the Air Force and the government does know about UFOs. Reportedly, a spaceship landed. It was all hushed up. I called Curtis LeMay and said, 'General, I know we have a room at Wright-Patterson where you put all this secret stuff. Can I go in there?' I've never heard General LeMay get mad, but he got madder than hell at me, cussed me out, and said, 'Don't ever ask me that question again!'"

—Senator Barry M. Goldwater on CNN's *Larry King Show*, October 1, 1994

Senator Barry Goldwater is probably best remembered as the 1964 Republican candidate for president of the United States who was in the wrong place at the wrong time when a tidal wave of sympathy for a recently assassinated president swept over him and his party, and deposited the Democratic candidate, Lyndon B. Johnson, into the presidency with a landslide victory. For Republicans everywhere, it was a "Year of the Blue Snow." It is hard to believe that out of the rubble of that election, its losing standard-bearer, Senator Barry M. Goldwater of Arizona, would lead a successful, conservative transformation of his party that lasts to this very day.

First elected to the U.S. Senate in 1952 at the age of 43 during Eisenhower's presidency, Senator Goldwater served under five presidents, retiring in 1987 under Jimmy Carter. Goldwater's senate seat has been occupied ever since by Arizona Senator John McCain. During his Senate tenure, Goldwater served on a number of important committees: the Armed Services Committee, the Aeronautical and Space Sciences Committee, the Strategic Nuclear Forces Committee (Chair), the Tactical Warfare Committee (Chair), the Communications and Transportation Committee (Chair), the Indian Affairs Committee, and in 1981 he became the Chairman of the Senate Intelligence Committee under President Reagan. As if that wasn't enough, Goldwater also served his country by joining the Army Air Corps when America entered World War II in 1941. By the end of the war, he had become a command pilot, having flown in the European Theater and the India/China/Burma Theater.[1] He remained in the Air Force Reserve after the war and founded the Arizona Air National Guard. He was also a leading proponent of creating the United States Air Force Academy in Colorado Springs.[2] Goldwater ended his military service with retirement on January 1, 1969, with two stars on his shoulder—the rank of major general in the U.S. Air Force Reserve. In his spare time, he created his own amateur radio station, which became part of the Military Affiliate Radio System (MARS) and, oh yes, he appeared on the cover of *Time* magazine on June 12, 1964. He died on May 29, 1998, at the age of 89.

Although he says he never saw one, the soft-spoken and respected senator from Arizona had a longstanding interest in the subject of UFOs.[3] He wisely kept this interest pretty much to himself and hidden from public knowledge as best he could until after he retired from public life in 1987. It is axiomatic even today that, for public officials, professional people, as well as a host of others who depend upon their "credibility" for their livelihoods and stations in life, the subject of UFOs is poison. For these people, to let it be known that one had an interest in UFOs or may have experienced a sighting is to lose credibility in the public's mind and eventually maybe one's job. The reader need look no further back than to the 2008 Democratic presidential primary for a high-profile example: When it got out in a book written by actress Shirley MacLaine that Ohio congressman and presidential candidate Dennis Kucinich had had a dramatic, close-encounter sighting of a triangular-shaped UFO in the 1980s while visiting the actress at her home in Washington State, his "credibility" for higher office plummeted to the low single-digits. His alleged sighting then seemed to follow him around wherever he went and in every interview he did, and, although he tried to make a joke of it, he quickly dropped out of the race. He is also no longer a congressman. This thinking is also the reason that the so-called "disclosure projects" that have come and gone throughout the years without disclosure will continue to go nowhere. With all of the problems facing the country and the world that require the attention and energies of whoever is president, the subject of UFOs is at the bottom of the list. Without a public mandate for UFO disclosure, it won't happen. Equally important is the knowledge that if it ever got out that an administration was expending any time or resources on UFOs, that administration would know with certainty that it would not only become the butt of jokes on *The Daily Show* with Jon Stewart, but it would also be booted out of office in the next election.

Considering his station in life, as a sitting U.S. senator and a member or chair of a number of senatorial committees dealing with military matters, as well as being an Air Force general himself, Goldwater traveled in and was accepted in the highest government and military circles. In his 30-year senate career, which occurred in two phases, separated by his run for the presidency, Goldwater developed many friends both in government and the military. One of these was another Air Force general by the name of William "Butch" Blanchard, whom Goldwater described as a "very close friend."[4] Back in 1947, then-Colonel Blanchard had been the commanding officer of the 509th Bomb Group and the Roswell Army Air Field when the Roswell Incident occurred. By the mid-1960s, Blanchard had become a four-star general and the vice chief of staff of the Air Force at the Pentagon in Washington, DC. He unfortunately died suddenly of a massive heart attack at his desk in the Pentagon in 1966 at age 50. There is no doubt it was Blanchard from whom Goldwater learned about Roswell and the "certain places" at Wright-Patterson where UFO "artifacts" were stored.

Another friend of Goldwater's was fellow Air Force General Curtis "Bombs Away" LeMay who, as commander of the 20th Air Force in the Pacific during World War II, was known for his fire-bombing of Japan prior to the dropping of the atomic bombs that ended the war. He is perhaps best remembered as the charismatic, cigar-chomping leader of "SAC," the Strategic Air Command (1948–57). (In a 1955 major motion picture of the same name, his character was played by actor Frank Lovejoy.) LeMay retired from the Air Force as a "four star" as well as its chief of staff (1961–65). He briefly entered world politics when he ran unsuccessfully for vice president of the United States as a third-party candidate on the American Independent Party ticket with George Wallace in the turbulent year of 1968. He died in 1990 at age 83.

Given his "longtime interest in UFOs" and who his "friends in high places" were, Senator Goldwater decided to make his move on the "Blue Room" sometime in the 1963–65 time frame, according to the best available evidence,[5] during a stopover at Wright-Patterson AFB in conjunction with other official duties for one of his Senate committees.[6] And what better way to cut red tape and get right to it than to call up his old friend, General Curtis LeMay, who just happened to be the Air Force's chief of staff at the time? Goldwater had to be taken aback—way aback—at the harsh tone of LeMay's response to a sitting U.S. Senator, a fellow Air Force General, and a friend as well. In telling this story on several occasions, Goldwater has used different words to describe LeMay's rebuff. In addition to the response described in the opening paragraph of this chapter, LeMay was also said to have reprimanded

General Curtis LeMay.

Goldwater with, **"Hell no! And, not only *no*, but if you ask me again, I'll have you court-marshaled!"** Or, **"Hell no! I can't go. You can't go. And don't ever ask me again!"**[7] Whichever it was, Goldwater, being a circumspect, respectful, and gracious man, never bothered LeMay about it again, and finally gave up his quest to find out what was behind the blue door. In a 1981 letter to researcher Lee Graham, Goldwater laments his fate on the matter: **"[I] have long ago given up acquiring access to the so-called 'Blue Room' at Wright-Patterson, as I have had one long string of denials from chief after chief. So I have given up.... This thing has gotten so highly classified, it is just impossible to get anything on it."**[8] Elsewhere, Goldwater further stated his conclusions that the artifacts in the "Blue Room" were classified above top secret[9] and that he did not know who controlled what was in—and who got to go into—the "Blue Room."[10]

The "Blue Room" at Wright-Patterson was said to be where alien "artifacts," including "little bodies," were stored.

Despite Senator Goldwater's discretion, word eventually got out regarding the "Blue Room" and his aborted attempts to gain its secrets. Leonard Stringfield, living in Cincinnati, heard the rumors emanating from Wright-Patterson and in 1974 exchanged letters with Senator Goldwater regarding them. In his 1977 book, *Situation Red: The UFO Siege*, Stringfield made perhaps the first public mention of Senator Goldwater's story and, in a series of eight, limited-circulation monographs published during the 1978–94 time period, Stringfield mentions the story in several of his "updates." For instance, in a 1979 monograph, Stringfield simply mentions Goldwater's failed attempt to get into a "room" at Wright-Patterson where the "information" was stored.[11] No further details were given, and the phrase "Blue Room" was not used. It was also not used in a 1980 follow-up monograph, wherein Stringfield expanded the Goldwater story to include several letters he had received from private researchers. Coincidentally, they were some of the same letters described in this chapter. One very interesting sidebar was brought to light, however, that has not been mentioned elsewhere to our knowledge: Stringfield's source was a friend of his son, whom Stringfield identified only as "JK." In a "long discussion" in 1978, according to Stringfield, JK revealed to him that he had been stationed at Wright-Patterson when Goldwater visited the base hoping, among other things, to see the UFO material stored there. According to JK, when word got around that Goldwater had been turned down by General LeMay, "This refusal caused quite a fiasco on the base."[12]

The decade of the 1980s witnessed the emergence of the name "Roswell" in the public's consciousness with the airing of several TV shows concerning the alleged crash. Shows such as the popular *In Search Of* with host Leonard Nimoy, *Unsolved Mysteries* with host Robert Stack, and an HBO special, *UFOs—What's Happening?*, all featured segments about Roswell. The decade also gave us the first book about the Roswell crash, the title of which has become the iconic reference for the 1947 event—*The Roswell Incident*, in 1980. More pertinent for our purposes in this chapter, that book devotes two pages to the Goldwater story. Of note is the fact that the phrase "Blue Room" is used in conjunction with the story for the first time in a public venue to describe the repository of UFO artifacts at Wright-Patterson.[13] When asked to comment by a private researcher on the Wright-Patterson account described in *The Roswell Incident*, Senator Goldwater responded that it was "essentially correct."[14] As a result of the burgeoning attention being given to the case and to his role in its unfolding narrative, in 1988 Goldwater made his first public appearance to discuss it on Larry King's radio show. By the decade's end, Goldwater was averaging 100 or more phone calls a year asking for more information and urging him to look into the Roswell case and the "Blue Room."[15]

U.S. Senator Barry Goldwater, also an Air Force Reserve
Major General, attempted to enter the "Blue Room."

In March of 2012 the personal letters of Barry Goldwater were
made available to the public by the Arizona State University Historical
Foundation. Included among them are more than a hundred letters concerning UFOs, and among these are a number that deal with the notion
of a location where UFO-crash artifacts might be stored and Goldwater's
attempt to find it at Wright-Patterson. UFO researcher Grant Cameron
has done perhaps the most comprehensive job of making sense of and
cataloging these letters on his "Presidential UFO" Internet site.[16] The
Goldwater "UFO letters" cover a 30-year period from 1966 to 1996
(Goldwater suffered a stroke in 1996, which ended his letter writing,
and he died three years later), and are nicely summarized sequentially
by the date of the letter. They reflect a man who was clearly frustrated
and conflicted about what he felt he could tell people on the subject of
UFOs and his search for UFO artifacts at Wright-Patterson. He tried to
be responsive to the people who wrote to him while observing his patri-
otic duty not to give away any national secrets. Regarding the subject of
UFOs in general, his position was that he didn't know any more than
the "man on the street," and that the subject was above top secret (thus
validating a similar statement made in 1950 by Canadian government

official Wilbert Smith).[17] In the mid-1970s, with the election of President Jimmy Carter, Goldwater started closing his letters with the hope that full disclosure regarding UFOs was just around the corner. This was no doubt based on the (false, as it turned out) belief that the new president would fulfill his campaign promise to release "unsettling disclosures" regarding UFOs.

After his assumption of the chair of the Senate Intelligence Committee concomitant with the election of President Ronald Reagan in 1980, Goldwater's responses to those inquiring about UFOs and his Wright-Patterson experience changed subtly but enough to suggest that he may have finally been briefed on these matters. In one letter he states that, although he did not get to see the "material," he didn't blame the Air Force for preventing him: **"I think it should be kept secret."**[18] That response begs the question: How would the senator know that something should be kept secret if he didn't know what that something was? Then, in a May 1981 letter he states that the reason he went to Wright-Patterson that day "...was not to see any remains, because **I don't know of any UFO that supposedly crashed."**[19] He must have forgotten about his old, "very close friend" General Blanchard. This remarkable statement was nothing short of a bold-face lie, which he would later correct in his interviews with Larry King. Finally, in a July 15, 1981, letter to a fellow ham operator on his radio network, Goldwater edges toward anger in a response to a question of whether the details of his attempt to gain entrance to the "Blue Room" at Wright-Patterson as recounted in *The Roswell Incident* were true or not: **"[T]hey are partially true, but not completely. I can't give you any other answer than that, so *please don't push it*"**[20] (authors' emphasis). In other words, "I know a lot more, but I can't tell you, and I don't want to have to lie about it." We've all been there at one time or another. Fortunately for us, after he retired, Goldwater had the honesty and courage to publicly correct his "Blue Room" story. The posthumous release of his personal letters on the matter, however, added little of substance to what we already knew.

The first Freedom of Information Act (FOIA) requests seeking information from the Air Force about the "Blue Room" were filed shortly after publication of *The Roswell Incident* in 1980. These were directed to the Foreign Technology Division (FTD) at Wright-Patterson. If a "Blue Room" ever existed, it would have been located somewhere within FTD, which was the intelligence entity at Wright-Patt. At the time of the Roswell events in 1947, it was known as T-2 (Intelligence), and it has undergone several name changes since then. In answer to his December 1980 FOIA request, William Moore, coauthor of *The Roswell Incident*, received a response from FTD that no information or records could be found regarding a "Project Blue Room."[21] A year later in 1982, researcher Lee Graham received a similar response from FTD that they were unable to locate "documents, film or any information about the [Blue Room]." Graham was sent on his way with the boiler-plate suggestion to contact the National Archives for further information. Curiously, the response to Graham also included a statement that **"Senator Barry Goldwater had visited FTD earlier that year and received a technology update briefing!"**[22] A decade later, researcher Brian Parks, who was a friend of William Moore's and had access to some of his files, came across an archival record card that referenced a 35 MM film taken inside the "Blue Room" at Wright-Patterson in 1955.[23] Parks was ultimately advised to direct his FOIA request for information about the film to the Department of Defense's film archival facility located at Norton AFB in California through the Air Force's Director of Information Management located at Scott AFB in Illinois. In an October 9, 1991, response to Parks, the Air Force confirmed the existence of the film by noting that it had a specific ID Number and a Project Number, and was titled **"Blue Room, Wright Patterson AFB OH, 1955."** The response also stated that the film had been destroyed on "9 September 1965."[24] (NOTE: This would have right around the time that Senator Goldwater was knocking on the "Blue Room" door at Wright-Patterson.) Coincidence?

In April of 2012, specifically citing the 35 MM "Blue Room" film record and the response by Brian Parks to his FOIA request in 1991, researcher Anthony Bragalia submitted a FOIA request of his own to the Air Force for information relating to the "Blue Room" and/or the 35 MM film of it. It worked. Less than a month later, Bragalia received a short but remarkable, and perhaps unwitting (as noted by Bragalia) reply from the FOIA analyst at Wright-Patterson AFB: **"[T]he office of record for BLUE ROOM is NASIC—the National Air and Space Intelligence Center** [also located at Wright-Patterson]."[25] Bragalia's

FOIA request was then forwarded to NASIC for a direct response. As it turns out, not surprisingly, NASIC is the immediate successor of the previously mentioned FTD, the very place where UFO wreckage, bodies, and artifacts have been rumored for years to have been stored and analyzed! NASIC's current mission, according to Bragalia's research, is **"to gather and analyze specialized global intelligence on current threats from the air and space realms."**[26] A few days later, Bragalia received an equally remarkable—if not shameless—response from the NASIC FOIA manager at Wright-Patterson. Coming full circle, thus proving that the runaround is indeed round, Bragalia received the same perfunctory "no records" response to his request that William Moore had received to his FOIA request 30 years earlier. The "stone wall" was obviously back up—but too late! As matters stand at this writing, Bragalia has appealed this response as being "non-responsive" and has promised to consider litigation if he is not satisfied with the response to his appeal.

Perhaps our only peek inside the "Blue Room" comes to us from the late Leonard Stringfield. In a 1991 update of his crashed-UFO series of monographs, Stringfield reprinted a secondhand account of such a visit as told to him by a high-ranking Army officer.[27] In it, Stringfield referred to the "Blue Room" as the "Inner Sanctum," a place that was **"a veritable museum holding the artifacts of crashed saucers and the retrieved cadavers from Roswell"**[28] (original emphasis). The following is an abridged version of the Army officer's account, as told to him by his friend. As was his usual practice at the time to protect his sources, Stringfield withheld the names of both the Army officer and his friend.

> **In 1955, my friend was working as a scientific research analyst in Texas, working on radar equipment. One evening at home, an MP pulled up to his house and informed my friend that he had to accompany him. He was taken to a local AFB and held in a secure area with others involved in various fields of research. The first order of business was the signing of Secrecy Non-Disclosure papers. Then they were frisked and their pockets emptied into marked envelopes. They were then led to an aircraft and seated along**

with armed guards wearing uniforms with no ID labels or identifiable insignias. The flight lasted several hours, and it was dark when they landed. They were led blindfolded from the plane, and after a short walk they stopped. They then heard a hangar door brought down behind them and were told to remove their blindfolds. At this point, my friend's voice always quivered when he tells me the story.

When they removed their blindfolds, they were inside a converted aircraft hangar—*the floor and walls were entirely painted blue*. Around the room were tables, shelves, and fixtures holding thousands of artifacts, none of which were immediately recognizable. They were told that they were to study each object and determine its purpose, operating parameters, and whether or not it could be duplicated. Looking back, he now recognizes many things, such as lasers, integrated circuits, printed circuit boards of now commonplace design (including microprocessors and surface-mount components, etc.). When someone finally asked where the artifacts came from, they were led to a small, locked room that they had heretofore not seen and shown four large aquariums filled with a pink solution. Each contained a small body with gray skin, oversized cranium, huge eyes, and no hair. In the back of this room were pieces of metal, ranging from little slivers to very large twisted chunks. The curator then related the story of the Roswell crash.

When they had been debriefed days later, they were told that they could return anytime to discuss the objects [within certain specified parameters]. A year or so ago [this would have been around 1990], my friend contacted the group and asked if the offer was still good. He was told that indeed it was, *and that the collection had grown tremendously* [authors' emphasis].[29]

What had specifically inspired Goldwater's interest in UFOs no doubt stemmed from his friendship with "Butch" Blanchard. Unfortunately for us and for history, Goldwater was never so vocal on details. Yet he clearly had inside information about the Blue Room. It has always been surmised that there was a connection to Project Blue Book, but no one at Blue Book ever gave the slightest indication that they knew the truth, or were aware that physical evidence existed (see Chapter 19). The descriptions of the Blue Room indicate that it was where the physical UFO evidence was kept. Why else would a good friend in the person of Air Force General Curtis LeMay threaten Goldwater, as was claimed? Even if it merely housed relevant UFO *documents* that have since "disappeared," the alleged, mysterious disappearance of documents requested by the GAO in 1993 concerning Roswell becomes a worn cliché. Lest we forget that the man in charge of the Roswell cover-up, Air Force General Hoyt Vandenberg, in 1948 ordered the final report of Project Sign—which concluded that UFOs were real and probably represented

General Hoyt Vandenberg.

extraterrestrial craft—be burned. All of which smacks of flushing the incriminating evidence down the toilet.

Though he never got to look inside the Blue Room, we can thank Barry Goldwater for bringing the notion of such a location to the public consciousness. When a well-respected person of his stature speaks of something, whatever that *something* is, it is immediately accorded a credibility factor that might not be obtained otherwise. Because of Barry Goldwater's moment of benign effrontery that day at Wright-Patterson, and the subsequent efforts of researchers dedicated to getting the truth, there can be little doubt now that there still exists somewhere a most secret room in the most secret building, in the most secret base in the U.S. Air Force, wherein lies...well, as Barry Goldwater stated so eloquently, **"I'm a firm believer that there is something that can fly around here that the Wright brothers didn't have anything to do with."**[30]

CHAPTER 6

Aliens on Ice?

"You mean we got a 'Man from Mars?' On-ice, Buddy...On-ice!"
—The Thing from Another World

For decades, reports have suggested that the material wreckage recovered by the officers and men from Roswell Army Airfield in early July of 1947 went to Wright Field (later Wright-Patterson Air Force Base) in Dayton, Ohio. Pilots allegedly flew plane-loads of wreckage there from a crashed flying saucer on a number of flights emanating from Roswell, including two special, unscheduled flights that were carried out with the utmost secrecy. Two flights that were said to have transported *something else*. After all, the logical extension of the crashed-disc theory was that the craft also contained a flight crew. An FBI document dated July 8, 1947, refers to the very first flight out of Roswell carrying wreckage to Wright Field—the flight the 8th Air Force commander in Fort Worth, Texas, General Roger M. Ramey, dramatically "cancelled" for the benefit of the press that same day in order to kill the burgeoning Roswell crash story.[1] It states that the *"disc" and balloon* (contrary to General Ramey's proclamation to the press) *were being flown to Wright Field by special transport for examination.*[2] The second untruth told by Ramey that day was not something that he said, but rather something that he did not say *something else* that he and the news releases about the incident dared not disclose: that strange *little bodies* were also found among the wreckage.

It should be noted that in 1947 Lieutenant General Nathan F. Twining was the commanding officer of the Air Materiel Command at Wright-Patterson, which controlled the Air Force's intelligence functions. Known as "T-2 Intelligence" at that time, it later became the Air Technical Intelligence Center (ATIC) in 1951, then the Foreign Technology Division (FTD) in 1961, and today it is known as the National Air & Space Intelligence Center (NASIC). It was this military organization that was primarily responsible for analyzing any and all foreign, new, or unknown aerial technology that came into the possession of the United States by whatever means. After World War II, it was logically assumed that most such material devices would be of Russian origin.

Numerous flights had originated either from Wright Field to retrieve wreckage from the Roswell crash or, as in the case of Captain Oliver W. "Pappy" Henderson, from the airbase in Roswell. In utmost secrecy, Henderson piloted a plane filled with wreckage and *something else* non-stop directly from Roswell Army Air Field to Wright (Army Air) Field, as it was then called, on July 8, 1947, which was the second day of the recovery operation taking place in the New Mexico desert. He kept this special flight a secret from everyone, including his wife, Sappho, for years, until the early 1980s, when he saw the Roswell story featured on the cover of a supermarket tabloid and figured that, if the story was out in the public domain, it was all right for him to talk about it.[3]

Henderson, who passed away in 1986, told his wife that he had wanted to tell her about it for years. He told her that he knew flying saucers were real because he had flown a planeload of such wreckage to Wright Field back in the 1940s. He didn't tell her much about it except that the debris was strange. And, according to Sappho, he never told her about the *something else*—the little bodies—he had transported in addition to the wreckage. The flight's destination had been Dayton, Ohio, and then back to Roswell again in a C-54 *Skymaster* transport plane. Henderson was a member of the First Air Transport Unit, known as the "Green Hornets," which was assigned to Roswell Army Air Field at the time. He would go on to tell his wife that it was a routine flight except

Captain Oliver "Pappy Henderson told close friends and
family that he flew strange wreckage and "little creatures"
from Roswell to Wright Field in early July 1947.

for its high classification status.[4] Our investigation has been able to identify and locate one of the crew members on this flight: Tech Sergeant
David Ackroyd. His widow, when asked whether her husband had ever
discussed this flight with her, responded in the affirmative: "All I remember about it is that this one day during this [UFO] thing he came
home early in a big rush and told me, '**I need to get some things. I have
to go on a special flight with Pappy back east. I'll be home in a day
or two.**' That was all he said."[5] Unfortunately, we have been unable to
locate any other crew members on this flight, but given the fact that,
according to Ackroyd's wife, her husband's flight took place during the
time frame of the Roswell recovery, there is no doubt that it was Oliver
"Pappy" Henderson's flight to Wright-Patterson on July 8, 1947.

Pappy kept the secret as long as he thought it was required of him,
but once some of the preliminary information was published, he started
to open up to his friends as well as his wife. In 1982, at a reunion of
his B-17 flight crew from World War II, the subject of Roswell came up

when he told them of piloting the wreckage of the spacecraft. There, at the reunion, he described how he flew the very aircraft they had been talking about from Roswell to Wright Field. He also mentioned for the first time the little humanoid bodies he observed lying on the hangar floor before his flight departed.[6] A former World War II bomber crew member by the name of Vere McCarty was also in attendance at the reunion. In a letter written in 1989, he recalled that Henderson was extremely serious in recounting his story for them that night, after which the discussion went on to other UFO sightings. **"The captain made comments about flying saucers on other occasions,"** he said, **"always telling his listeners that he believed in them because so many other pilots reported seeing them. He never broke his silence about his own role until the last few years before he died."**[7]

Sappho remembered that, sometime after the incident when they were still living in Roswell, her husband had been outside with their daughter Mary Katherine staring up into the night sky. When asked by his daughter what he was doing, he told her, **"Looking for flying saucers. They're real, you know."**[8] Pappy was able to tell his daughter that fact with a certainty that few others possessed. The more amazing part of Henderson's reasoning at the time—why he *knew* they were real— had yet to be told.

Corroboration of the Henderson story comes from a former B-29 pilot from WWII stationed in Amarillo, Texas, in the summer of 1947: Captain Joseph Toth. He was sent to Wright Field at the time of the Roswell incident to undergo a complete physical exam to determine whether he could maintain his flight status. While waiting for medical tests, he strolled outside for a quick smoke and saw that a C-54 transport plane had just arrived and taxied up close to the base hospital, where a hasty unloading then took place. Toth immediately noticed men removing and carrying several stretchers from the hold of the aircraft with bodies of short, large-headed corpses and quickly taking them into the building. Later, he remembered hearing the excited scuttlebutt back in Amarillo about the activity that had taken place over in Roswell, and he especially recalled that much of the talk at the Wright-Patterson base that day was about what had arrived in the C-54 that he had fortuitously observed.[9]

When asked if the bodies recovered from the crash at Roswell went to Wright Field, Brigadier General Arthur Exon said, **"That's my** information. **But one of them went to a mortuary outfit...I think at that time it was [Lowry Air Force Base] in Denver. But the strongest information was that they were brought to Wright-Patt.**"[10] General Exon had been a lieutenant colonel and an administration student at Wright-Patt at the time of the Roswell incident, and in the mid-1960s became the base's commanding officer.

General Exon was not alone in his beliefs that the bodies had been brought to Dayton. Former First Lieutenant Raymond A. Madson said that he and his wife, who both worked at Wright-Patterson, had heard rumors of bodies stored there.[11] And Norma Gardner, an employee at the military facility until 1959 when she had to retire due to health reasons, would often hint to friends that she knew more about the "flying saucer situation" than the government was saying or was comfortable with her knowing about. A typist with top security clearance, she had been given the duty of logging in all UFO-related material, which included parts of the interior of a spacecraft that had been brought to the base prior to her employment there. Everything had to be photographed and tagged and labeled, and all the documentation had to be filed by someone. Norma Gardner had that task.[12] At one point, she saw two bodies as they were being moved from one location to another. The bodies had been preserved in some kind of **chemical solution**. She said that they were small, about 4 feet tall, but with large heads and slanted eyes, and **"obviously were not human."** In the course of her duties, she also typed the autopsy reports of the remains. All of this, according to her, was done while she was employed at Wright-Patterson.[13] Norma Gardner died shortly after recounting her story, which would in effect make it the equivalent of a "deathbed confession." Such statements are accorded a special status in "truth-telling" in courts of law throughout the land.

Support for Norma Gardner's reports regarding alleged alien autopsies came some years later via Leonard Stringfield. As we've mentioned, he developed numerous contacts with military and civilian personnel who were or had been employed at Wright-Patterson Air Force Base, or had contact with the base in some form or other. One of these was a doctor described by Stringfield as his "prime medical contact" for information regarding the alien bodies recovered from Roswell. From this source, Stringfield received detailed descriptions of the body structure of the recovered crash victims.[14] Given all of the medical information at his disposal, Stringfield felt that he had enough data to try to illustrate how the Roswell aliens must have looked morphologically. This led to several attempts by Stringfield at line-sketching an alien, each of which was submitted to his medical source and returned to him with comments as to its accuracy. In 1978, after many tries, he was finally able to put together a composite sketch that was accepted by his medical source as being an accurate depiction of an alien entity that had crashed at Roswell and was autopsied at Wright-Patterson.[15]

A former Air Force major by the name of Truman Weaver provided additional information. He displayed to researchers a letter from a friend by the name of Robert Thompson who was a technician at Wright-Patterson in the early 1950s and claimed to have worked across the alley from the building where the bodies were kept. Thompson said by 1953 there were 13 of them stored in a room on the third floor there. He claimed that on some days a strong odor drifted across the alley, and when he asked about it he was told that it was embalming fluid. According to Thompson, **"This was before air conditioning was installed, and with the windows open I could smell the strong odor of formaldehyde. It was sickening."**[16] The strong smell of formaldehyde at Wright-Patterson isn't enough to suggest that alien bodies—or bodies of any kind—were there at all. Thompson went on, however, explaining that his boss, a man named McAdams, showed him a report that confirmed the rumors that there were bodies and a captured saucer being stored at Wright-Patterson. The next day, according to Thompson, the paper report was taken from McAdams, and officials later denied that it even existed.[17] In April 1979, Thompson wrote Stringfield, who had received the story from Richard Hall, then the editor of the *MUFON UFO Journal*, confirming the original story but with a notable addendum: **"The building number [where the bodies were stored] was 18F, 3rd floor. The 13 bodies and 2 saucers are at a small air base [Langley Air Force Base] at Hampton Roads, Virginia, if they have not been moved again."**[18]

John G. Tiffany reported that his father was stationed at Wright Field in 1947 and that his unit, as part of their assignment, supported the 509th Bomb Group in Roswell. According to Tiffany, his father, along with his crew, had been flown to a "destination in the southwest." There they picked up strange, metallic debris and a large cylinder that reminded him of a "giant thermos bottle" for transport back to Wright Field. Tiffany was told by his father that the metal was very lightweight but very tough. It was smooth, had a "glass-like" surface, and everything that the flight crew had attempted to deform it—mark it, bend it, or break it—failed. But what bothered the airmen most was the unusual cylinder and its unknown contents. Tiffany wasn't sure if his father had actually seen anything resembling bodies firsthand, but he did state that **"two of the corpses were intact,"** which suggests that he had. After the flight, the crew started to experience a strange sensation—a feeling that they were somehow "contaminated." According to Tiffany, "They couldn't get over **[the feeling of] handling something that foreign."**[19]

Once they arrived at Wright Field, everything was off-loaded, including the giant, thermos-like capsule. The entire cargo was loaded into

Building 18F at Wright-Patterson contained "cold-storage rooms" fom which pungent, formaldehyde-like smells would emanate on warm, summer days.

trucks, and once the vehicles departed, the flight crew was debriefed by a high-ranking official who told them that the just-completed flight never took place.[20] Was this the second body-flight, which originated as a large wooden crate in Roswell, then was flown to Fort Worth Army Air Field, Texas, on July 9, 1947, under armed guard in the bomb bay of a B-29 named the *Straight Flush*? The large, hermetically sealed, thermos-like device aboard Tiffany's aircraft suggests that something very out of the ordinary, something that was possibly epidemiologically harmful to humans—or simply smelled bad—was being transported (recall the crew members' strange feelings after the flight). Tiffany's father told him that they picked up the capsule in *Texas!*[21]

A similar feeling of uneasiness regarding the bodies also overcame the aforementioned Captain Oliver "Pappy" Henderson when he told a close friend and fellow military officer, Dr. John Kromschroeder, about them. According to Kromschroeder, he and Henderson were sharing stories while on a fishing trip, and after a few hours Henderson mentioned that he had seen the bodies of alien visitors and the remains of their craft. Kromschroeder said that Henderson was nervous about it. "He was clearly **uncomfortable talking about it**."[22] Henderson, according to Kromschroeder, did not like being around the dead or injured and wanted to get away from them as quickly as he could. Kromschroeder quoted Henderson as saying, "I couldn't really look at them." But he did see enough to say that **they were "kinda little guys."**[23] He also told Kromschroeder that the bodies had been put into the deep freeze and that, as late as 1986, he thought that they were still at Wright-Patterson Air Force Base.[24] Naturally Kromschroeder wanted to know more about it, but Henderson would only repeat the descriptions (gray little men with big heads, slanted eyes, and tiny mouths) and then ended the conversation with **"I just can't talk about it."**[25]

Helen Wachter said that she had been a nursing student at a school in Dayton, Ohio, in the summer of 1947. According to her, she was visiting a friend who had just given birth. While Wachter was in their small studio apartment, the husband of the new mother returned home in an agitated state. He dragged his wife into the single bedroom and told her, in a voice that could be easily overheard, that something of a top-secret nature had happened at the base that day. Bodies of "alien creatures" had arrived at the base—four of them. He knew because he had been one of the guards posted when the plane arrived with them. That was all that was said about it: Four bodies had come onto the base one day during the summer of 1947.[26]

Could one of the other guards posted that day have been a famous stage, screen, and recording star from the 1940s, 1950s, and 1960s? Hard to believe, we know, but...

An interesting story of a similar nature involving famed stage, screen, and recording star Gordon MacRae (*Oklahoma!*, *Carousel*) comes to us from his former wife, actress Sheila MacRae (*The HoneyMooners*, *Petticoat Junction*). According to her, back in the 1940s her former husband was an armed security guard who had stood guard over a wooden pallet at Wright-Patterson AFB. On the pallet was something that was completely covered by a canvas tarpaulin. Told not to let anyone near the pallet and not to look under the tarp himself, MacRae complied with the first part of the order but not the second. When his chance arrived, he peeled back the tarp to receive the shock of his young life—for on the pallet lay small, large-headed creatures from another world!

His story was told publicly on a late-night TV talk show by Sheila MacRae shortly after Gordon passed away in 1986. In a chance meeting following a stage show in New York City a few years ago, respected UFO researcher Peter Robbins heard the story directly from Sheila MacRae herself.[27] In 2010, with Robbins's help, we attempted to arrange an interview with Sheila MacRae to confirm, deny, or learn additional details of the story as described to us. We also wanted to find out just how it was that her former husband came to view the aliens at Wright-Patterson, as we knew that Gordon MacRae had been in the Air Corps during World War II, but by 1947 he was already on the Broadway stage and presumably a full-fledged civilian citizen. These questions remain unanswered. After an initial period of apparent cooperation, the MacRae family stopped communicating with us, and the interview with their mother never took place. The family knew of the story about their iconic father and have not denied its veracity, but they will no longer discuss it. We have since learned that Gordon MacRae may have recounted the episode himself on a TV talk show, perhaps *The Mike Douglas Show*, in the 1970s. His widow, Sheila, is still living but is understandably no longer available to us for an interview.[28]

In 1957 a military photographer confided to his son that he was stationed at Wright Field in 1947, where he was assigned to the base photo lab. One day, an officer instructed him and another camera man to follow him after grabbing two 16-millimeter cameras. They were led to a heavily guarded hangar, stopped briefly outside, and then allowed to enter. Inside, the two men observed a heavily damaged circular craft, and the floor covered with wreckage of a similar metal, all of which were on top of a canvas tarpaulin. The officer directed them to immediately start filming the unknown craft and debris. Upon completion, they were taken to the back of the building where a refrigeration unit was housed. Inside the unit was a "museum case" containing the remains of two small, thin, grayish creatures with "large eyes." One was notably severely injured, and the other body was apparently not. A guard was told to open the case so that the two men and their cameras could get a clear view. Beyond the shock of witnessing the two bodies was the strong odor. "[It was like] the smell **of dead fish**," added the photographer to his son. Both men's cameras were confiscated and they were warned of the consequences of ever repeating what they had just filmed. The man's son commented that, "My father was a true patriot and a very religious man"[29]—ideals that must have been put to the test on that fateful day!

The late reporter Carl Day, a newsman with the FOX affiliate in Dayton, interviewed two MPs in May 1991. They both described **"frozen bodies, wreckage, and a ship"** that were kept in Building 21, which they guarded. All of which they said had been transported to the base (Wright-Patterson) on planes many years before.[30]

UFO researcher Thomas Blann interviewed a retired Wright-Patterson colonel off the record who said, "In the earlier years, they had taken some bodies to this base, but later on, it depended where they were found. They had a hell of a time setting up **procedures for this operation** [most likely "Operation Blue Fly" and/or "Project Moon Dust"], **as well as getting the craft out of the area without being observed. Usually, this was done at nighttime."**[31]

Yanic Ritger (a pseudonym) retired from the military on a medical pension. During World War II, he had served as a driver for none other than General George S. Patton. After his service, he worked for General Electric but was forced to go on permanent leave due to radiation exposure—an exposure that was suffered in a most unusual circumstance.

In the early 1950s Ritger was employed at Wright-Patterson AFB in a civilian capacity and lived in Dayton during that tenure. His wife (now deceased) remembered how he was on special assignment at the base, which lasted for an entire week. He was unable to give her any details about his secret work. It was only many years later that he related any specifics about the missing week to his daughter. Like so many others sworn to perform clandestine work for the government, Ritger feared the loss of his medical pension, which he depended upon for his special care. The following is the account he reluctantly expressed to his daughter.[32]

As his work had never required on other occasions, this job involved the installation of a nuclear device located on a secret underground level. In fact, everything about the job was strange. He and a coworker were blindfolded, driven to an unknown destination, taken into a building, and placed into what obviously (to them) was an elevator shaft, which then descended to their worksite. Their eye coverings were then pulled away, and guards escorted the two men into another chamber. What then immediately became evident to them was the cold temperature, and—worse—the repugnant smell. One of the supervisors there gave them detailed instructions for the task at hand. But something remained uncomfortable about the very room in which the job was taking place. For there, out of the corner of Ritger's eye, he witnessed a sight he had only heard about in rumors. At the rear of the chamber was a row of glass cases, and inside of each was the corpse of something that did not appear to be human.[33] Each structure was on a stone slab, and his occasional glimpses revealed bodies that were short, with large heads and "clammy skin."[34] Metal coils were attached to each case, and at times the glass would fog up. One of the guards present noticed the distraction and quickly drew back a cover over the glass containers. Nothing was said, and no other reaction was noted.

For the balance of the week, Ritger and his work assistant were kept overnight in what was, for all intents and purposes, a jail cell, as no outside communication of any kind was permitted. The one feature that stood out was the overwhelming stench, which burned their noses.[35] Upon completion of the project, both men were checked for aftereffects of radiation exposure and were required to have regular check-ups. Once he finished the job at Wright-Patterson and returned home, Ritger told his family of the pungent odor in the cold room. His daughter said that she remembered her father's clothes having a strong odor of ammonia on them. Later, first his assistant, then Ritger, too, died of cancer.[36] Sadly for Ritger, the rumors became a reality and also left a lasting impression with his daughter. It was quite a price to pay for a brief encounter with some of the hidden secrets at Wright-Patterson. Was this an encounter with the long-rumored "aliens on ice" allegedly stored at Wright-Patterson? Sounds like it to us.

It should be clear from all these testimonies that, in addition to physical crash wreckage, bodies from another world were brought to and stored at Wright-Patterson, beginning with the Roswell crash in July of 1947. The evidence suggests that the bodies were preserved in clear containers in a state of cryogenic suspension by some combination of low temperature ("on ice") and cryogenic gas or solution. At least some of the bodies still continued to emit a foul odor, even under these conditions, which was first noted before the bodies left Roswell. No doubt the bodies were stored in Wright-Patterson's AeroMedical facility, at least during the time that they were under examination and dissection. Long-term storage ("on ice") was at another location on the base. Are they still there? We don't know for sure, but we do know that they were "loaned" to other airbases around the country throughout the years for

Wright-Patterson's AeroMedical Center.

examination.[37] We believe that the they were still at Wright-Patterson at least through the 1970s, because of a recent development. A reliable source who is employed in the U.S. rocket program approached us in 2012 regarding a surprising conversation he had in 1976 with a former chief of Wright-Patterson's AeroMedical Laboratory. Both men lived in Dayton, Ohio, at the time, and our source also worked at Wright-Patterson at the time. During the conversation the AeroMed chief told our source that he had something of interest to tell him. Knowing that our source had an interest in UFOs, he confirmed for him what he knew about the reality of visiting extraterrestrials by stating, "The Air Force has *little fellows* **stashed away at Wright-Patterson.**"[38] The only thing he forgot to do was add the ice.

CHAPTER 7

"My Name Is June Crain"

"I'm 72 years old. I've outlived two husbands and survived cancer twice. What are they going to do—shoot me or put me in prison?"
—*Tell My Story: June Crain, the Air Force & UFO's,* James E. Clarkson

Sarah Holcomb knew that the bodies had arrived at Wright-Patterson. Employed at the base in a sensitive secretarial position, she was able to supply various documents that confirmed her security clearances as well as her presence on the base during three separate periods of employment from 1942 to 1952. According to her, a sergeant she knew who had the proper authority to get into her office where she worked told her that he'd just come in on a special flight. He told her and the others in the office that they had brought in bodies from a flying saucer crash. He was telling them in no uncertain terms that the flying saucers everyone else in the country had been talking about were real. Having seen the strange little bodies himself, there was no question about it. Not long after the sergeant departed, the base commander appeared with a statement for them all to sign. He advised them, including Holcomb, that there was no truth to the story that the sergeant had been spreading, but they were nevertheless never to talk about it, or even mention it, under penalty of 20 years in prison and a $20,000 fine![1]

Years later when civilian UFO investigators came calling, Holcomb wanted to know if she was still obligated to abide by the security oath she had signed four decades previous, fearing at this late date that the military and the government might still prosecute her for talking. She was extremely cautious but decided that—with information about the Roswell crash starting to come out—information about the bodies should be released as well.[2]

In reality, the name "Sarah Holcomb" was a pseudonym. She had initially requested anonymity when Kevin Randle and Don Schmitt first interviewed her in 1990.[3] A version of her story appeared under her pseudonym in the 1994 Randle and Schmitt book, *The Truth About the UFO Crash at Roswell*, for the purpose of connecting the Roswell crash-retrieval to Wright Field. With apparently nothing further to pursue at that point, Randle and Schmitt then closed their "Sarah Holcomb" file.

Three years later, in 1993, an Aberdeen, Washington, police officer by the name of James Clarkson, who also happened to be a private UFO investigator as well as the Washington State Section Director for the Mutual UFO Network (MUFON), entered the scene. Part of any MUFON State Section Director's function is to promote the organization in one's home state by giving presentations and the like. As any UFO investigator knows, it is at such presentations and conferences that contacts are made, some of them unexpected—such was the case with

Former police detective and security officer James Clarkson obtained June Crain's story shortly before she passed away in the late 1990s.

James Clarkson and "Sarah Holcomb." At the conclusion of his presentation one evening on the subject of UFOs at a local library in the seaside town of Ocean Shores, Washington, Clarkson was approached by 68-year old "Sarah Holcomb." She told Clarkson that she *knew* he was right about our government's knowing much more about UFOs than they were telling the people. When asked by Clarkson how she knew this, Holcomb simply but forcefully replied, "Because I worked there." Behaving now like the trained investigator that he certainly was and still is, Clarkson asked for some details to back up her statement. **"I can't tell you—they'll come and arrest me"** was Holcomb's response.[4] Clarkson did not know it at the time, but he later learned that she had signed a nondisclosure agreement in 1952 when she left the employ of the U.S. Air Force. The document threatened her with a fine and a prison sentence if she ever disclosed what she knew.[5] Discussing this case years later in 2013, Clarkson revealed to coauthor Tom Carey that he felt at the time that this witness was afraid that he, being a police officer, might arrest her, and that was the reason she was not forthcoming with any details.[6] Clarkson then gave Holcomb his business card and hoped for the best, although every UFO investigator knows that the chances that a reluctant witness will ever call back—even after promising to do so on a stack of Bibles—is no better than one in 10. Still, Clarkson sensed that there was something special about Holcomb; she came across as a serious person and not just some UFO buff trying to impress a speaker of the moment.[7]

Four years later, in 1997, which was the 50th anniversary of the Roswell UFO crash, the U.S. Air Force released its fourth and final official "explanation" for the Roswell incident—parachuting mannequins[8]—and a CNN reporter glibly instructed his audience not to give UFOs another thought. For Sarah Holcomb, that was the tipping point. She had heard enough. And so she contacted James Clarkson and defiantly rejected the "balloon and dummy" explanations of the Air Force by calling them "damned lies." Years later, Clarkson recalled the conversation: He had barely answered, "Hello?" when he heard an outraged woman's voice on the other end of the line exclaim, **"It's a damned lie! Have you been watching CNN? It's the damned balloon lie. They used it before."** And regarding the Air Force's "dummies from the sky" explanation, she said, **"There had to be something there to attach them to...if they drop a dummy with a parachute, then the parachute should** be there. **Any normal person would say, 'Okay, that got dropped by a parachute.' There's nothing extraordinary about that."**[9] How did she know? Because her real name was June M. Crain, and she worked at Wright-Patterson AFB when the UFO wreckage and bodies arrived. She told Clarkson, **"I'm 72 years old. I've outlived two husbands and survived cancer twice. What are they going to do—shoot me or put me in prison?**[10] Fortunately for history's sake, June Crain had kept James Clarkson's business card and was the "one in 10" who felt compelled to take action and called back. Because of that, here is what we know about June Crain.

Employed at Wright-Patterson originally by the U.S. War Department, Crain was present at the base off and on three times from 1942 through 1952.[11] While there she worked as a secretary with security clearances that allowed her access to highly sensitive technical military data. Because of this status, she encountered numerous scientists and engineers who openly displayed personal knowledge of a number of flying saucer crashes and the fact that wreckage and bodies had been brought to the base. For example, one colleague mentioned to her how the bodies from New Mexico were "put in the ice box"—more specifically, the Aero Medical Lab there. He described them as **"Two dead little men about 4 feet tall and greenish-blue in color."**[12] (We have heard a number of witnesses who claimed to have seen the bodies from the Roswell crash describe to us the color of the bodies as "greenish-blue." Others have described different colorations, suggesting that the state of decay when the witnesses viewed the bodies might have accounted for the variations in coloration.)

In a 1990 handwritten letter to Kevin Randle that was reproduced in James Clarkson's book, June Crain described the "buzz" on the base at the time the bodies came in. Everyone was in a high state of excitement. Soon after the person who spoke of the bodies from New Mexico—a master sergeant whose first name was Clarence (June could not remember his last name)—left the office, a memo was hand-carried around the office that each person was made to read and sign. In essence the memo stated that the story the master sergeant had just told about alien bodies having just been flown in from New Mexico and allegedly residing in Wright-Patterson's Aero Medical facility was not true. It further stated that **"Anyone repeating this rumor will be liable for dismissal and/**

June Crain was a clerk-typist at the Foreign Technology Division at Wright-Patterson. Because of her high security classification, she was in a position to see and hear some of the base's deepest secrets.

or a $20,000 fine and 20 years in prison as punishment for unlawful disclosure." According to June, **"This memo was over the signature of the base commander. Needless to say, all talk stopped immediately, and I never heard anything about it again."** Outside of the nondisclosure agreement that June signed when she left her employment at the base, it was the only other time she was made to sign a document such as that, suggesting that something of great uniqueness and importance, something that had to be quashed immediately in its tracks before it went any farther, had just occurred.

Because this incident took place in the 1951–52 time frame, during June's third period of employment at the base, it is unlikely that the bodies in question were from the 1947 Roswell crash. June was certain, however, that three known crashes of UFOs had taken place up to that point in time: the one at Roswell and two others. She could not remember the two others but had learned of the crashes from the conversations of scientists and engineers in whose proximity she had worked on a daily basis. According to June, "Engineers are sort of wacky. They don't tell lies. They don't have jokes. And so when they say something, they know it had better be the truth."[13] This incident suggests that, although it may or may not have involved the Roswell crash, the final destination of choice for UFO wreckage and bodies was always Wright-Patterson AFB in Dayton, Ohio. It also begs the question that, if there was no truth to a tall story being spun over morning coffee by a master sergeant named "Clarence," why take the extraordinary step of threatening people with fines, prison, or loss of their jobs to remain silent forever about a rumor when they already knew not to discuss such things as a condition of their employment? It makes no sense, unless...

An interesting corollary to the memo incident occurred just a few days later. According to June, it was right after the bodies had been brought to the base.[14] It involved a project curiously code-named Project Caucasian—a project so sensitive that June was the only person in her job classification ("Clerk-Typist/Stenographer") allowed to work on it. This was because June carried a top-secret "Q" security classification, with the "Q" part of it clearing her to work administratively on matters involving atomic research, atomic weaponry like the H-Bomb, or requests emanating from the Atomic Energy Commission. The "Q" clearance was the highest security level on the base at the time. Here is how June described it for James Clarkson:

June: *Now I was cleared for Q, and it was so secret that I wasn't allowed to read the whole thing. I had a very small portion of it, I'd say a paragraph that I read and then had to add another paragraph onto that. Then I had to take it out of my typewriter. I left a piece of carbon paper in the drawer and got in trouble over it. But it was very secret. To this day I don't remember what that paragraph was. I remember it was a forwarding paragraph was all I added to it.*

James: What makes you think that *Project Caucasian* may have been related to the bodies?

June: *Well, it was right after they brought the bodies to the base. Also, I tried to get my direct boss to tell me what it was. And he looked at me like he was scared. I mean he looked like he was frightened. And he says, "June,*

I can't talk about it." I mean that he would not talk about it, and normally he would tell me anything I wanted to know. I even knew that he had a girlfriend.

James: And if I understand this Q clearance right, if it had been your job to work on the atomic bomb, a Q clearance would have gotten you in and out of that place...

June: *Yeah.*

James: So whatever this was, it was classified higher...

June: *Higher than me.*

James: ...than a Q clearance...

June: *Yep. It had to be.*[15]

This exchange between June Crain and James Clarkson suggests that even though June possessed a security clearance of the highest order on the base, a top-secret "Q" clearance, it still was not quite high enough to work with full knowledge on *Project Caucasian*. She was cleared to work on any project or matter that Wright-Patterson could throw at her—even those involving atomic secrets—except *Project Caucasian*. June thought, not unreasonably, that it must have had something to do with the alien bodies that had arrived at the base a few days prior.

Unknown to June, the answer to her conundrum may have been provided several years earlier in 1950 by a Canadian governmental engineer. Wilbert B. Smith headed up the Canadian government's first top-secret investigation of UFOs. After a meeting in Washington, DC, with physicist Robert Sarbacher of the U.S. Defense Department's Research & Development Board under Dr. Vannevar Bush, a meeting that included the subject of UFOs, Smith returned to Canada with some startling information for his superiors. In a top-secret government memorandum, Smith stated that as far as the United States government was concerned, regarding UFOs, **"The matter is the most highly classified subject in the United States Government, rating higher even than the H-bomb."**[16] And higher, we should add, than June Crain's "Q" clearance.

On another occasion, June Crain observed an officer who casually displayed a piece of what has come to be known as "memory material" that had been recovered from a UFO crash site. Tossing it on her desk, he teased her by telling her, **"Go ahead. Try to tear it up!"** Having the rare opportunity to actually handle it, she described it as "light as a feather," and no matter what attempts she made to inflict damage to the metal-like artifact, all such efforts failed. Exasperated, she finally asked the officer, "Well, what is it?" **"It's a piece of a spaceship,"** he said. **"I just came back from New Mexico, and I brought it back with me."**[17] June remembered the name of the officer only as a "Captain Wheeler." (NOTE: Our associate, Anthony Bragalia, was able to search and find a reference to a "Richard V. Wheeler" at Wright-Patterson AFB in the 1950 time frame. He worked in the Air Materiel Command's Engineering Division–Parachute Branch—the same branch as June Crain!)[18]

June described for Clarkson how she tried to cut the small, aluminum-colored piece of metal with a pair of scissors, but the scissors would just slide off without leaving so much as a scratch. She folded it every which way trying to tear it, but all it did was go back to its original shape. **"I tried everything I could to tear it up, and I couldn't tear it. I couldn't make a dent on it. I couldn't make a mark on it. It had a funny slick feel to it. Didn't feel like any metal I've ever felt. I have yet to see anything that would have those properties. And, so *light*!"**[19] She just couldn't get over how something so light could be so strong. Then, when someone else entered the room, Captain Wheeler quickly jammed the piece of metal into his pocket, suggesting that others did not know he had it and that he wasn't supposed to have it in his possession.[20] It also suggests that several years after the Roswell incident itself there were "souvenirs" from the crash still in circulation "beneath the radar" and reach of the authorities. As for June Crain, she was one of the lucky few to have had an up-close and personal encounter with a piece of Roswell's *Holy Grail*, something for which we are still searching.

Crain also described having had the rare experience of taking dictation from eminent German rocket scientist Werner Von Braun, one of the world's most important rocket scientists and the champion of modern-day space exploration; he was the chief architect of the Saturn 5 rocket, which successfully put our Apollo astronauts on the moon. It can be documented that von Braun was in Roswell on a number of occasions at the time of the 1947 crash. When June Crain worked with him, he told her that he knew of *three* crashes of extraterrestrial origin. Von Braun was under military escort at that time from Fort Bliss in El Paso, Texas (where some 200 German rocket scientists who had been brought to the United States after World War II under the auspices of a secret program known as "Operation Paperclip" were then being housed), indicating the importance of the matter and his trip to Dayton. Others have also testified that the famous scientist had confirmed to them of having a firsthand knowledge of the Roswell crash.[21] He would later state in 1959, **"We find ourselves faced by powers which are far stronger than we had hitherto assumed, and whose base of operation is at present unknown to us."**[22] It should be pointed out here that White Sands Missile Range, near Alamogordo, New Mexico, where early rocket development and testing were carried out, was just a short flight from Roswell and the 1947 UFO crash site. His presence at Wright-Patterson, as well as that of other "Paperclip" Germans, has also been confirmed.[23] According to Crain, the reality of UFOs and crashes was "common knowledge" among the scientists and engineers at Wright-Patterson. **"It was a matter of fact. I mean they talked like everybody knew it, that they were crashing... they said that there was no doubt about there being a, you know, a flying saucer—whatever you want to call them—there was no doubt about that."**[24]

So, as a historical witness, what are we to make of June Crain? On the negative side was the fact that, of the 10-year period bracketing her three employment stints at Wright-Patterson, she was actually employed there for a total of only two and a half years, and none of those was during the time of the Roswell incident. On the positive side of the equation, however, was the fact that June quickly became a respected and highly valued employee, as evidenced by her being entrusted with a top-secret "Q" security clearance. She was, therefore, in a position to see, hear, and know about the events she has described. She also provided documentation to back up her times and positions of employment at Wright-Patterson. But what about her story?

Throughout the years we have encountered a number of alleged witnesses to the Roswell events of 1947 who were propitiously situated in both time and place so as to permit them to falsely plug themselves into the Roswell narrative as participants when such was not the case. These are the most difficult alleged witnesses to try to verify because, knowing the landscape as they do, they sound as though they know what they are talking about. In some cases, it has taken years to expose them. The experience, skill, and determination of the investigator is critical in ferreting out the truth, and we must rely upon these investigators in order to reach the proper conclusions.

With that in mind, let's take a look at James Clarkson. He is a retired police officer of the Aberdeen, Washington police department; at least half of his career there was spent as a detective sergeant. Before that, Clarkson was a U.S. Army plainclothes Military Police investigator. He has been employed for the past eight years as a fraud investigator in the Department of Licensing for the State of Washington, and is now the MUFON State Director for the state of Washington. Adding up these positions, Clarkson has spent more than 30 years investigating, interviewing, and making judgments about people regarding their honesty, guilt, and innocence. His judgments about June Crain, therefore, carry exceptional clarity and weight, and can be relied upon, in our opinion.

June (Crain) Kaba died of cancer at age 73 in 1998, a little more than a year after contacting James Clarkson for the second time and giving him permission to go public with her story. Unlike confabulators and fabricators of tall tales, June's story remained unchanged from the time she first contacted Randle and Schmitt back in 1990. According to Clarkson, **"She was very careful to tell me when she could not remember a detail. She wanted to tell me what she remembered as true—that and only that. I think June knew that she was settling the accounts of her life. She decided to end her silence. There is not a court in the world that does not lend additional credence to those who believe that they do not have long to live."**[25] We have referred to these situations elsewhere as "deathbed confessions." Using a more legalistic definition, James Clarkson refers to it as a "Dying Declaration," especially noting its exception to the "hearsay rule" that normally excludes second-hand testimony in court proceedings.[26] This doctrine would apply, in June's case, to her second-hand accounts of overhearing others in her shop talking about crashed UFOs and little bodies at her place of employment. At the end of the day, June was a straight shooter who, according to James Clarkson, "was torn between her patriotism and her no-nonsense commitment never to suffer liars, fools, and hypocrites."[27] As she put it, **"I lead a very clean life and always have. I'm a fighter, and I believe in the truth. And I don't like when I think somebody is trying to pull something over on me."**[28]

No, June Crain is not a "smoking gun" witness, but she is a significant corroborating "inside" witness to Wright-Patterson's secret history. Rest in peace, June.

CHAPTER 8

The Fighter Ace Meets Something *Squiggly*

"It was alive. But we killed it!"

—*Nightfighter: Radar Intercept Killer*, Mark A. Magruder

He looked for all the world like a young Tyrone Power decked out in his flight gear getting ready to take on the Luftwaffe in 1941's *A Yank in the RAF*, or like the similarly situated and motivated Robert Stack in 1942's *Eagle Squadron*. In a case of reality imitating art, instead of vice versa, such movie plots were real life for Lieutenant Colonel Marion Milton "Black Mac" Magruder. After developing tactics he had learned from night-fighting with the British, he would go on to become an "ace" fighter pilot and squadron commander of the legendary "Black Mac's Killers" in World War II. For sweeping the night skies of Japanese aircraft over Okinawa in 1945, the biggest and bloodiest battle in the Pacific during the war, his squadron would win a Presidential Unit Citation. Additionally, "Black Mac" would be awarded two Bronze Stars, the Air Medal with Gold Stars, the American Defense Service Medal with Base Clasp, the European-African-Middle Eastern Area Campaign Medal, the American Area Campaign Medal, the World War II Victory Medal, and the National Defense Service Medal.[1]

The summer of 1947 found 36-year-old Magruder in class at the Air War College (AWC) at Maxwell Field in Montgomery, Alabama. This

Getting ready for business, WWII night-fighter and
squadron leader Marion "Black Mac" Magruder hitches
up his flight gear somewhere near Okinawa.

was the second such class to commence after the war,[2] and Magruder
would have the honor of becoming the first Marine officer to attend and
graduate from the Air University of the Air War College.[3] The class was
filled with officers whose ranks ranged from general down to lieutenant
colonel, which was the lowest rank permitted in the program. The officers chosen for the class were deemed to represent the "best and brightest" in their respective branches of the military destined to become the
future leaders of U.S. military doctrine heading into the post-war era.

Magruder's class at the Air War College was scheduled to last for approximately one year, from July of 1947 to June of 1948, during which
time the officers would receive advanced training in military history, de-
cision-making, and geo-political strategy. The class had been in session
for nine months when, in April of 1948, all class members were flown

up to the newly merged Wright-Patterson Air Force Base for a week's worth of classes and on-site training.[4] The class's "opinion" was desired on a matter of utmost urgency and importance. According to Mark Magruder, Marion's son, the military wanted the class's feedback on a strategic decision regarding military and political planning. "Basically, the higher-ups in the military were looking for guidance on a critical decision they had to make."[5]

Not knowing what to expect, the curious officers were led into a room where they were told about the recovery to then–Wright Field of an extraterrestrial spaceship that had crashed near the town of Roswell, New Mexico, the previous summer.[6] Most of the officers had not been aware of the crash and were puzzled when some of the strange wreckage was brought out for them to examine.[7] According to Mark, his father described the wreckage as being "out of this world." The most interesting item was a piece of what his father described as "metallic cloth," which was light and strong, and which could be folded up into a ball and, when released, would resume its original flat shape. His father also used the term "foil-like" to describe it. (We, of course, would today call it a piece of "memory metal.") His father also talked about handling pieces of wreckage that had strange markings inscribed on them, which he referred to as "hieroglyphics," for want of a better term, that he could not make sense of.[8] Marion also told his son that his group was shown photographs of the craft that had crashed, and that it was definitely not crescent-shaped (as Kenneth Arnold had described what he witnessed near Mt. Rainier in June 1947) or triangle-shaped (as described by discredited dissembler Frank Kaufmann in the early 1990s), but was more like a disk. To "Black Mac," the stuff that he had closely examined was clearly "otherworldly" and like nothing he had ever seen or handled before.[9]

The real shocker, however, was yet to come. After everyone had a chance to examine and handle the strange wreckage, they were led into another room. There, they were shown *something else* that would haunt Marion Magruder for the rest of his life.[10] He somehow managed to keep what he saw there to himself for the next 20 years. But on July 20, 1969—the day that Neil Armstrong and Buzz Aldrin first landed on the moon in *Apollo 11*—"Black Mac" Magruder finally confessed to his five sons—Mark, Mike, Merritt, Marshall, and Marion, Jr.—that he knew from an experience in his past that ET was real. And in response to the obligatory question from one of his sons about "little green men," he matter-of-factly replied, **"They weren't green."**[11] Black Mac did not expand upon his statements to his sons as to how their father *knew* these things at that point, but in the ensuing quarter century, especially after the books and TV shows about Roswell started appearing in the 1980s and 1990s, he gradually overcame his reluctance to discuss with them "the rest of the story" of what he and his Air War College class had learned on a trip to Wright-Patterson Air force Base back in 1948.[12]

While lying on his deathbed many years later, "Black Mac" Magruder recalled the otherworldly encounter he had on his trip to Wright-Patterson with his Air War College class in 1948: After being told about the Roswell crash/recovery and having examined some of the wreckage, the class was told that there was a *survivor* from the crash, and they were then led into another room. As had his four brothers, Magruder's son Mike had heard the story before, but this telling was meant for Mike's daughter, Natalie, who was interested in UFOs.[13] Marion told her that the "creature," as he referred to it, was about 4 feet tall, humanoid in general appearance, but with long, thin arms and an oversized head for its small frame. Its other features, as described by Mark Magruder, were also similar to the descriptions of others who have claimed to have witnessed the Roswell bodies: a thin, one-inch slit for a mouth, just two small orifices where the nose should be, a small orifice on each side of the head instead of ears, and large, wide-set eyes.[14] One big difference from most other descriptions, however, was the color of the creature's skin. Not only was it not green, as Black Mac had previously stated, but it wasn't gray, either. According to Mark Magruder, his father stated that the being's skin had a "flesh-tone" color to it.[15] (NOTE: The pink-ish color might be explained by the fact that this being was still alive, whereas most other witnesses who have described the color of the skin had viewed bodies in various stages of decomposition.) Seeing the crea-ture again in his memory, Magruder stated that, although he did not converse with it, some sort of connection was made at the time, in that he felt great empathy for it. As a result, throughout the years he made sure to emphasize the "human-like" qualities of the small, child-like be-ing.[16] A similar feeling was reported by another eyewitness who had had a close encounter with the live Roswell alien being: Roswell fireman

Dan Dwyer had gotten to the crash site just before the military when he came face to face with a living, ambulatory alien entity. He told his family that, although he did not talk to the being, it talked to him "in his head," and he was overcome by a strong sense of sympathy for it as it was obviously stranded alone on a strange planet.[17] In his final reminiscence for his granddaughter, however, Black Mac nevertheless allowed to her that, despite its human-like qualities, the creature he saw looked *squiggly* (rubbery) to him, and there was no question that "**[I]t clearly was not from this planet.**"[18]

Unknown to Colonel Magruder, even on his deathbed, where he passed away peacefully on his 86th birthday on June 27, 1997, the same general terms he had used to describe the Roswell "survivor" were also used by other military officers years earlier who had had a chance to see the bodies from the Roswell crash close-up. The year prior to Magruder's class trip to Dayton, Captain Oliver "Pappy" Henderson had flown not just wreckage but also the first group of alien bodies to then–Wright Field on July 8, 1947 (see Chapter 6). Having viewed the bodies lying on the floor of the hangar just prior to loading them for the flight, Captain Henderson would later describe their appearance as reminding him of the cartoon character "Casper the Ghost."[19] Major Jesse Marcel, Sr., the Roswell base intelligence officer who was dispatched to the crash site on July 6, 1947, and who reignited interest in the Roswell story 30 years later by breaking his silence regarding it, told a subordinate of his that the Roswell aliens had the appearance of "white, rubbery figures."[20] It would not be too much of a stretch here to suggest that all three men were simply using their own perspective and respective terms to describe the same thing.

According to Mike Magruder, his father later learned that the military had been conducting experiments on the being he saw, but that it had died in the process. To Black Mac Magruder, his eyes tearing up at the thought of the small extraterrestrial he had seen at Wright-Patterson, "**It was a shameful thing that the military destroyed this creature by conducting tests on it.... They killed it!**"[21]

Marion "Black Mac" Magruder graduated from the Air War College in June 1948, for which he coauthored the thesis "The Impact and Role of Missiles in a War During the Foreseeable Future (5–10 years)." In 1950, Magruder was personally selected and sent by the Secretary of the

Navy to Germany. As the only Marine in the European Theater, he was tasked with drawing up a plan for the use of tactical nuclear weapons in case of a Russian attack, and the plan remained in force during the Cold War.[22] In 1954–55, he attended and graduated from the National War College, where his thesis, "Nuclear Weapons—An Instrument of National Policy," won special honors for its future strategic implications. Along the upward trajectory of his military career, he also handled a number of prestigious special assignments all over the world, including serving as chief of staff, G-4 Fleet Marine Force Pacific, as well as becoming the commanding officer of the Marine Air Station at Kaneohe, Oahu, Hawaii. In the latter capacity, he hosted President Eisenhower for a five-day visit.[23] By 1961, Magruder had been a "full bird" colonel for 10 years, but with a Commandant of the Marine Corps harboring a

AIR WAR COLLEGE - CLASS 1947-48 - GROUP 1

The 1947–48 Air War College Class at Maxwell Air Force Base in Montgomery, Alabama. Marine Lt. Col. Magruder is standing in the exact middle of the first row.

petty grudge, he concluded that he would never achieve flag (general) rank. So, on August 31, 1961, after 26 years of exemplary service to his beloved Marine Corps and his country, Marion M. "Black Mac" Magruder retired.[24]

Not content to just sit back and live off his military pension, now-civilian Mac Magruder entered the world of high business with the same skill, aggressiveness, and professionalism that he displayed when he was ridding the skies over the Pacific Theater of Japanese *Zeros*. Deciding fairly quickly that he would rather be a private businessman than work for someone else, he purchased a McDonald's franchise in the state of Colorado. Before he retired for a second time, he owned as many as 30 McDonald's franchises in the states of Colorado, Arizona, and California.[25] Given Mac Magruder's self-confidence, his foresight, his personal skills, and his commitment to success, Mac Magruder's civilian achievements came as no surprise to anyone who knew him.

The larger point to be made regarding the Air War College's class trip to Wright-Patterson in April 1948 is that, by that point in time, the Air Force, acting in consort with the government, still had not decided how to proceed with the secret they were keeping from the citizens they were serving as well as from those within their own ranks. Having killed the Roswell story and a potentially chaotic situation nine months earlier by denying everything, the Air Force had finally caught its breath and was looking to its upcoming "best and brightest" for some sage advice. How would soldiers react to the knowledge that they were not alone in the universe? Would they panic, or, as some officers did down in Roswell, just "lose it"? Could they be trusted with that knowledge, and, most importantly, would they still keep it secret from everybody else? We do not know the AWC class consensus regarding these questions, but Magruder told his sons that the military was looking for the class members' opinions on what to do. Strategically (and sociologically), what did they think would be the best course to follow, and could the class members themselves handle this truth? [26]

The Air Force and/or the government apparently were *still* not quite sure how to proceed, as the next Air War College class—the class of 1948–49—was also invited up to Wright-Patterson to examine the Roswell wreckage and to meet ET.[27] Kevin Randle, a Roswell researcher of note and a former Army intelligence officer himself, notes, "[I]n the military, when you are presented with an already cleared, talented, and senior group, you might well take advantage of that expertise because it is...well, there."[28] This would be the second and last AWC class to make that trip. A decision had been reached: The Air Force and U.S. government would continue to keep "The Secret" secret from everybody, deny that the Roswell incident (as a crash and retrieval of a UFO and crew) was anything more than a balloon and a dime-store mannequin, and deny that UFOs exist until one lands on the White House lawn.

The Magruder family has provided ample and convincing evidence in the form of documentation that their father was where he said he was at the time he said he was with his Air War College class during the first week of April 1948. Skeptics would say that, although that may be true, it still doesn't prove that the ET part of the story is true. For the skeptics, only an authenticated photo of "Black Mac" shaking hands with ET, or a notation in the AWC's class schedule stating "Field Trip to Wright-Patterson AFB to meet ET," will suffice. For the rest of us, the veracity of the story, given the documentation in hand, turns on the type of person that "Black Mac" Magruder was in life and the credibility of his surviving family members. In the cases of past hoaxers, an agenda for telling tall tales usually becomes apparent at some point in the investigation, one that normally involves attention-getting in the hope of a monetary reward at the end of the rainbow. Given his wartime military record, coupled with his post-military business success, neither *attention-grabbing* nor *hope of financial gain* would seem to apply in this case. Having divested themselves of their father's "McDonald's Empire," the Magruder family is more than well off today. Experience also tells us that surviving family members of the "rich and famous" and notables of all stripes like to preserve a positive memory of dignity and respect for their departed in the minds of the public, and the word "UFO" is not a word they want attached to that memory or seen in an obituary. So, given what we know about the principal and the surviving family members in this case, there is no logical reason for them to make up a story, like the one discussed in this chapter, about their beloved father. As it was, Black Mac's real life needed no embellishing, and he would not have approved it. Being one of the *greatest* of America's "Greatest Generation" will do that for you.

CHAPTER 9

Project Sign:
"The Estimate of the Situation"

On September 23, 1947, Lt. Gen. Nathan Twining drafted a letter to Brigadier General George Schulgen stating that the "saucers" were real. In the historic memo, Twining outlined the first official verdict on the subject of UFOs. Essentially:

1. The phenomenon is something real and not hallucinatory, hoaxed, or misperceived natural phenomena—"something is really flying around."
2. The surface of the objects is metallic or made of some other reflective substance.
3. The objects rarely leave a trail except perhaps in high-performance operations.
4. The objects are circular or elliptical, flat on the bottom with a low dome on top.
5. Flights may occur in well-ordered, well-kept formations in numbers of three to nine disks.
6. Speeds are estimated in excess of 300 knots.
7. Sizes are estimated to be as large as "man-made" aircraft.[1]

What is not generally known, even within UFO circles, is that at the end of the letter, handwritten, is the listing of high-ranking officers and scientists who "coordinated" the memo—specifically, people from the aircraft, propeller, and power plant labs, and the engineering division T-3 at Wright Field. After full consultation, his lead aeronautical engineers at Wright Field had essentially said, **"The phenomenon is real and it isn't ours."** Therefore, Twining clearly demonstrated his knowledge of the reality of the flying saucers. What did the general know that his intelligence advisors did not have access to? What had happened during that time that forced the top brass at the Pentagon and Wright Field to put out such a definitive statement as to acknowledge the reality of UFOs? Mind you, this conclusion was arrived at within the course of a few months. As described, investigations were lackluster, photographic evidence was rare, and most sightings went unattended. Only physical evidence could have provided incontrovertible proof. Only an event such as the recovery of such physical evidence... A weather balloon would hardly fill that need. Clearly, something extraordinary had happened in New Mexico two months before Twining's amazing assessment. And where had the wreckage from the alleged flying saucer crash been taken? Wright Field—where Twining was headquartered.

Twining's memo must have shocked nearly everyone in Air Force intelligence outside of Wright Field—especially its recipient, Brig. Gen. Schulgen, who expected to hear that everything was under control and that it was our own classified aircraft. Far from recommending that future inquiry be suspended, Twining elevated the concern to an official, centralized, secret project to gather UFO information. More importantly, it was not only censored from the public and the media, but also from the intelligence agents in the field collecting the data on the true nature of the new phenomenon. The classified information gathered would be provided to appropriate persons in all branches of the military, the Atomic Energy Commission, the joint Research and Development Board, the Air Force Scientific Advisory Group, the National Advisory Committee on Aeronautics (NACA, the predecessor of NASA), the RAND (Research and Development) Project, and the Nuclear Energy for Propulsion of Aircraft (NEPA) Project. Each one of these projects had the distinction of being top-level and highly classified; they also had the best government scientists, all experts in their respective fields, which clearly demonstrates how urgent was the need for answers on the part of the Pentagon and the Air Materiel Command (AMC) at Wright Field.

One of those top-level scientists was civilian Alfred C. Loedding, an aeronautical engineer who started the first Jet Propulsion Laboratory at Wright Field. An expert in aviation, Loedding had worked at Bellanca Aircraft Company before taking the position in T-3 (engineering) at Wright Field in 1938. From all indications, in that capacity, he was especially intrigued by the wave of UFO sightings the summer of 1947, and became anxious to interview witnesses. Soon, he would find himself a principal investigator of such incidents. At that time, throughout the two-week surge of sightings leading up to the crash of the unknown object in New Mexico, reports went to the Air Force Office of Intelligence at the Pentagon.[2]

General Howard McCoy would order one of Loedding's colleagues, civilian engineer George W. Towles, to Roswell to investigate the crash "material" and be sure to get the "whole story."[3] Numerous military witnesses at the RAAF described all the "suits" overseeing the recovery operation, Towles cataloged the debris and crash material and helped to prepare it for transport to Wright Field. High-ranking officers as well as intelligence men and Secret Service agents arrived in Roswell, from not only Wright Field but also Washington, Los Alamos, and White Sands Proving Grounds. As Earl Zimmerman, who was assigned at that time to the base radio shack, remarked, "Something unusually important was taking place."[4]

Another unscheduled arrival in Roswell was Major General Laurence C. Craige, chief of the Army Air Force's Research and Engineering Division under LeMay's R&D department at the Pentagon. Craige was sent from Wright Field by LeMay to get the "full story" himself. After spending a number of hours at the base in Roswell, Craige was flown directly to DC where he and LeMay provided a detailed account to President Truman. It was immediately after this briefing that the oval office called a flurry of meetings apparently discussing what had just transpired in New Mexico.[5] From all appearances, the events in Roswell had breached national security and the Pentagon was desperately searching for any answers. LeMay told the press, **The Army Air Force has no project with the characteristics similar to those which have been associated with the flying discs."**

SECRET
C O P Y

TSDIN/HMM/ig/6-4100

23 September 1947

TSDIN

SUBJECT: AMC Opinion Concerning "Flying Discs"

TO: Commanding General
          Army Air Forces
          Washington 25, D. C.
          ATTENTION: Brig. General George Schulgen
                      AC/AS-2

     1. As requested by AC/AS-2 there is presented below the considered opinion of this Command concerning the so-called "Flying Discs". This opinion is based on interrogation report data furnished by AC/AS-2 and preliminary studies by personnel of T-2 and Aircraft Laboratory, Engineering Division T-3. This opinion was arrived at in a conference between personnel from the Air Institute of Technology, Intelligence T-2, Office, Chief of Engineering Division, and the Aircraft, Power Plant and Propeller Laboratories of Engineering Division T-3.

     2. It is the opinion that:

        a. The phenomenon reported is something real and not visionary or fictitious.

        b. There are objects probably approximating the shape of a disc, of such appreciable size as to appear to be as large as man-made aircraft.

        c. There is a possibility that some of the incidents may be caused by natural phenomena, such as meteors.

        d. The reported operating characteristics such as extreme rates of climb, maneuverability (particularly in roll), and action which must be considered evasive when sighted or contacted by friendly aircraft and radar, lend belief to the possibility that some of the objects are controlled either manually, automatically or remotely.

        e. The apparent common description of the objects is as follows:

           (1) Metallic or light reflecting surface.

Incl. #1

SECRET
C O P Y

U-39552

Twining letter, page 1.

Authority NND700188
By HS NARA Date 7.30.03

SECRET

Basic Ltr fr CG, AMC, WF to CG, AAF, Wash. D.C. subj "AMC Opinion Concerning "Flying Discs".

        (2) Absence of trail, except in a few instances when the object apparently was operating under high performance conditions.

        (3) Circular or elliptical in shape, flat on bottom and domed on top.

        (4) Several reports of well kept formation flights varying from three to nine objects.

        (5) Normally no associated sound, except in three instances a substantial rumbling roar was noted.

        (6) Level flight speeds normally above 300 knots are estimated.

    f. It is possible within the present U. S. knowledge -- provided extensive detailed development is undertaken -- to construct a piloted aircraft which has the general description of the object in subparagraph (e) above which would be capable of an approximate range of 7000 miles at subsonic speeds.

    g. Any developments in this country along the lines indicated would be extremely expensive, time consuming and at the considerable expense of current projects and therefore, if directed, should be set up independently of existing projects.

    h. Due consideration must be given the following:-

        (1) The possibility that these objects are of domestic origin - the product of some high security project not known to AC/AS-2 or this Command.

        (2) The lack of physical evidence in the shape of crash recovered exhibits which would undeniably prove the existence of these objects.

        (3) The possibility that some foreign nation has a form of propulsion possibly nuclear, which is outside of our domestic knowledge.

  3. It is recommended that:-

    a. Headquarters, Army Air Forces issue a directive assigning a priority, security classification and Code Name for a detailed study of this matter to include the preparation of complete sets of all available and pertinent data which will then be made available to the Army, Navy, Atomic Energy Commission, JRDB, the Air Force Scientific Advisory Group, NACA, and the RAND and NEPA projects for comments and recommendations, with a preliminary report to be forwarded within 15 days of receipt of the data and a detailed report thereafter every 30 days as the investi-

  C O P Y

SECRET

U-39552

Twining letter, page 2.

SECRET
COPY

Basic Ltr fr CG, AMC, WF to CG, AAF, Wash. D.C. Subj "AMC Opinion Concerning "Flying Discs"

gation develope. A complete interchange of data should be effected.

    4. Awaiting a specific directive AMC will continue the investi-
gation within its current resources in order to more closely define the
nature of the pehnomenon. Detailed Essential Elements of Information
will be formulated immediately for transmittal thru channels.

                        N. F. TWINING
                        Lieutenant General, U.S.".
                        Commanding

This letter was coordinated by:
    Col. Moore - Ch. Aircraft Lab
    Mr. DA Dicky - Ch Propeller Lab
    Gen D.L. Putt - Engr Div
    Col. Minty - Ch Power Plant Lab
    Gen Brentnall - T-3.

SECRET
COPY   U-39552

Twining letter, page 3.

General Nathan Twining.   General George Schulgen.

All would return to normal—as far as the press and the public were concerned—on the afternoon of Tuesday, July 8th, as military officials put out the fire at Roswell with the balloon explanation. Ironically, the next day, Wright Field started to receive firsthand flying disc reports while T-2 made every effort to determine whether the phenomenon had anything to do with Soviet technology. Major Victor H. Bilek, assistant chief, ATIC, and assistant chief of analysis at T-2, would acknowledge the crash and the recovery of bodies.[6] In the aftermath of Roswell, "foreign origin" would become the code term for "extraterrestrial" at Wright Field. Further damage control for the events at Roswell reduced the level of public attention down to a trickle, and by July 12th, sighting reports fell off sharply. However, behind closed doors, T-2 frantically tried to determine the source of the "craft of unknown origin" from Roswell.

Loedding was one of the scientists who convinced General Twining to call for an official Air Force investigation just two months after the crash in Roswell. General Craige, now the head of USAF R&D, ordered the establishment of the Air Force's first official study of UFOs, Project Sign. Loedding was quick to convince the Pentagon to transfer most of their flying disc reports to Wright Field, and greatly influenced T-2 to become specifically involved in the reports, which demonstrated flight aerodynamics.[7]

According to Ruppelt, only the very top people at ATIC were assigned to Sign, and their main mission was to determine whether UFOs were Soviet or interplanetary. Clearly, he was not in the inner loop and was not aware that the Soviet element had already been dismissed. Still, regarding a possible Russian technology, he states, "Classified orders came down to investigate all UFO sightings. Get every detail and send it direct to ATIC at Wright Field. The order carried no explanation as to why the information was wanted. The lack of an explanation and the fact that the information was to be sent directly to a high-powered intelligence group within Air Force Headquarters stirred the imagination...."[8]

Project Sign's duty was to "collect, collate, evaluate, and distribute to interested government agencies and contractors all information concerning sightings and phenomena in the atmosphere which can be construed to be of concern to the national security." Captain Robert R. Sneider served as chief officer, under the command of General McCoy and T-2. As the civilian liaison, Loedding reported to Colonel Albert Bonnell Deyarmond, who had worked with McCoy in establishing the technical database at Wright Field after WWII. Then a civilian, he was recalled specifically by McCoy as a personal favor. Project Sign was given a 2A priority rating—1A being the highest in the Air Force—and was often called Project Saucer by those both inside and outside the program.[9]

The Air Materiel Command under General Twining at Wright-Patterson was tasked with enabling the full completion of the project. The cooperation of the Army, Navy, Coast Guard, and FBI was also encouraged in order to expedite the forwarding and investigation of all reports. A memorandum dated August 6, 1948, under the title "Flying Saucers," required the Air Intelligence Division to examine the tactics pattern of reported UFOs and develop conclusions as to their probability.[10]

The driving force in the AMC investigation remained Loedding throughout the tenure of Sign. Cooperating with the Pentagon, he would report at meetings with both General Schulgen and Dr. Charles Carroll, a mathematics and missile expert. It was Loedding and Carroll who had drafted the focus by which Sign would conduct its investigation.

Sighting reports were categorized into four sections:

1. Flying disks.
2. Cigar/torpedo-shaped craft.
3. Balloon/spherical craft.
4. Balls of light.

Clearly, Sign was investigating, as Hynek would describe it, "the properties of a phenomenon."[11] It's curious that the scientists at Wright-Patterson were not looking for a psychological explanation. Rather, whether American, Russian, or Martian, they were investigating hardware that was cavorting through U.S. airspace. However, as Loedding at times noted, they were not getting much support from the military. This would be especially evident when he would assist in writing one of the most mysterious documents in U.S. history: the ill-fated "Estimate of the Situation," penned mostly by Loedding and Sign director Sneider around September 1947—two months after the Roswell incident.[12] According to Ruppelt, "The situation was the UFOs; the estimate was that they were interplanetary."[13] Most of the project's personnel had arrived at the very same interpretation of the data, and, from all accounts, relying strictly on eyewitness testimony, a number of photographs, and a far-reaching hope that we were truly dealing with an advanced technology.

Skeptics point out that such technical thinkers were not investigators, nor were they trained at discerning prosaic explanations. To skeptics, the entire subject remains relegated to the "mental health" fringe. But what is more telling than anything else is that immediately after the Roswell Incident the subject attracted the very scientific, "nuts and bolts" crowd that one would expect. They sought out the technological advances that such a phenomenon could provide. Again, Sign was not a psychological study of any kind.

Finally, there is absolutely no reason to believe that any of the researchers at Sign had any access to the Roswell material evidence. If T-2 had physical proof, it was too sensitive to share with anyone outside of the highest ranks of authority. The attitude at the Pentagon was, *We have a wreck*; the task for Sign was to demonstrate how the wrecked craft worked, and, more importantly, are they a threat?[14]

Loedding and Sneider's "Estimate of the Situation" made its way up the official chain of command in September/October 1948, and was approved by Colonel McCoy and his number-two man at T-2, Intelligence Chief William Clingerman. It was also approved by the chief of Air Force Intelligence at the Pentagon, Major General Charles P. Cabell.[15] One is inclined to ask, just as the original "straw man" was created with the first pronouncement at Roswell and the press release about the capture of a "flying disk," was "Estimate" intended to create the same effect? Namely: first, admit it, and then tear it down. And that is exactly what General Vandenberg did when the report crossed his desk. He immediately stated that it lacked evidence, but rather than rescind the report and have it resubmitted in a style more to his liking, he did a most curious thing: He ordered the report destroyed.[16] The question remains: Why did Cabell, McCoy, and the other officers send it upstairs with their endorsement, unless they knew that their boss would shut down the growing UFO crescendo at Wright-Patterson? All that was left to do now was dismantle the project and quiet the ET advocates who were too inclined to yell *fire* when all the Pentagon would accept was smoke.

Colonel Howard "Mac" McCoy.

A more acceptable final summation was written by Deyarmond and Truettner, and was released in February of 1949. The new, sanitized version stated that although some unidentified aerial objects appeared to represent actual aircraft, there was not enough data to determine their origin.[17] As ardently as the project tried to chase down the facts through 1948, the more advisable recourse was to again (figuratively) substitute a weather balloon for the truth. "Anything but extraterrestrial" became the immediate fallback answer. However, many of the key players at Sign remained unconvinced by another official denial. Curiously, in one of the report's appendices, waxing more philosophical than authoritative was a paper written by a member of the Air Force's oversight committee, Dr. George E. Valley, Jr., a physicist and the project supervisor and senior staff member of the Radiation Laboratory at MIT. He said, " If there is an **extraterrestrial civilization which can make objects as are reported, then it is most probable that its development is far in advance of ours...such a civilization might observe that on earth we now have atomic bombs and are fast developing rockets. In view of the past history of mankind, they would be alarmed. We should therefore, expect at this time above all to behold such visitations.**"[18]

Nevertheless, their time was passing and they were about to be made irrelevant because their results did not subscribe to the official position. The "nuts and bolts" crowd was becoming too vociferous at Wright-Patterson and the fire needed to be doused before it reached a particular hangar.

Alfred Loedding's brother Fred visited him in the year after the summer of 1947 at the base in Dayton. While they were walking around the facility, Alfred made a rather telling comment to his brother. Fred asked him what he thought "this flying saucer business is all about." Alfred pleaded ignorance but at the same time pointed out one of the hangars. He paused, and then in a tone of frustration, mentioned that he had no idea what was inside, just that it was off limits even to him. It was Alfred's understanding that the answer to the flying saucer mystery was locked inside.[19]

CHAPTER 10

Project Grudge Grounds the Saucers

Renowned German Philosopher Dr. Arthur Schopenhauer is noted for stating, "All truth passes through three stages. First it is ridiculed; second, it is violently opposed; and third, it is accepted as self-evident."[1] With the disbanding of Project Sign, the Air Force had strategically moved to Schopenhauer's Stage 1.

Let us examine the history of Project Sign's post-existential UFO edict and the metamorphosis at Wright-Patterson that would transform a serious, proactive inquiry into its antithesis, appropriately named Grudge. Its lasting impact has created a self-perpetuating ridicule factor when dealing with the subject of UFOs that is still manifesting today.

The second official UFO study at Wright-Patterson (after Project Sign) was so reduced in scope that it was not even a special project anymore. Code-named Project Grudge, the new, understaffed, and underfunded response to its predecessor amounted to the total abandonment of any attempt at an objective investigation of the flying-saucer situation. The immediate concern of the intelligence community was flying-disk hysteria at Wright-Patterson and the Pentagon, and whether their research was becoming too interplanetary. The final summation of Sign, the new thought went, demonstrated a direction that had to be disparaged and shut down quickly. This necessitated the summary dismissal of almost all the pro-UFO personnel on the project. In place of them were assigned trained military masters of the art of debunkery. This in itself would establish an entirely new theme at the newly named Grudge. Ruppelt himself would remark, "Weird things are taking place."[2]

A reduced number of civilians from Sign remained, such as Deyarmond, Loedding, and Towles. Dissension, whether planned or the end result, made for total impotence of the former Sign scientists. The open level of hostility toward them and other believers created a period of no investigations, progress, or hope of any resolution regarding the subject. Ruppelt would accurately label the tenure of Grudge as the "Dark Ages" of USAF UFO investigations.[3]

For J. Allen Hynek, the military's scientific advisor on all their UFO studies, the question always came back to this: Why stay on with a project that has a desire to fail? Fortunately for him, he still had his full-time employment at Ohio State, and his involvement with Grudge was a sideline—a sideline that was about to become a circus.

Grudge clearly had one agenda: deflating the true nature of the phenomenon until it disappeared. The reader need only ask the question, *Why?* The project had no intention of conducting any legitimate investigation. Sign had concluded that the UFO phenomenon was real and that the craft were not manufactured on planet Earth, but suddenly Grudge torpedoed the very notion without a counter-investigation or any substantive opposing evidence of any kind

As part of the inside joke on any serious continuation on the Sign theme, Pentagon officials announced that Grudge would resume the same policies. However, as Ruppelt observed, **"In doing this, standard intelligence procedures would be used. This normally means an unbiased evaluation of intelligence data. However, it does not take a great deal of study of the old UFO files to see that Project Grudge was not following standard intelligence procedures. Everything was being evaluated on the premise that UFOs couldn't exist. No matter what you see or hear, don't believe it."[4]**

Ruppelt also pointed out that some of ATIC's most influential intelligence specialists, so committed to an unbiased approach with Sign, were nowhere to be seen with Grudge. Some even went so far as to become outspoken critics of the reality of the enigma. With promotions and future pensions at stake military officers follow orders, and the new

General Charles Cabell.

official attitude was that UFOs needed to be played down with the hope that it would all just go away. At the Pentagon, the analysis officer assigned to UFO reports, Major Aaron J. Boggs, and intelligence chief Colonel Harold Watson at AMC at Wright-Patterson, were publicly presenting the position that the entire UFO business was nonsense. As a result, Grudge became nothing more than a front to debunk the subject, and T-2 Intelligence wrote the book on evading the truth. In fact, Major Boggs was so exuberant in his anti-UFO campaign that General Cabell at the Pentagon ordered that a more "respectful" atmosphere be created even in the midst of their true agenda—to discredit the subject into obscurity. Only later would Cabell learn that those deceived extended all the way to his own office.[5]

Next to the infamous press conference in General Ramey's office held to explain away the entire Roswell affair as nothing but a downed weather balloon, an article in the April 30, 1949, *Saturday Evening Post* titled "What You Can Believe About Flying Saucers" by Sidney Shalett constituted the greatest attempt by the Air Force to shut down the subject. The *Post* at that time was the most read magazine in the country and carried more weight than any other major newspaper. A May 7, 1949, article presented the position that most UFO sightings could be readily explained in prosaic terms and were simply misidentifications by the inexperienced public. It also suggested that the root cause was mass hysteria encouraged by the media. Shalett also made the fallacious accusation that pranksters and hoaxers made up the vast majority of such reporters. To slam down the lid even tighter, military luminaries such as LeMay, Vandenberg, Norstad, and McCoy peppered the biased article with every negative remark they could muster. Shalett also went out of his way to exculpate the Air Force by writing that they never would have taken such a controversial subject seriously if not for all the pressure from the public for a rational explanation.

For some people at least, the article left the door open a crack with its mention of a minuscule fraction of UFO cases that remained unexplained. Indeed, in spite of Grudge's efforts to explain away all the sighting reports that crossed its desk, a trickle of cases still cried out for legitimate investigation. This left the project with no other recourse than to release its own "official" summation of the Air Force's ongoing investigation of the UFO phenomenon: Authored by civilian George Towles and Lt. Howard Smith in August 1949, the 600-page release announced that the case was closed and its mission accomplished in dismissing the entire enigma. What the press missed was that it took hundreds of pages of the same propaganda it was fed over the previous year to draw such a conclusion. General Cabell was not amused, and he referred to the study as "tripe." Many other high-ranking officers at the Pentagon were surprised at the rejection of the entire subject. Nonetheless, as flawed and ineffectual as Grudge was, its formal statement was widely accepted by the media. It read:

> **There is no evidence that objects reported upon are the result of an advanced scientific foreign development; and, therefore they constitute no direct threat to the national security. In view of this, it is recommended that the investigation and study of reports of unidentified flying objects be reduced in scope. Headquarters at AMC [Air Materiel Command, Wright Patterson] will continue to investigate reports in which realistic technical applications are clearly indicated. NOTE: It is apparent that further study along present lines would only confirm the findings presented herein. It is further recommended that pertinent collection**

directives be revised to reflect the contemplated change in policy. All evidence and analysis indicate that reports of unidentified flying objects are the result of: Misinterpretation of various conventional objects. A mild form of mass-hysteria and war nerves. Individuals who fabricate such reports to perpetrate a hoax or to seek publicity. Psychopathological persons.[6]

With zero fanfare, Lt. Gerry Cumming was appointed the new project director, and for the next two years, he mainly provided a statement or two for any remaining curious reporters. One just happened to be Robert Ginna of *LIFE* magazine who traveled from New York to Wright-Patterson to peruse the Grudge files. In short order he observed, "the project's manifest shortcomings." Files of publicized cases were missing, and sighting reports were not attended to—all by design. Ginna found no flying saucers in the dysfunctional Grudge reports. So he sought answers at the Pentagon, and it would be another year before he broke his eye-opening story, "Have We Visitors from Space?" in *LIFE*.[7] This piece was by far the most pro-UFO media investigation to date—considering Project Grudge provided nothing substantive for their report. Ruppelt was compelled to respond to the article: "I knew that the Air Force had unofficially inspired the *LIFE* article. The 'maybe they're interplanetary' with the 'maybe' bordering on 'they are' was the personal opinion of several very high-ranking officers at the Pentagon—so high that their opinion was almost policy. I knew the men and I knew that one of them, a general, had passed his opinions on to Bob Ginna."[8] However, for the bewildered Grudge, the bottom had yet to drop out.

Grudge was ordered by the Pentagon to report the results of one of the rare investigations it actually attempted concerning a UFO report of September 10, 1951, in Fort Monmouth, New Jersey. The head of Air Force Intelligence at the Pentagon, General Cabell, was not pleased. He accused project personnel of outright debunking and sabotaging procedures. Cabell believed the subject deserved serious attention, and in his eyes, Grudge was an embarrassment to the Air Force. He was especially upset by Grudge's portrayal of having zero respect for civilian witnesses. Project director Cumming addressed the forum stating that every UFO report was taken as a "huge joke" and that Grudge had become all but irrelevant. Cabell immediately lashed out at both Grudge and the AMC, both headquartered at Wright-Patterson. Angrily, he stated, "I want an open mind; in fact, I order an open mind! Anyone who doesn't keep an open mind can get out now! Why do I have to stir up the action? Anyone can see that we do not have a satisfactory answer to the saucer question."

At a subsequent meeting of high-ranking officers, Cabell charged, "I've been lied to, and lied to, and lied to. I want it to stop. I want the answer to the saucers and I **want a good answer.**"[9] Cabell had no desire to publicly voice his personal position on the subject, and he likewise maintained that although the project should move forward more seriously, it should remain nondescript in the eyes of the press and public.

Theoretically, Project Grudge practiced the policy of preemption as defined by Russian novelist Leo Tolstoy. He stated, "The most difficult subjects can be explained to the most slow-witted man if he has not formed any idea of them already; but the simplest thing cannot be made clear to the most intelligent man if he is firmly persuaded that he knows already without a shadow of doubt what is laid before him."[10] Just four years after Roswell, the press and people's minds remained uneducated regarding the subject of unidentified flying objects. They relied strictly on officialdom to convey to them the most truthful, most reassuring solution to this increasingly perplexing mystery. Whatever the answers— or lack thereof—someone decided not on restraint, not on caution, but rather on intentional deception. Someone who knew the truth...

But let the game continue.

Within the next few months, 1st Lt. Edward J. Ruppelt took over as the new head of Grudge. In earnest, he upgraded the effort with the creation of the Aerial Phenomenon Branch.[11] The official investigation of UFOs was about to become respectful again, and the new director did not intend to lie to the general, who continued to watch from Washington.

Alas, the green light to openly search for the truth would be all too short.

CHAPTER 11

Project Stork:
The Secret Project That Never Existed

On December 26, 1951, the newly appointed Ruppelt and ATIC's Technical Analysis Division Chief, Colonel S .H. Kirkland, met with administrators at Battelle to propose a new study. The topic of discussion was whether there was sufficient data to conduct a statistical analysis of the growing number of UFO sighting reports. Under the contention that "some type of unusual object or phenomena" was being observed, Battelle was contracted to put together a panel of consultants in astronomy, psychology, physics, and other disciplines to establish patterns and trends pertaining to the subject. This project's code name was Stork.[1]

On the surface, Project Stork was assigned the mission of determining the capabilities of the Soviet Union in a technological confrontation. The obvious question is: Why would ATIC at Wright-Patterson enroll Battelle in such a study, which was clearly outside their purview? Simply stated, Stork was a funding vehicle for something outside of the public domain. After all, the project was classified top secret, which even prevented most military officers from having any knowledge of its presence. As far as military historians are concerned, for many decades after the last UFO case was cataloged by the secret study, it never existed.

The preliminary status report on Project Stork was sent to ATIC at Wright-Patterson on April 25, 1952. It was stamped "Secret." In it, Battelle included the following:

- A listing of proposed consultants who would analyze the existing UFO reports.
- Plans to subscribe to a print-media clipping service to monitor civilian reports.
- Plans to compose a Technical Observer's Interrogation Form.
- A pledge to update ATIC on a monthly basis.

During one of his assignments with the secret project, J. Allen Hynek conducted interviews with professional and amateur astronomy groups with these purposes:

- To learn if any competent people in this profession have made sightings that have not been reported.
- To summarize the opinion of the competent people in this field relative to the broad subject of unidentified flying objects.
- To obtain information and suggestions that may be useful in carrying out future phases of the work on the investigations.[2]

Hynek submitted a Special Report on Conferences with Astronomers on Unidentified Aerial Objects to ATIC at WPAFB on August 6, 1952. Contrary to Air Force press information, astronomers were seeing unknowns during the course of there professional observations. This fact should have carried considerable weight among the other sciences. However, it was not only ignored, but other astronomers refuted it.[3]

One of the more renowned astronomers mentioned in the report was Dr. Lincoln LaPaz, the director of the Institute of Meteoritics at the University of New Mexico in Albuquerque. Not only had LaPaz been secretly involved with the Manhattan Project, but also, and more importantly to this story, he had been assigned from Washington, DC, in September 1947 to investigate the Roswell crash and determine the "speed and trajectory" of the unknown craft.[4] At the time of Hynek's report, LaPaz was in his home state researching mysterious sightings of "green fireballs," a type of unidentified flying object that were all too often observed around top-secret military bases, particularly in the Southwest. Hynek remarked, **"The discussion of green fireballs with many astronomers disclosed that most of them were of the opinion that those were natural phenomenon. However, close questioning revealed that they knew nothing of the actual sightings, of their**

Dr. Lincoln LaPaz.

frequency or anything much about them and therefore cannot be taken seriously."

He added, **"This is characteristic of scientists in general when speaking about subjects which are not in the immediate field of concern."** After giving a detailed account of the numerous sightings from New Mexico, Hynek then deduced that they were quite unlike meteors, which, upon entry into the Earth's atmosphere, are typically observed over a wide area—even thousands of miles. He explains, **"There is no reason that they should all show up in New Mexico.... If the data reported by LaPaz are correct, then we do have a strange phenomena here indeed."**[5]

Prior to this research, Hynek had already conducted his own private polling among his colleagues and had obtained "interesting information" from professional astronomers who, in some cases, also witnessed the "green fireballs." To maintain the upper hand, the Air Force pulled from its hat one of its own heavyweights: astrophysicist Dr. Donald Menzel of the Harvard Observatory, who, according to Hynek, had a habit of labeling some of the more spectacular films of UFOs flying in formation as "Birds...just birds." Menzel would publicly decry the lack of accessibility to sighting reports and in the next breath debunk all UFO sightings as nonsense.[6] This encouraged one of Hynek's colleagues at Ohio State, Dr. Paul M. Fitts, professor of psychology and director of aviation, along with a few associates, to revise the Stork sighting form to gain maximum information regarding future sightings. There was then an attempt to analyze existing sighting reports, including those dating back to 1948.

Aside from a more systematic report form, Hynek also recommended the following procedural change to the Air Force:

> ...the problem of unidentified aerial objects should be given the status of a scientific problem. Therefore, it is proposed that some reputable group of scientists be asked to examine recent sightings, which have already gone through one or two screenings. If this group becomes convinced that the data are worthy of being treated as a scientific problem, that is, that the sightings are valid and that unexplained phenomena really do exist, then they should be asked to vouch that these data are worthy of being admitted into court.[7]

He continued,

> There is much confusion in the public mind as to what is being done about the situation, and a great deal of needless criticism is being directed toward the Air Force for "trying to cover-up" or "dismissing the whole thing." The considered statement to the public press that the problem is being referred to competent scientists in various fields should do a very great deal in satisfying the public clamor.

Moreover, Hynek ran into the same roadblock as before: The Air Force was not looking for scientific validation of UFOs; quite the contrary, they continually sought the support of scientists who not only had negative attitudes toward the subject, but who also excoriated their own colleagues for displaying any inquisitiveness about the subject. Donald Menzel best exemplified this policy. Though skeptical by nature, Hynek was the one of the few scientists who demonstrated the principle character of the scientific mind: curiosity. He continued to argue that such a study within Stork should not be difficult to overcome, because **"the number of truly puzzling incidents is now impressive."** The part of the equation that Hynek realized would take a great more time and effort was "to **determine with great accuracy what the phenomena to be explained really are and to establish their reality beyond all question."**

Finally, Hynek encouraged the eventual publication of the findings of the scientific panel. In doing so, he tacitly dismissed the conclusion from Grudge, which erroneously claimed that flying saucer sightings had dropped off. He refuted Grudge by saying, "**...the flying-saucer sightings have not died down, as was confidently predicted some years ago when the first deluge of sightings was regarded as mass hysteria."** He reiterated that we must "try to understand it."[8]

Project Stork (designated project no. 9974) officially began on March 31, 1952, as four scientists were assigned to the secret UFO project at Battelle. The study would be the most sophisticated analysis of sighting reports ever conducted by any research group heretofore. This was accomplished utilizing new IBM data-processing machines, which encoded the entered data. The sighting reports would be broken down into separate classifications—"known," unknown," and "insufficient information." Each case would also be rated from "excellent" to "poor" in quality. Seven status reports were sent to ATIC at Wright-Patterson, which included soil and vegetation samples collected at UFO landing sites. Radiation readings were also included—hard science in search of physical evidence. During this time, 168 sighting questionnaires were completed by witnesses and assigned a battery of 30 specific characteristics of UFO sightings. These were combined with the bulk of reports provided by the Air Force since 1948. Stork computerized more than 3,000 case reports that, based on the code system, were kicked out as "unknown" or "insufficient data."[9] More importantly, the final results demonstrated that UFOs were not of any foreign earthly (in other words, Russian) design. ATIC expected a final report in the fall of 1953, though analysis at Battelle continued through 1954, evidently in an attempt to force the data to more closely resemble the information the Air Force was providing the public.

As a former secretary to Hynek and employee of Battelle, Jennie Zeidman remarked, **"Battelle's involvement with the fringe subject of UFOs was therefore a source of great embarrassment to it—a family secret, a skeleton in the closet equivalent to Grandpa's alcoholism or Uncle Ray's penchant for little boys. One absolutely did not mention Battelle in connection with UFOs."** As enthusiastic as Hynek was to have an independent scientific study of the phenomenon outside of the barriers established at Wright-Patterson, the U.S. government heavily contracted Battelle. Subsequently, Stork had little chance of making any breakthroughs and found itself marginalized by the quality of the data provided by the Air Force.[10]

After months of delay, Stork's final UFO study was released on October 25, 1955, as Bluebook Special Report 14. The report's introduction explained that it was commissioned by the Air Force **"to determine if 'flying saucers' represented technological developments not known in this country."** The greatest portion of the report debunked the topic as "natural phenomena that are not completely understood, psychological phenomena, or intruder aircraft of a type that may be possessed by some source in large enough numbers so that more than one independent mission may have been flown and reported."[11] Hynek had once again been taken out to the woodshed and left to ponder just how entering UFO data onto punch cards at Battelle had solved the entire mystery. Ruppelt wrote at the time, **"This was a shock to me because I was the one that had this study made...the answer was, statistical methods were no good for a study like this. They didn't prove a thing...I had written it off as worthless."** The Air Force would claim that only 3 percent of the cases examined by Stork remained unexplained. This was a total fabrication on their part as the actual percentage was 22. It should also be pointed out that the more available the information and the higher the quality of the individual cases, the more likely they were to be classed as unidentified.

Jennie Zeidman met with Lincoln LaPaz at his university office at that time and briefed him on Hynek's efforts, which included Project Stork. Zeidman vividly recalled how the formidable scientist "pinned me with a solemn stare." **"UFOs are the Fifth Horseman of the Apocalypse,"** he said.[12] Pestilence, war, famine, death, and UFOs?

CHAPTER 12

Project Blue Book's Fall to Irrelevance

After the early demise of Project Grudge, Project Blue Book was established with the intention of enacting a renewed academic study of the phenomenon. In an attempt to bring respectability back to the study, its director, Captain Edward Ruppelt, decreed that "flying saucers" and "flying disks" were now to be called "Unidentified Flying Objects."[1] From late 1951 through the middle part of 1953, under Ruppelt's leadership, UFO investigation would see its last legitimate public analysis. The late astrophysicist Dr. James E. McDonald once said, **"The Ruppelt era was a heroic period...the one interval during which UFOs were seriously and relatively vigorously investigated."**[2]

Originally, Ruppelt's agenda was to play down the negative public stigma associated with the subject. The general public was once again encouraged to report their personal experiences to their friendly neighborhood Air Force base. Blue Book would assign investigators to facilities throughout the nation. There would be a concerted effort to add civilian sightings to the daily roster, and field reports would all end up at Wright-Patterson for evaluation and possible follow-up. Ruppelt would even create the very first investigation questionnaire, with all the raw data accessed and computerized at Battelle Institute. Objectivity was required and personal opinions were better left unspoken. The new study was looking for answers and hired numerous scientists from different respective fields, while J. Allen Hynek remained the head scientific

Captain Edward Ruppelt.

consultant. A more open-door policy was provided to the media, and Hynek was holding regular meetings to update the press on current sighting investigations. "We're on it," became the new order of the day, and Ruppelt was the man in charge—or so he was led to believe.

Project Blue Book simplified the official study of the phenomenon down to two basic goals:

1. Determine if UFOs are a threat to national security.

2. Scientifically analyze UFO reports.[3]

The groundwork was completed, Grudge was the little train that failed, and Ruppelt had promised General Cabell to bring him "answers." Predictably, others at the Pentagon envisioned a continuation of the same old tactics for the project; they just needed the right set of circumstances to unveil the old Grudge under the new Blue Book banner. As long as sightings remained manageable and nothing extraordinary happened, officials at both the Pentagon and the AMC at Wright-Patterson would continue looking for solutions outside of public scrutiny. Grudge had experienced three full years of "all's quiet." Nothing major happened on the flying disc front to renew any media coverage—all while Battelle Institute, Rand Corporation, Hughs Aircraft, General Electric and The Bureau of Standards, just to name a few, all frantically attempted to decipher the debris recovered at Roswell. Time was not on their side.

The summer of 1952, similar to that of 1947, witnessed one of the greatest waves of UFO activity America has ever seen. Aside from many of the civilian reports, Air Force bases throughout the country were observing and tracking infiltrations of unknowns beginning in May, and on two consecutive Saturdays in July, the unexpected took place: Not only did the UFOs return *en masse* but also, on both nights they literally buzzed the White House. F-94 Fighters were urgently scrambled from Andrews AFB to pursue as many as eight aerial invaders, and what next ensued was a public demonstration of who possessed the superior technology. Experienced pilots attempted in vain to intercept the violators while radar operators watched as our fastest jets were completely outperformed. Over the nation's very capital, the situation had risen well beyond the auspices of Blue Book and Captain Ruppelt. For the first time, UFOs had reached our most senior defenders of national security and, at best, all we managed to do was chase them away. According to all accounts, the UFOs were doing the chasing and eventually gave up on the cat and mouse shenanigans. Banner headlines after the first night's drama beat out coverage of the Republican presidential convention, so the Pentagon had to move fast to allay the worst fears of the public.

"The Washington Nationals," as the UFOs were dubbed by the media, forced an immediate return back to the tactics of Project Grudge. Despite the best intentions of Ruppelt, who authorized the interviewing of all key personnel involved with the incident, with no obligation to the chain of command, AF Intelligence at the Pentagon moved in quickly. Witnesses were coerced to change their testimony; films, photographs, and official reports were confiscated. But through Ruppelt's independent investigation, he discovered a rather startling fact:

We found out that the UFOs frequently visited Washington. On May 23 [1952] 50 targets had been tracked from 8:00 p.m. 'til midnight. They were back on the Wednesday between the two famous Saturday-night sightings, the following Sunday night, and the night of the press conference [held on Tuesday, July 29, at the Pentagon, where Major General John A. Samford, Chief of Air Force Intelligence, dismissed the "Washington Nationals" as natural phenomena]; then during August they were seen eight more times. On several occasions, military and civilian pilots saw lights where the radar showed the UFOs to be."[4]

There were additional UFO incidents recorded during that wave at 24 military bases throughout America. Once again, the situation was getting completely out of hand and the Pentagon sounded the alarm. The subject of UFOs was under lockdown. Overnight, Project Blue Book morphed into the very study group it was assigned to bury. The Dark Ages had returned and the project would never recover. Time had run out and any hope of a legitimate investigation was quickly scrubbed.

Enter the CIA: After an extended period of many unexplained reports, the Air Force was in a major quandary—the media was demanding answers, which were still unavailable. Riding in on a big black horse, the CIA ordered the Office of Scientific Intelligence (OSI) to review the files on UFO reports at Wright-Patterson and make a recommendation. Continuing the methodology of Ruppelt's tenure at Blue Book, the OSI recommended that further study into UFOs was required. Taking that suggestion, the CIA convened a special panel under the directorship of Dr. Howard P. Robertson, a physicist from the California Institute of Technology.[5] The prestigious group consisted of other physicists, meteor scientists, engineers, and one astronomer: Hynek, who, along with Ruppelt, presented their best evidence of a genuine phenomenon. Undoubtedly, the remainder of the staged panel listened to a summation of six years of UFO data with a skeptical mindset. Hynek would later lament, "It didn't matter what evidence was presented...it was though I wasn't even in the room."[6]

After a total of 12 hours in four days of study from January 14 through 17, 1953, the Robertson Panel was able to accomplish what the Air Force was unable to do in five years: explain away most of the sightings. The remainders were dismissed as "raw, unevaluated reports." The panel made three recommendations: **"That the national security agencies take immediate steps to strip the Unidentified Flying Objects of the special status they have been given and the aura of mystery they have unfortunately acquired."** They also expressed the concern that low-grade reports were "overloading" standard military (intelligence) channels and as a result were more threatening to our national security than the actual phenomenon. The emphasis shift, or return, was for the Air Force to again "debunk" the subject through the media using psychological solutions to ridicule the witnesses and explain their reports. Civilian UFO groups were to be labeled crackpots and the very term *UFO* was to conjure images of uneducated, wide-eyed believers seeking attention for their mental instabilities. Nonetheless, the panel suggested that such groups should be monitored.[7]

In just four days the greatest mystery of all time was resolved by a handful of men.

In reality, the Air Force had enlisted the CIA for an intelligence bail-out, and, once again, the media headed for the tall grass. Within days of the final recommendation, Chairman Robertson wrote in a letter to the assistant director of scientific intelligence, Dr. H. Marshall Chadwell, who provided much of the UFO data to the panel, **"Perhaps that'll take care of the Forteans [supporters of Charles Fort, a pioneer in UFO studies] for a while."**[8]

CIA director Allen Dulles summed it up best: **"If you want to keep a secret, then pretend to share it."** Dulles is best remembered for actively establishing a recruiting and cover capacity within the highest levels of journalistic institutions; since the inception of the CIA, it has succeeded in manipulating the media. In fact, since the early 1950s, more than 400 American journalists have worked either directly for or informally for the CIA.[9] Former British MI6 agent John le Carré reminded us in his best-selling book *The Spy Who Came in From the Cold*, "Most people would be absolutely amazed if they knew how many people in the American Intelligence community were sitting around doing nothing but thinking about ways to influence public opinion."

So that would take care of the press and the public. In stark contrast, the Air Force immediately implemented regulation 200-2 and JANAP

Former CIA Director Allen Dulles.

146, which would make it a crime for any military personnel to disclose information about UFOs.[10] Total containment of the subject was now complete.

Prior to the Robertson Panel, the renewed attitude of Project Blue Book with Ruppelt at the helm was to conduct a serious, no-nonsense investigation of the UFO matter. During the first five years, through the end of 1952, there were 394 unidentified sightings in the project files. In the remaining 15 years up until the close of the study in 1969, only 308 more cases were added to the unexplained list. After advisement by the CIA panel, Blue Book was completely demoralized and thoroughly stripped of its investigative duties. Air Force regulation 200-2 instructed officers to discuss openly only "identified" sightings; those that remained unsolved were to be completely withheld from the public. As Hynek described, **"When the Air Force could explain away a sighting,**

they would jump handsprings to get it out to the public." He also added, "All the hardcore cases were going upstairs [at that time]. We didn't have access to any of the important cases any longer." Blue Book was only assigned the more mundane sighting reports.[11] The newly formed 4602nd Air Intelligence Squadron (AISS) of the Air Defense Command, which investigated reports that were even more serious, took all investigative responsibilities away. This secret unit was located at Ent Air Force Base in Colorado Springs, Colorado. The mission of the 4602nd was to:

1. Retrieve downed enemy aircrew.

2. Retrieve downed enemy material.

3. Retrieve downed enemy documents.[12]

Subsection (a) of regulation 200-2 states that all personnel in the Air Force may conduct initial investigations, but warns that additional inquiry "should not be carried beyond this point unless such action is requested by the 4602nd AISS."[13]

In a subsequent report, dated January 3, 1953, Air Force Regulation 24-4 described specific training of the 4602nd as "general intelligence procedures, written and spoken foreign languages, technical intelligence investigation, photography and photo interpretation, and such other activities as may be necessary for the accomplishment of the mission." One of their directives stated, "In case of any physical [UFO] evidence, you are to safeguard it and notify us. We will tell you what to do with it."[14]

Blue Book was also restricted by Air Force regulation 200-2 and could only release information on explained UFO investigations. All the while the media was misled to believe that Project Blue Book was still conducting actual, legitimate investigations, when in reality it quickly became merely a public relations front and debunking tool for the Air Force. Longtime Hynek associate and fellow astronomer Walter N. Webb commented, "...the Roswell revelations now furnish ample evidence for the existence of an ultra-secret UFO study coexisting with Blue Book."[15] A great analogy to describe the final years of Blue Book was provided by author and State Department analyst Douglas P. Horne when addressing a similar topic: "[It's like] if you have a five-hundred piece puzzle, then someone throws out 250 of the pieces, and next, someone else substitutes 250 pieces from another puzzle." Such was the total obfuscation of the UFO enigma by the post-Ruppelt project.

With his funding and public support reduced to an ineffective shadow of what Blue Book promised to be, Ruppelt resigned. He felt a sense of foreboding because of how much of the truth even he was not told. As King Arthur bemoaned at the falling of Camelot, "Those dreary dark days we had sought to put to rest were once again upon us." Meanwhile, Blue Book returned to those dreary, dark days of Grudge that Ruppelt had tried to end. Hynek lamented, "**Everything would go in [to Blue Book] and nothing would come out.**" The Air Force had little need for its chief scientist during this time. When Captain Joseph Cybulski flew in to Wright-Patterson from 4602nd Headquarters, Hynek threatened to resign. He expressed, "**I have not been able to get support from the Air Force. It seems that they all think this is a hot subject...they want to drop it...don't want to have anything to do with it. No one wants to be quoted.**"[16] After assurances from Cybulski that things were about to change for the better, Hynek threw away his resignation paper. And things did change—for the worse.

In the wings was hardnosed skeptic Captain George T. Gregory, who personally felt it was unfair that the Air Force had to compete with civilian UFO organizations. After all, how could they explain away all of the sightings if such outside groups were consistently publicizing well-investigated, very puzzling cases. Because of "personal impressions and interpretations" of the witnesses reporting experiences to these non-military researchers, he said, "**it is doubtful that the number of 'unknowns' will ever be reduced to zero.**"[17] Ironically, Hynek saw this as an excellent opportunity and started to correspond with such outside researchers, who, because of their more serious nature, attracted many new cases unknown to the scientist.[18] Nonetheless, Blue Book was dropped as a special project and sightings were to be classed as "identified" regardless of the facts—all while the physical evidence was right below their feet at Wright-Patterson. Air Force Intelligence still needed more time to determine the facts, and Blue Book's new role was to run interference.

By 1955, the Pentagon had decided that the mission of the project was not to investigate the UFO phenomenon but rather to reduce the number of unknowns. Their new function was to play damage control for any suggestion of a legitimate sighting that had leaked to the public. At the same time, the 4602nd was dissolved and replaced by the 1066th Air Intelligence Service Squadron, who would maintain the true inquiry.[19] However, the Pentagon was not through with Blue Book. In 1956, chief officer Captain Gregory revised AFR-200-2 to explain all previous reports with the insertion of the words "possible" and "probable." The all-out attack on the validity of the very suggestion that UFOs might represent an intelligence from off the planet had to be squashed and relegated to the ranks of the funny farm. Toward the end of 1956, unexplained cases were down to a mere 2 percent, and 1.4 percent by the end of 1957.[20]

The Air Force had spectroscopic cameras, telescopes, and other sophisticated instruments available to track unknown aircraft, but it was not until 1953 and the early part of 1954 that such instrument recordings were attempted. Gregory would claim to Walter Webb in an interview in 1956, "**We have scientists working for us [Blue Book] all over the U.S.**" In reality, Hynek was the only paid scientific consultant to the project at that time.[21]

After Gregory, another low-ranking officer, Captain Charles Hardin, would take charge, who, as later described by Ruppelt, "**...thinks anyone who is even interested [in UFOs] is crazy.**" Historian Dr. David Jacobs added, "**During [Hardin's] tenure, he made the most strenuous efforts of any Blue Book leader to identify UFO reports regardless of the information they contained.**" When they had to deal with specific reports that were not so readily explained, it became standard Blue Book procedure to dump them into the "insufficient data" hopper.[22]

Time ran out for the Air Force once again as a major wave of UFO sightings began in November of 1957. In response, the Assistant Air Force Secretary Richard Horner said, "**The Air Force is not hiding any UFO information, and I do not qualify this in any way.**"[23] Sightings were called "misidentified natural phenomena," but still, whenever an exceptional case reached the news media, they ran with it. The Air Force found itself again the target of public scrutiny and bad publicity. Therefore, there was an attempt to transfer Project Blue Book to some other Air Force Agency, specifically to the Secretary of the Air Force, Office of Information (SAFOI), a government public-relations group. Other documentation, such as a letter to the Pentagon from project science advisor A. Francis Arcier in April of 1960 commented on a memo written by Colonel Philip Evans, a senior officer at ATIC at Wright-Patterson. He said, "...**[I] have tried to get Blue Book out of ATIC for 10 years...and do not agree that the loss of prestige to the UFO project is a disadvantage.**"[24]

No matter what high-ranking officials wanted to believe about the public persona of the floundering Air Force investigation, the next Blue Book director, Major Robert Friend, recommended to his bosses that the program be turned over to a civilian agency. The plan to turn the Air Force study over to a civilian committee started to take root in 1962, but the trick would be to have them draw the same conclusions as the military did, all while totally exculpating the Air Force of any mishandling of the present UFO situation.[25] The search for the "way out" had begun, though it was just a matter of time before another batch of sightings would begin.

Major Hector Quintanilla would replace Friend in 1963 and serve out the final years of the project. With a lone enlisted man at his side, Quintanilla was an arrogant, nasty officer—perfect to usher in the final demolition of Blue Book. His custom was to respond to an eyewitness account over the phone this way: **"Tell me about the mirage you saw."** He had an automatic reaction to twist and manipulate the testimony of witnesses and distort the facts—in keeping with the official policy of the doomed Blue Book.[26] Nonetheless, the phenomena always seemed to go against the plans of the Air Force.

The UFOs did return once again *en masse* during the summer of 1964 into 1968. Many other books recount the most famous cases of that period, which would include the Socorro, New Mexico, landing and the Dexter/Ann Arbor, Michigan, sightings. In each of these, not only was the malnourished Blue Book in way over its head, but local law enforcement and even the FBI were also at a loss to resolve either incident. Regarding Socorro, it was the first time that an Air Force report referred to the police-witnessed UFO as an actual "vehicle"[27]—hardly a word one would use to define something imaginary or fictitious. However, the Michigan sightings attracted the most contempt on the part of the media. As so often in the past, Hynek was trotted out to offer a conventional explanation. He found himself overwhelmed as cameramen and newspaper reporters literally pulled on him for a statement. He described the circus: "**Everyone was clamoring for a single, spectacular explanation of the sightings. They wanted little green men.**" When the scientist suggested that *one* of the sightings might have resulted from "swamp gas," it spawned an outrage from the press and public, and also elicited accusations from none other than Michigan congressional representative Gerald Ford.[28]

In an unprecedented move, there were even preliminary talks scheduled on Capitol Hill: Congress entertained a motion to conduct open hearings to address the ongoing situation and the persistence of the sightings. This was all contrary to what the Pentagon and Blue Book were publicly stating. Talk of a cover-up was getting out of hand and the American media was tasting blood. In April 1966, the House Armed Services Committee urged the Air Force to contract a university to conduct a scientific study into the matter.[29] This allowed the Air Force to fall back on their original plan: to allow an unbiased, civilian group of scientists to examine the official files and make an independent evaluation and final decision on the entire UFO picture.

By October 1966, an agreement was completed with the University of Colorado at Boulder to conduct this private inquiry. Unlike the Robertson Panel, which convened for a total of four days, this study would last for the next 18 months.[30] Congress really did not want to tackle the UFO malaise in the first place. In their eyes, it was a military concern and they were responsible for the national defense. If UFOs represented a threat to the nation's security, certainly the Pentagon and the official UFO study at Wright-Patterson would have told Congress. Certainly, if they knew that UFOs represented a technology from off the planet, they would have told the press. At the very least, if they still did not have any answers and they too remained ignorant of the truth, they would tell the public. That is, *if* there was nothing to hide. In 1967, Senator Barry Goldwater of Arizona told a reporter of the *Bradenton Herald* in Florida, "**The policy of the Air Force is to allow no one to see the UFO files at Wright-Patterson.**"[31]

CHAPTER 13

A General Exposes the Air Force's True Agenda

"...everyone from Truman on down knew what we had found was not of this world within twenty-four hours of our finding it."

—General Arthur Exon

Most of the military veterans from the Roswell Army Air Field who had been part of the recovery knew or had heard from others that the wreckage from the crash had gone to Wright Field in Dayton, Ohio. Small amounts may have gone to other locations in New Mexico (such as Alamogordo AAF, Kirtland AAF, or Los Alamos) or a base in Florida, but the bulk of it went "back East," as some referred to Wright Field. We know that Captain Oliver "Pappy" Henderson flew a cargo planeload of wreckage (and perhaps *something else*) there.[1] Colonel Thomas DuBose, General Roger Ramey's adjutant at Fort Worth AAF in Texas, who had ordered some of the strange wreckage that rancher Mack Brazel had brought with him into Roswell to be flown to Washington, DC, for a quick look-see by the higher-ups ASAP, told us that the final destination for the sealed "package" was Wright Field.[2] And a teletyped FBI memorandum sent to J. Edgar Hoover on the same day of the weather balloon press conference orchestrated by General Ramey stated that both the weather balloon and the [real] wreckage were headed to Wright Field for examination.[3]

In 1980, *The Roswell Incident* book suggested that the bodies from the crash were transported by rail to Muroc AAF—now known as Edwards Air Force Base—in California. But after interviewing hundreds of witnesses since then, we found that almost everyone who knew anything about the bodies suggested that the super-secret military facility at Wright Field in Dayton, Ohio, was the ultimate destination for the remains. The pilot of the first of two suspected "body flights" from Roswell told his close friends that he flew them there nonstop.[4] John Tiffany said his father was dispatched from Wright Field to pick up strange bodies at Fort Worth after what we now know as the second "body flight" from Roswell had deposited them there.[5] And there were those like Norma Gardner and June Crain who suggested that the bodies were in Ohio years later. A welter of circumstantial evidence had accumulated, and a growing number of first- and secondhand witnesses had been found. But the proof was still far from conclusive. Enter Brigadier General Arthur E. Exon.

Exon was a pilot who flew 135 combat missions and had more than 300 hours of combat flying time in the European Theater during World War II. When his aircraft was severely damaged by an exploding ammunition dump he had just bombed, he was forced to bail out over enemy territory and was captured. He spent more than a year in several German POW camps before he was liberated in April 1945. His decorations include the Distinguished Service Cross, Legion of Merit, Distinguished Flying Cross, Air Medal with 15 Oak Leaf Clusters, Air Force Commendation Medal with Oak Leaf Cluster, British Distinguished Flying Cross, and the French Croix de Guerre with Palm and Star.[6]

After the war, he completed a two-year industrial administration course at the Air Force Institute of Technology (AFIT) in 1948 and was then assigned for the next three years to Air Materiel Command (AMC) headquarters, both located at the newly named Wright-Patterson Air Force Base.[7] Lieutenant General Nathan F. Twining was the commanding officer of the Air Materiel Command, which was responsible for the Air Force's intelligence functions, known as T-2 in 1947, which later became the Air Technical Intelligence Center (ATIC) in 1951, and then the Foreign Technology Division (FTD) in 1961.

Throughout the course of several years, Exon held a variety of positions, and attended the Air War College at Maxwell AFB in Montgomery,

The late General Arthur Exon in a photo taken by Tom Carey circa 2000. By this time, the general was more reluctant to speak about his days as commandng officer at Wright-Patterson.

Alabama, finally arriving at the Pentagon as a "full bird" colonel in 1955, where he would remain for the next five years. In 1960, he became the chief of ballistic missiles and was responsible for establishing the Jupiter Ballistic Missile System for NATO in Italy and Turkey. In July of 1963, he left Europe for an assignment at Olmsted Air Force Base in Pennsylvania. In August of 1964, he was appointed as base commander of Wright-Patterson Air Force Base, followed a year later by promotion to flag rank as a brigadier general.[8] It can be established, therefore, that General Exon had a most impressive military career. Officers are not promoted to flag rank (general officer) without having proven themselves as being totally competent. Those who make it while on active duty (in other words, those who are not simply "rewarded" with the promotion upon their retirement) are a small minority. Only the top officers achieve the privilege of wearing stars. General Exon was, therefore, in a position to know things. For instance, even if he did not have firsthand access to the Roswell artifacts, he knew people who did.

In 1988 Whitley Strieber, the author of *Communion, Transformation, Breakthrough,* and *Majestic* (a fictionalized rendition of the Roswell crash), among other books, was introduced to an "old friend" of one of his uncles, a retired Air Force general by the name of Art Exon who had been the "commandant" of Wright-Patterson AFB.[9] Strieber had a number of conversations with the general about Roswell, during which he learned that:

1. The Air Force had not really gotten out of the UFO business with the publication of the 1969 *Condon Report*.

2. There was still a scientific effort in progress since the crash at trying to understand the Roswell debris.

3. Other UFO materials had been obtained since then.[10]

The year 1988 was also when Kevin Randle and Don Schmitt re-opened the Roswell case and began a full-scale re-investigation of it. Word of Strieber's discussions with General Exon got around, and by 1990 Randle and Schmitt were conducting their own interviews with the general. They learned that Exon had been a lieutenant colonel and a student participating in a two-year industrial administration course on the base (Wright Field) at the time of the Roswell events in 1947. According to Exon, **"We heard that the [Roswell] material was coming to Wright Field. Testing was done in various labs—everything from chemical**

Author Whitley Strieber was the first researcher to interview Arthur Exon, as Exon was a good friend of Strieber's uncle.

analysis, stress tests, compression tests, and flexing. It was brought into our material evaluation labs. I don't know how it arrived, but the boys who tested it said it was very unusual."[11]

Exon also described the material: "[Some of it] could be easily ripped or changed.... There were other parts of it that were very thin but awfully strong and couldn't be dented with heavy hammers.... It was flexible to a degree." Further, according to him, "Some of it was flimsy but tougher than hell, and the [rest of it] was almost like foil but strong. It had them pretty puzzled." The lab chiefs at Wright Field set up a special project for the testing of the material. "They knew they had something new in their hands. The metal and material were unknown to anyone I talked to. Whatever they found, I never heard what the results were. A couple of guys thought it might be Russian, but the overall consensus was that the pieces were from space.[12] Everyone from the White House on down knew that what we had found was not of this world within 24 hours of our finding it."[13] When asked about the wreckage's physical makeup, he said that he didn't know if it was titanium or some other metal that we knew but that the *processing* of it was different (see Chapter 4).

Remember that John Tiffany reported that his father was stationed at Wright Field at the time of the incident and that his unit, as part of their assignment, supported the 509th Bomb Group located in Roswell as well as its parent organization, the 8th Air Force headquartered at Fort Worth Army Air Field in Texas. As we learned in a previous chapter, according to Tiffany, his father had been sent to a destination in Texas (most likely, it was Fort Worth AAF). There they picked up strange metallic wreckage and a large cylindrical container that reminded him of a giant thermos bottle. Tiffany described the metal as being lightweight and tough. It had a smooth, glass-like surface, and everything the crew did on the flight back to Wright to mark it, bend it, or break it had failed.[14]

When asked about the bodies, Exon said, "I know people who were involved in photographing some of the residue from the New Mexico affair near Roswell. There was another location [this would be the Impact Site, which is distinct from the Debris Field Site on the Foster Ranch] where apparently the main body of the spacecraft was... where they did say there were bodies. They were all found, apparently, outside the craft itself in fairly good condition. **In other words, they weren't broken up a lot."**[15] In an over-flight of the area a few months after the incident, Exon said that he was able to identify two distinct but related sites by the trail of many tire tracks leading up to them. He also told of seeing the "obvious gouges in the terrain" that were reported to us by Bill Brazel, Bud Payne, and others.[16] When asked specifically if the bodies recovered from the crash at Roswell went to Wright Field, Exon said, **"That's my information. But one of them went to a mortuary outfit...I think at that time it was in Denver. But the strongest information was that they were brought to Wright-Patt. People I have known were involved with that."**[17] Regarding the bodies, John Tiffany said that the large, unusual cylinder and its unknown contents bothered the flight crew the entire way on its flight back from Fort Worth to Wright Field. After the flight, the crew felt somehow contaminated; as though they could not get clean. They could not "get over handling something that foreign." At some point during or shortly after the trip, Tiffany's father must have seen what was inside the cylinder, because he later told his son that two [of the bodies] were intact. Once they arrived at Wright Field, everything was off-loaded, including the giant jug, and put on trucks. Once the trucks were gone, the flight crew was debriefed by a high-ranking official who told them that the flight never happened.[18]

Exon was apparently not aware of the alien that was purported to have been recovered alive from the Roswell crash, as he never spoke of it. There are any number of stories out there, however, that have it either being taken to White Sands or Los Alamos, or even staying in Roswell for a period of time. In short, its immediate whereabouts post-recovery are still a mystery, but it ultimately turned up at Wright-Patterson in 1948 (see Chapter 8).

When we interviewed General Exon in the 1990s, he was sure that at least some of the extraterrestrial "space material" was still being housed at Wright-Patterson. He told us there would still be reports, probably filed in the Foreign Technology (FTD) Building, which would describe everything learned in the past 60-plus years of studying the exotic materials. There would also be photographs logging each and every aspect of the crash, including retrievals from multiple sites, the transporting of the remains, all the recovery-related activities at the base in Roswell, and the final disposition of all physical evidence.[19] In short, everything needed to prove that Roswell represented the crash of an extraterrestrial spacecraft and its crew was at one time housed at Wright-Patterson AFB—and it still may be.[20] After all, after more than 60 years of rumors and whispers, the base remains shrouded in mystery. And like all former Strategic Air Command bases (those bases with nuclear strike forces), Wright-Patt is an underground maze of secret vaults, tunnels, and multi-level hangars. At ground level, newly poured concrete has sealed off entrances and resurfaced hanger floors long suspected of securing the base's biggest secrets (e.g., most notably, Hangar 23). Former base commanders have told us that there were specific areas that were even off-limits to them. One of these was General Arthur Exon.

Students of Roswell will know that the cover-up started down in Roswell on the very first day that it became a story in the national news media. Even before General Ramey's infamous weather balloon press conference, it started on the Roswell base itself when the people to whom the media would be looking for answers about the crash all "got out of Dodge" as quickly as possible: Major Jesse Marcel, the first military person at the crash site, was sent off to Fort Worth, Texas; Lieutenant Walter Haut, the Roswell base public information officer who issued the initial press release announcing the RAAF's "capture" of a flying saucer, was ordered home to hide out; and the base commander, Colonel William Blanchard, announced that he was going on leave.[21] Because he knew Blanchard, Exon said, "Blanchard's leave was a screen. It was his duty to go to the [crash] site and make a determination. Blanchard couldn't have cared less about a weather balloon."[22] Unknown to Exon, someone else had told us the same thing. According to retired Colonel Joe Briley, who was an operations officer at the Roswell base in 1947, **"Blanchard's leave was a blind. He was actually setting up a base of operation at the crash site north of town."**[23] Exon also pointed out that there were no secret balloon or weather devices that could account for the wreckage that he heard about. **"The lab men and officers at Wright Field, because it was their job, would have known if the debris fit into those categories."**[24] Except for his own *ad hoc* flight over the Roswell crash sites, Exon made it clear that he was repeating what he had been told by his friends and colleagues at Wright-Patterson.

Exon knew of the UFO cover-up, starting with the one that originated at Roswell. **"I know that at the time [it] happened, it went to General Ramey...and he, along with the people out at Roswell, decided to change the story while they got their act together and got the information into the Pentagon and to the president."**[25] According to Exon, the instant they knew the nature of the find, Ramey (after being notified by Colonel Blanchard in Roswell) would have alerted the chief of staff, General Eisenhower. (This would not have been done directly by Ramey, but by going up the ladder through his direct chain of command.) Once they had the information in Washington, control of the operation would have come from the Pentagon. The men in Roswell would have been tasked with the cleanup because they were there on the site, but the responsibility for it would have moved up the chain of command to the Pentagon and the White House. We now know that this scenario described by Exon is exactly what happened, according to the sealed statement of the former Roswell base public information officer in 1947, the late Walter Haut.[26] The men of the 509th Bomb Group located at the Roswell Army Air Field were indeed dispatched to the boondocks to effect the cleanup, which included the recovery of wreckage and bodies, while the entire operation, including press releases, was directed out of the Pentagon by the Air Force's deputy chief of staff, Lieutenant General Hoyt Vandenberg.[27]

The outgrowth of all this, according to Exon, was the formation of an official oversight committee to study the phenomenon and control access to the wreckage, bodies, and information regarding the Roswell crash. He referred to this group as the "Unholy Thirteen," only because he did not know the actual name of the group.[28] Its responsibility would also be to protect the data developed, to control access to it, and to design studies to exploit it. Exon supplied us with the names of some of the members of this group—names that students of American history of the late 1940s would recognize, like Truman, Eisenhower, Symington, and Hillenkoetter. According to Exon, "...**a top intelligence echelon was represented, the President's office was represented and the Secretary of Defense's office was represented....**" One thing that Exon made clear was that no elected officials, other than the president, were ever included. Elected officials were excluded from knowing anything about it.[29]

This policy would explain why Barry Goldwater was denied entry to the "Blue Room" at Wright-Patterson in the 1960s when he asked to look inside and see the UFO artifacts rumored to be stored there. Although Goldwater was at the time a major general in the Air Force Reserve and a good friend of the Air Force chief of staff, General Curtis LeMay, he was also a sitting United States *senator* and therefore disqualified from ever entering the room or knowing what was in it (see Chapter 5).

At the time of our interviews with Exon in the early 1990s, he was sure that most if not all of the Roswell material was still being housed at Wright-Patterson. In addition to the physical wreckage and bodies, he believed there would be reports filed in the FTD building that described everything learned up to that point in time. There would be photographs from the debris field, the Impact Site, the Dee Proctor Body Site, and of the bodies and the autopsies.[30] Since then, it is possible that some or most of the Roswell material has been dispersed to other locations throughout the country because of the publicity surrounding the case and the focus upon Wright-Patterson as destination of choice for the material. And because we *really* do not know for sure, it is equally possible that it is all still quietly tucked away in the "Blue Room."

While Exon was a colonel at the Pentagon from 1955 to 1960, he ran into the controlling/oversight committee that was formed after the Roswell Incident. They were still in operation and still concerned with UFOs. And when he moved back to Wright-Patterson as the base commander sporting the single star of a brigadier general in 1964, UFOs were apparently still of major interest to the committee in Washington. He said that he would receive calls from Washington that teams of 8–15 uniformed officers would be arriving at Wright-Patterson on a certain date, and that appropriate aircraft should be made ready for them to take off on secret missions to unknown destinations that usually lasted from three days to a week. **"We were never informed about any reports [regarding these missions]. They all went to Washington."**[31] It was Exon's belief that the committee in Washington not only controlled all access to Roswell but also all highly classified UFO reports. As J. Allen Hynek, Project Blue Book's scientific consultant, once informed us, "All of the hardcore cases were going upstairs [to Washington]." Exon assumed that the head of Project Blue Book, which was still operating out of Wright-Patterson at the time, would have been aware of, if not part of, the committee in Washington. (They were, in fact, parts of different operational Air Force commands.) Exon ultimately came to the conclusion that the real UFO investigations were being controlled from Washington and not Wright-Patterson, where Blue Book was headquartered. The latter entity, Exon felt, had assumed more of a public-relations function than that of an investigative arm.[32] This major revelation totally contradicts our government's public position on UFOs. Exon's startling testimony confirms what many researchers have always believed: that Project Blue Book was simply a front for the actual UFO investigation being conducted elsewhere, and that a special committee was created to control access to and study of the Roswell remains. Exon's brush with the control committee—he didn't know its name or code word—was limited, but it was the first outside confirmation of such a committee that had been found.

Exon's beliefs and conclusions regarding the handling of UFO matters proved correct. We now know that in 1953 a secret project was created to investigate the UFO phenomenon that had nothing to do with Project Blue Book.[33] Located at Ent AFB, in Colorado Springs, Colorado, the 4602nd Air Intelligence Service Squadron, with its "Project Moon Dust" and "Operation Blue Fly," was designed with the retrieval of UFO material in mind.[34] No doubt such teams were from Moon Dust for whom Exon was tasked to prepare aircraft when he was the C.O. of Wright-Patt. All UFO reports of whatever nature were to go to the 4602nd first rather than to Project Blue Book. After 1953, and until it was closed down in 1969, Blue Book became nothing more than a public relations outfit. Ever since then, the Air Force has been misleading the public when it says that it no longer investigates UFOs. While the left hand was in Ohio handing out benign press releases that it was "out of business," the right hand was in Colorado continuing the investigation of UFOs under a cloak of secrecy. Those documents that have been pried loose from government agencies clearly show a pattern of suppression, deception, and misinformation about a topic that the Air Force and the government would like us to believe doesn't exist.[35]

Because of how publicly outspoken Exon—a high-ranking Air Force officer—was about the Roswell incident, we anticipated some sort of reaction in Washington. During the federal General Accounting Office's investigation in 1994–95, Exon was interviewed by a number of high-level congressional staff members. One of the discussions took place at his home on December 2, 1994. Exon was extremely guard-ed during these talks, and one of the staff members entered into his report, **"General Exon is afraid. He was afraid that he was being monitored at that point. He was probably afraid that his whole house was bugged."**[36] We last visited with General Exon and his lovely wife at their retirement home in Irvine, California, in 2000. With us was Jesse Marcel, Sr.'s granddaughter, Denise. Even with the granddaughter of one of the major players in the Roswell story present, it was clear to us from the very first that the general, by that point in time, was willing to discuss any subject under the sun—except Roswell. In spite of our dis-appointment, the lunch was good.

Similar to others who had been involved in the crash-retrieval of a craft and bodies of unknown origin, Exon's consistent testimony has typically pointed to Wright-Patterson Air Force Base as the final reposi-tory of such "artifacts." And Arthur Exon was *there* on the receiving end back at the time of the Roswell incident. He was, according to available documentation and his own words, in a position to hear of the crash and learn that its remains were arriving for analysis. He also learned of the Air Force's secret UFO study operating in Washington, which continues to this very day. In short, he was in the right place at the right time. Most importantly for us today, however, is the fact that Air Force General Arthur Exon, unlike so many others of rank before and after him, was not afraid to talk on the historical record about what he knew to be the truth. Until the day he died on July 23, 2005, he remained thoroughly convinced that the truth was *something not manufactured on this earth*. At the end of the day, according to the general, **"Roswell was the recov-ery of a craft from space."**[37]

CHAPTER 14

The Air Force Washes Its Hands

In 1966, a special Air Force–funded committee was formed at the University of Colorado at Boulder to study reports of the UFO phenomenon from Project Blue Book and civilian research organizations such as NICAP (National Investigations Committee on Aerial Phenomena) and assess whether any further in-depth study of UFOs would be worthwhile. Its director was distinguished UC physicist Dr. Edward Condon.

At a cost to the American taxpayer of $525,905, the infamous Condon Report was completed two years later, in 1968, weighing in at 1,485 pages. The so-called Condon Committee's conclusion was that that **"[f]inal extensive study cannot be justified...nothing has come from the study of UFOs in the past 21 years that has added to scientific knowledge"**—despite the fact that the committee was admittedly unable to explain 25 percent of the cases it examined. Condon praised the Air Force for its noble 22-year effort and proclaimed that the effort had run its course, having provided no reason to justify further study. Project Blue Book was officially closed that December with the release of a single-page statement. It stated that **"[n]o UFO reported, investigated and evaluated by the Air Force was ever an indicated threat to our national security. There was no evidence submitted to or discovered by the Air Force that sightings categorized as 'unidentified' represented technological developments or principles beyond the range of** modern scientific knowledge. There was no evidence indicating that sightings categorized as 'unidentified' were extraterrestrial vehicles."

Dr. Edward Condon.

One of the civilian groups, the National Investigations Committee on Aerial Phenomenon (NICAP), under the directorship of Major Donald Keyhoe, provided what they called their "best evidence" to the Condon Committee. These case studies often occurred around and concerned military facilities and trained personnel. Many were some of the most profound UFO sightings, which demonstrated the classic superiority over our own conventional aircraft. It was NICAP's opportunity to take its case to court, but few if any of these significant reports were ever considered.[1] The committee was not looking for physical evidence, but rather who was making such outlandish claims, and why. Whereas a legitimate court or study would acknowledge an evidentiary phase of the hearings, Condon and his committee refused even to recognize the possible legitimacy of such reports. Instead, they relied strictly on a stock sampling of mundane Air Force cases. The higher-ups at the Pentagon had no intention of airing their "best evidence" no matter what the true agenda of the project. Look, but don't look too closely. Think, but don't think too loud.

For the record, the Condon Committee was the vehicle, but the Air Force was driving the car. It was maneuvered, steered, and driven precisely to the predetermined destination desired by the Pentagon. And just as when General Ramey staged the substituted weather balloon to get the press off his back regarding the Roswell incident, now that it had a mundane answer, the press could go back to covering stories like city budgets and road construction. The creation of the "straw man" had worked once again. We would have to wait eight more years for the declassification of the Blue Book files to discover just how much obfuscation the project employed.

For example, many of the most well-known and highly publicized cases are somehow missing from the Condon Committee's files. This in itself does not suggest incompetence. What it does support is the contention that this was all a well-coordinated and well-conceived cover-up. Many of the filed reports simply have passing references to UFOs, and the "identified" UFO cases demonstrate blatant attempts to deceive the public.[2] And yet, the media didn't seem to notice.

As was certainly the plan, the exorbitant length of the Condon Report and the technical jargon in which it was written discouraged most of the press from studying its pages. Only die-hard civilian investigators cried foul as they waded through the report, looking for a reason why its "unexplained" ratio was higher than that of the Air Force. This ratio was hardly consistent with the conclusions of the study—that there's nothing to see here...move along—and suggests a well-coordinated and well-conceived cover-up of the true nature of UFOs. Think of the inconsistency this way: An outside group, appointed by the Commissioner of Major League Baseball, to investigate reports of the use of performance-enhancing substances, does not discover that 25 percent are possibly using such supplements, and then concludes that no one is using them, so nothing need be investigated further. This analogy to the Condon Report cannot be stated any clearer.

When one realizes the amount of spectacular UFO cases that could and should have been provided to Dr. Condon and his colleagues, there should have been a log-jam of evidence too overwhelming for the panel to ignore. For example, Project Blue Book mentions no less than 20 separate interceptor gun camera films in their files, yet in the master index, it says they do not exist.[3] Specifically, the report says **"...and a section of gun camera spectrographic film furnished by the Air Force for analysis was examined by experts on spectroscopy."** This would suggest that special filters were mounted on the gun cameras in an attempt to film UFOs while in pursuit by U.S. aircraft. Historically, such efforts originated in the summer of 1947 with newspaper accounts of P-51 Mustang pilots configuring 35-millimeter cameras on the nose of their planes. There were a total of *zero* such films provided to Condon for examination. It is one thing for the Air Force to provide only sources and methods to the panel for review, but deliberately withholding film footage known to be mentioned in specific military UFO cases either was an obstruction of the truth or its omission was part of the pre-agreement with the commission.

Throughout the Blue Book files, it produces press releases, which are there to remind everyone that there is no UFO secrecy—all within the same pages where entries have been altered or removed entirely.[4] Someone ordered these changes. Who, and for what purpose?

Noted UFO researcher Dr./Lt. Colonel Kevin D. Randle has pointed out a major argument exposing the Air Force lies and distortions and the culpability of the Condon Committee. He states, **"One other fact suggesting a cover-up becomes obvious when looking at the Blue Book files—almost no reports came from any of the other services. Hundreds of members of the Air Force reported sightings to Blue Book but the other services—the Army, Navy, and Marine Corps— are represented by only one or two listings. Does this mean that only Air Force personnel see objects they can't identify, or did the reports from the other services go elsewhere?"[5]**

The answer? Yes. Not only did the other branches have their own UFO projects with their own investigators, but Blue Book also references sending reports to both the Office of Naval Research and the Office of Naval Intelligence. Ironically, there is no mention of Army reports as defined by JANAP 146 and AFR 200-2. They were to be sent somewhere other than Blue Book. Need we remind the reader that the Roswell case was an Army incident?

When it was completed, Condon's report was first assigned for review to the National Academy of Sciences and the U.S. Department of Defense in November 1968. The academy appointed a Special Review Panel of 11 highly respected scientists with Dr. Gerald M. Clemance as the chair. Others were from Yale, the University of California, Stanford, Rockefeller University, the University of Rochester, and Michigan State University. After a standard procedural examination of the Condon Committee Study, Academy president Dr. Frederick Seitz sent a review copy to the Honorable Dr. Alexander H. Flax, assistant secretary of the Air Force. Dr. Seitz stated:

> **The Academy accepted this task because of its belief in the importance of making available to the Government and the public a careful assessment of the scientific significance of the UFO phenomena which have been variously interpreted both in this country and abroad. Substantial questions have been raised as to the adequacy of our research and investigation programs to explain or to determine the nature of these puzzling reports of observed phenomena. It is my hope that the Colorado report, together with our panel of review, will be helpful to you and other responsible officials in determining the nature and scope of any continuing research effort in this area.**

This would be the last card played to the public on the subject of UFOs. The chairman of the panel, Dr. Seitz, was the former scientific director of the U.S. Naval Observatory. Dr. James E. McDonald was one of the few scientists who voiced opposition at the time. His concern was that **"[the panel was] not adequately prepared to assess the Condon Report."** The panel never investigated the UFO phenomena; it simply endorsed the conclusions of the Condon Committee.[6]

Dr. James McDonald.

The very same day the report was released in early 1969, it received a shocking rebuttal: Former Condon Committee member Dr. David R. Saunders released an explosive exposé entitled "**UFOs? Yes. Where the Condon Committee Went Wrong: The Inside Story by an Ex-Member of the Official Study Group**" that told the behind-the-scenes story about the true objective of the project.

Dr. Saunders, a professor of psychology and assistant director of the university's Department of Testing and Counseling, along with electrical engineer Dr. Norman E. Levine, had been fired for "incompetence" by Condon a year before the project was completed.[7] What had actually necessitated Condon's move was Saunders's and Levine's open disdain of an internal memo they uncovered in the project's files. Saunders and Levine made copies of the memo, which they sent to Dr. James McDonald.[8] In short order, they made their way to John Fuller of the *Saturday Review*. As a result, Fuller penned a feature story in *Look Magazine* entitled "Flying Saucer Fiasco."[9] That story so angered Condon and Robert L. Low, coordinator of the project, that pink slips were immediately handed out to Saunders and Levine. Members on

Capitol Hill were similarly not amused, and members of Congress wondered if the study was a waste of tax money.

The memo that had sparked such controversy, penned even before the university accepted the commission, questioned whether the subject of UFOs was good for the reputation of the school. Other campuses had been approached and refused the very notion, as Low realized that the majority of his colleagues considered the subject of UFOs unscientific and rather radioactive. But the Air Force was in desperate need of a scapegoat and had close ties specifically with Condon. Ostensibly, the plan was to select an apparently objective group in academia, outside of any government influence, to conduct an impartial study utilizing both Blue Book and civilian UFO group files. The group's final report was not supposed go back to the Air Force; rather, it would be released to the public. However, the hidden memo spelled out a more nefarious plot. It read:

> **The trick would be, I think, to describe the project so that, to the public, it would appear a totally objective study but, to the scientific community, would present the image of a group of nonbelievers trying their best to be objective but having an almost zero expectation of finding a saucer.**
>
> **One way to do this would be to stress investigation not of the physical phenomenon, but rather of the people who do the observing—psychology and sociology of persons and groups who report seeing UFOs.**
>
> **If the emphasis were put here, rather than on the examination of the old question of the physical reality of the saucer, I think the scientific community would quickly get the message.[10]**

With the cat out of the bag, Condon went even further to discredit Saunders. He ranted that he should be "ruined professionally." Moreover, why not throw Hynek in for good measure? Condon called him a "kook."

The plan had worked, and the Pentagon was privately celebrating never having to utter another public remark on the subject of UFOs again. The lights had finally been turned off on the Air Force's "Dark Ages." The government relishes the use of the term "Case Closed" as though it is some arbiter of the truth. Like Moses coming down from the Mount of Olives with the stone tablets, officialdom sets the rules—and often breaks them. Many labeled the Condon Report a "whitewash," and the case was closed before it ever started. The Air Force had its scapegoat.[11]

In the early years of the military's forays into UFO research, while Ruppelt was at the helm, there was a series of status reports numbering 1 through 14. Aside from Special Report 14, the others served as briefing summaries of sightings during that period, accept for one oddity that continues to this day: Report 13 is missing, and the Air Force has never posited a rational explanation for such an omission. Was it destroyed?[12] One might recall how General Vandenberg ordered the final report from Project Sign burned. Consider that Washington, DC alone is rife with secret vaults and storage rooms filled to the brim with classified documents. Experts estimate that more than 150 million unclassified papers exist at the CIA alone.[13] The very act of destroying, shredding, or burning any government document is an act of censorship, especially if it concerns the subject of UFOs. The reader should ask the question, *Why such a need for secrecy regarding a subject so castigated by the authorities? Are we dealing with something much more sinister in its implications?* Some unelected individuals have made it their business to ensure that certain truths are not disclosed no matter what. The existence of a clandestine government system using military personnel for its own purposes has been demonstrated since the National Security Act of 1947 was signed into law. In more recent times, during the Iran-Contra Senate Hearings in 1987, late Senator Daniel Inouye remarked, "**There exists a shadowy government with its own Air Force, its own Navy, its own fundraising mechanism, and the ability to pursue its own ideas of the national interest, free from all checks and balances, and free from the law itself.**"[14]

It could be argued that, especially during the 1960s when the Air Force unceremoniously left the UFO scene, Communism was a growing threat to democracy. During this time, government agencies and branches of the military, which were already not inclined to share information with each other, became even more secretive and deceptive. Within such a clandestine atmosphere, suspicions grew deeper as bureaucracies became even more compartmentalized. However, there was a record of accomplishment established very early on within the Air Force complex pertaining to UFOs: "Don't ask, don't tell," became policy long before gays in the military.

In short, Project Blue Book knowingly provided fraudulent evidence to the Condon Committee, withheld significant cases, changed names, and altered case conclusions, as proven by the disclosure of the files 10 years later.[15] Now we need to ask who Edward Uhler Condon was and what stake he may have had in sabotaging the true perception of UFOs to his scientific colleagues. Condon was a nuclear physicist and a pioneer in quantum mechanics. He was endorsed by none other than Albert Einstein and even has a crater on the moon named in his honor. After the Condon Committee report was released, when asked why he took on such a risky project, he answered, "On the basis of appeals to duty...to do a needed public service." We can now surmise that such duty extended all the way back to the time of Roswell: Back in 1947, samples of the actual wreckage were sent for analysis and identification to the National Bureau of Standards—under the directorship of Edward U. Condon. This was the same supposedly unbiased, objective, open-minded-to-the-evidence Edward Condon who stated publicly at the very beginning of the UFO project, at the Corning Glass Works, **"It is my inclination right now to recommend that the government get out of this business. My attitude right now is that there's nothing to it...but I'm not supposed to reach a conclusion for another year."**[16]

Within a couple of years after the final UFO report all but nailed the lid down on any future scientific interest on the subject of UFOs, J. Allen Hynek and Edward Condon would attend a banquet in Colorado. It was there that Mrs. Condon approached Mrs. Hynek and, much to her surprise, privately apologized to her. "For what?" asked Mimi Hynek. Mrs. Condon replied, **"I hope your husband understands that my husband was only doing what he was supposed to do."** Mimi graciously nodded and just smiled.[17] Did Mrs. Condon's husband know that in spite of his report, Hynek's work with the Air Force investigating UFOs was not quite over? The lid to the coffin was still very much open.

CHAPTER 15

Dr. J. Allen Hynek: Dupe or Accomplice?

Legendary folklorist Mark Twain was not the only famous American to be born in the year of Halley's Comet and die in the year of its next return. Like Halley's Comet, Dr. J. Allen Hynek traveled an astronomical path, and his story remains an important one in ufology—moving from a position of skepticism to an acknowledgment that something outside the ordinary was actually happening in the skies above us. Amazingly, his work as the scientific consultant to the study of UFOs undertaken by the U.S. Air Force (1948 to 1969) may have been an accident of geography: At the time of his selection, he was a professor of astronomy and physics at Ohio State in Columbus, Ohio. The university is really just down the road from Wright-Patterson AFB. That opportunity changed his life.

He always promoted the idea of scientific analysis of UFO reports, though initially he sought a psychological explanation. After a few years, he was scientific enough to realize that he would follow the evidence, wherever it led, and soon noted that many of the cases were not so easily explained. His emphasis on evidence first and investigating the "properties" of a phenomenon still influences many of his surviving colleagues today.

While employed by the government, Hynek realized that they were not sharing all the Pentagon knew about the true nature of the

Dr. J. Allen Hynek.

anomaly. He would often describe how he would peruse UFO reports at Blue Book, and how often none of the "hardcore" cases were present. Eyewitness accounts from seasoned SAC officers, military and commercial pilots, which he had filed himself, were all strangely absent from the files. The USAF found itself withholding such cases even from its own chief scientific spokesperson. That, in itself, should have alerted the scientific community. Their blinders were bought and paid for in the shape of government funding and special grants. Moreover, Hynek became all too familiar with the ridicule attached to any public study of the subject. He said, **"Ridicule is not part of the scientific method, and people should not be taught that it is."** To his colleagues, it was perfectly fine that the government should investigate UFOs for almost 20 years—after all, Washington does a lot of silly things. Yet, Hynek stood up to the tar and feathering of his associates who demonstrated relentlessly that, for some reason, the subject was beneath them. That reason was that the government told them it was all nonsense, and bribed them with grants and special funding. However, Hynek had access to the raw data and he begrudgingly heard a real "noise" within the phenomenon. On one occasion he confessed, **"I stretched far to give something a natural explanation, sometimes when it may not have really had it."**

As the reports persisted and Hynek's conviction of the reality of the UFO phenomenon grew, the Air Force's need to shift public attention did as well. Hynek was asking them repeatedly to increase funding and conduct outside studies, and—worse—in the final years of his tenure, was taking his case to the public. In the late 1960s, he became an outspoken critic of both Project Blue Book and the Condon Report. The writing was on the wall and he foresaw that the Air Force was about to throw in the towel, so he had nothing to lose.

After the demise of Blue Book, Hynek was free to search for the answers with his blinders off. He knew that not all of the hundreds of witnesses he personally interviewed could be liars. He knew better—and, more importantly, so did the U.S. government.

The first actual attempt at some form of public disclosure took place during Gerald Ford's administration following the resignation of Richard Nixon. Ford had previously taken an active interest in UFO reports while serving as a congressional representative for the state of Michigan because of the famous Dexter/Ann Arbor sightings in 1966. At that time, while with Blue Book, Hynek suggested that *one* of the numerous reports could be attributed to "swamp gas," and that phrase stuck with him for the rest of his life and colored perceptions of him both within and outside the UFO community. Ford, in particular, was not amused by the Air Force's nonchalant attitude and treatment of his own constituents, and the future president never forgot the scientist who made, in his eyes, such an outlandish suggestion.[1]

About five years after Blue Book lost what remaining credibility it had with the American public, partly due to such controversial explanations, Hynek met privately in Washington with then-President Ford's secretary of defense, Donald Rumsfeld. Hynek spoke plainly, and demanded to simply be told the truth after being dismissed with no answers from the Pentagon after 20 years of service. Hynek was of the opinion that he had faithfully maintained the Air Force's status quo and had earned the right to be told the truth. Clearly, the good professor felt he had intentionally been left out of the inner circle and that someone was controlling access to the truth about the UFO phenomenon. Not the least bit moved, Rumsfeld told Hynek that he **"had no right to know."**

At the least, Rumsfeld's remark can be interpreted that there remains "something to know."[2] The reprimand only fueled Hynek's desire for answers.

Former Secretary of Defense Donald Rumsfeld.

As a former government consultant on a subject as controversial as UFOs, Hynek stirred the pot enough to receive a phone call about a year later from a close friend within the Chicago media who had just been tipped off that an announcement pertaining to the subject was about to come out and they wanted Hynek in their TV studio for an immediate reaction. He waited a number of hours before this shocking invitation suddenly evaporated. No excuse was ever given, even after the original source was verified to have been someone with authority in the United States government. Further inquiries by the Chicago media failed to trace the tip to the original informant. It was either a false alarm or a possible test for some future action.[3] Hynek would have to remain patient.

The next possible opportunity surfaced a few years later, in 1977, under President Jimmy Carter. During his presidential campaign, Carter had stated on numerous occasions that, should he be elected, he would open the government's UFO files "if they did not threaten national security." As before, Hynek received an early evening call, but this time it was more direct and specific—and reliable. TV/radio station WGN (owned by the Tribune Company, which also publishes the *Chicago Tribune*) had received a call from a verified source in Washington and the word was that the president or a presidential representative was about to break into live TV and make a special announcement about UFOs! For the aging Hynek, always the curious scientist, this was another chance he could not resist. Within the hour, he was picked up by a cab and driven into downtown Chicago to sit and wait. And wait and wait, as the station remained on standby. As he waited, he wondered, if this was the real thing, why was he waiting with reporters in Chicago and not at a press conference at the Pentagon? Rumsfeld's words resounded once again in his head. After a number of hours passed, an exasperated Hynek was delivered back to his home in Evanston. The last word the TV studio received was, "It's all off. Forget about it."[4] Nevertheless, Hynek and certain powers in Washington would not forget.

The notion that the powers that be have at times considered disclosure rather than continuing secrecy is based on an old rumor that refuses to die: Anyone involved in the study of the UFO phenomenon is aware of the story that at one time Walt Disney was asked to produce a documentary about UFOs. The theory was that in the event the government would have come clean due to some unforeseen event, they would have something to immediately present to the public. This story has been around for 50 years, but when it is described in detail from a source who was one of Disney's closest employees, we should all take note—especially as it is in the context of the aforementioned Hynek experiences.

During his lifetime, one would be hard-pressed to name anyone else who symbolized not only the American dream but also the American way of life better than Walt Disney. Parents didn't have to worry about the impression a Disney production would leave on their children; Disney had a greater influence and lasting impression on the offspring of the World War II generation than anyone else. It is for that reason alone that we believe the U.S. government saw him the same way: as someone who could soften the blow of shocking information.

Walt Disney had his original and most gifted animators through the 1950s. He affectionately called them the "Nine Old Men." One of them, Ward Kimball, was the artist who drew Jiminy Cricket and would later do the animation in *Mary Poppins*. In 1955, Kimball was one of the illustrators for the documentary *Man in Space* that combined animation and live-action footage. As a demonstration of the influence a Disney production had at that time, 42 million viewers watched the special in their homes. If the American public could dream it, Disney could make it come true. And Kimball could make it come to life.

At the 1979 Mutual UFO Network Symposium in San Francisco, California, Kimball made a revelation that would substantiate the rumors about his former boss. He explained that Walt Disney was contacted by the Air Force in 1955–56 and asked to produce a special documentary on UFOs. Keep in mind, this was post–CIA Robertson Panel and post-Ruppelt. This was a time when the Air Force was in a renewed policy of "seek and destroy" for all apparently legitimate UFO reports. Were they enlisting Disney to do the same style of propaganda material he did so masterfully during WWII? Not according to Kimball, who would have been one of the animators on the project. It was his understanding that the Air Force would be providing them with footage that proved the existence of UFOs. In fact, Kimball overheard one discussion with Air Force officials who stated they had "plenty of UFO footage." Even as the animators, including Kimball, started to sketch out thumbnail drawings of purported aliens, the Air Force backed out without any fanfare. It was as though it never happened.[5]

Unlike Disney, Hynek, in many ways, was a statesman whose portfolio was full of UFOs. This was partly due to all the time he spent in Washington. In addition, like a diplomat, he had been forced to tolerate broken promises on so many occasions, and forced to maintain cool detachment when he felt anger. As a scientist, it must have been maddening to deal with uninformed bureaucrats and branches of the military, all controlled by that same bureaucracy. But he knew how the game worked and he reluctantly realized he had to actively campaign for his final research into this increasingly elusive new scientific endeavor. Now on the outside, he would no longer have access to official data. There would be no funding from Washington, and the scientific community regarded his association with the topic, even while he was a paid government consultant, as somewhat of a betrayal to their sacred "true science." UFO research was, and remains, fringe science to many people.

And so in 1973 the foremost authority on the subject of UFOs found himself spending more and more time soliciting funding and support for his newly founded Center for UFO Studies (CUFOS) in Chicago. His credentials, which included being head of the astronomy department, emeritus, at Northwestern University in Evanston, Illinois, helped. Still, without financial assistance, how could he possibly compete with the forces that had sold him out and withheld the truth from him after so many years of playing by their rules? The forces that had repaid his loyalty of 20 years with not so much as a token offering? In their eyes, he had no right to know anything about the subject he had devoted his life to studying. Betrayed, he knew he would have to do it on his own. "I'm an old man in a hurry," he said.[6]

This was his regular lament in those days when stress became an emotional tiger, which caused him to cast logic and reason aside at times, as he occasionally did. Too often, he would believe some of the most outlandish promises from individuals outside the UFO community who offered "funded research projects." The next entrepreneur was "just around the corner." And like a stuck record, the truth was always poised to come out "within the next year." In addition, with his own time dwindling, he was often naive to such false claims. But he wanted to be there. He deserved to be there. Like Mark Twain, he always believed that he had come with the comet and then he would go with the comet. Alas, he feared his time was running out.

He never gave up hope that some irrefutable case would finally reveal itself to the world or, as he had learned from all his years working with the people who had full access to the truth, maybe the truth was right here all along. Apparently, that was one of his reasons for becoming desperately curious in the whole UFO crash-retrieval phenomenon. Accepting his role strictly as a former consultant to Project Blue Book, which, as he would confess, was "fairly low on the scale of things," Hynek had no problem accepting the idea that high-ranking intelligence officers could possess knowledge of recovered UFOs. At one time, he had even suggested holding a press conference to enable firsthand witnesses to collectively step forward. "Then you would have something that nobody could deny," he would add. He started investigating Roswell back in the early 1980s, interviewing neighbors who lived near the famous site where a rancher claimed a UFO crashed back in 1947. Personal notes in his handwriting revealed a renewed "little-boy" enthusiasm from interviews he conducted with witnesses who provided him with hope he had almost lost. These individuals described to him the same characteristics we have long heard about the strange debris.[7] None of them told him tales about weather balloons. Still, he wisely realized that time was speeding past even then.

Character assassination, smear tactics, all the elements utilized by the skeptics and, tragically scientific colleagues who should have known better—Hynek had encountered them all. Nevertheless, the government remains their meal ticket with grants and special project funding. SETI, the "Search for Extra-Terrestrial Intelligence," is a principal example. Ironically, as just announced, the present economic climate cannot even save such sacred cows. Yet, throughout SETI's existence, if Hynek or anyone else should ever have solved the UFO mystery, they would have been out of business much sooner. It is quite that simple, and Hynek knew it better than most.

"Why can't they tell me now? Why can't they tell me the truth even now?" moaned the dying astronomer as he lay in the recovery room at the hospital, after having a brain tumor removed.[8] His plea fell on ears hardened by years of deceit and denial. Moreover, Hynek, like the rest of us, once trusted them. In similar fashion, Major Jesse Marcel had been told at Roswell, "Just be a good soldier for a few more years and it will all come out."

In his lifetime, J. Allen Hynek had seen the study of UFOs become a circus more than a few times. He observed some people he worked for as having more in common with P.T. Barnum than Abraham Lincoln, another son of Illinois like Hynek. He had been patient to a fault. Now, for the remaining months of his life, Hynek's family focused on fulfilling his one final request. He simply wanted to know the truth, to take to his grave a sense that his life had been lived well in the service of history.

He was denied. No secret documents anonymously arrived from parts unknown. There were no special couriers from Washington. No senior public official called with any final confessions. The Pentagon was just running out the clock.

Hynek's last wish was to **"[j]ust let me see the comet before it's too late."**[9] Those of us who worked with him had discussed a trip down to New Zealand to get the best possible look at the comet, but he was so weakened by chemotherapy treatment and the ravages of cancer itself that taking him on a prolonged trip for a better look was out of the question. He was quickly fading, sleeping nearly 23 hours a day.[10]

One night in 1986, a small party drove out into the black Arizona desert with the most heralded UFO authority in the world—not to look for the unknown but rather an old friend. The group stopped at a good open spot and gently helped the frail old scholar from the car. Then, leaning him against the side of the vehicle, they waited.[11]

The comet made its appearance at the appointed time, 76 years after it heralded the departure of Mark Twain and the arrival of Josef Allen Hynek. "Halley, my old traveling companion" is what he said as they lifted his head slightly so he could get a better look[12]. He nodded approval at the sight. Nothing else seemed to matter now. A tear trickled down his contented face.[12]

Too soon, it became time to head back. Dr. J. Allen Hynek was ready to go home.

CHAPTER 16

"They're Making Us Patsies All Over Again!"

Just for the sake of argument, let us suppose that the U.S. government has been telling us the truth about UFOs all along. After all, federal officials would have us believe that they have a perfect record of doing what is in the best interests of the American people. As former Speaker of the House Jim Wright liked to say, "We only want to help you." Now, for those of you who either earn a paycheck from Uncle Sam or just cannot imagine ever being deceived by our elected officials, it will not matter what the rest of this chapter says. But if you have occasionally had some doubts and have an open enough mind to consider that, more often than not, we are only told what "they" want us to know, read on.

Let us begin with the Roswell incident. Two days after the crash was reported to military authorities, including officials at the Pentagon, the Roswell Army Air Field released one of the most startling admissions the world has ever seen: They had in their possession an actual flying saucer. Within five hours all media attention was diverted away from Roswell as General Ramey in Fort Worth, Texas announced that the only atomic bomb squadron in the world at that time couldn't tell the difference between an off-the-shelf, rubber weather balloon and advanced technology, possibly from outer space. Witnesses were intimidated and ridiculed, and military officers, merely following orders, were made patsies to ensure that the secondary story would close the case.

Fast-forward to September 1994. The Pentagon, responding to pressure from the late congressman Steven Schiff of New Mexico, calls a rare "UFO" press conference to issue a new edict on Roswell. In it, Colonel Richard Weaver explained that back in 1947, the military was forced to lie about the situation to cover for another scenario. The new theory was that it was the same type of balloon, but it might have been part of a top-secret project called "Mogul" used to listen to upper-atmospheric shock waves should the Soviets detonate their first atomic bomb. It was the same off-the-shelf materials, just a secret project—but it sounded good to the media.[1]

Advance three more years to May 1997. At an event dubbed "The Roswell Report: Case Closed," the Air Force allowed that witnesses may have seen bodies in 1947, but that the occurrence was actually 5 to 10 years later, and the cause was anthropomorphic wooden crash dummies. This one *didn't* sound right even to the usually compliant press. A Pentagon spokesperson addressed the idea that the public would not accept the latest explanation: **"Then I guess we'll be back in another few years offering another one."**

Now let's illustrate the parallel explanations from the Air Force throughout its post-Roswell investigations and observe if there exist any patterns:

Within three months of the recovery at Roswell, General Twining received an assessment and educated position from his "top" engineers at T-3, who stated, **"The phenomenon was real."** Such highly experienced technicians would have been part of the effort to analyze the physical evidence to support such an assertion.

One year later, after a more prolonged investigation of the phenomenon, Project Sign submitted its final summation to the Pentagon for approval. From there, it was sent up to General Vandenberg for his blessing, whereupon he countermanded the Pentagon's conclusion and ordered the report destroyed.

Project Grudge was born out of the need to supply a counter-explanation to Sign. The new study was purged of just about all the pro-UFO researchers to ensure the alternative solution. As predicted, Grudge found that there is "nothing to see here." Flying saucers are nothing more than misidentified common aerial objects. This final assessment is widely publicized and accepted by the mainstream media.

After the UFO wave of 1952, the tone changed across the country as people again faced the possibility that something else was behind the mystery. Roswell was not yet a distant memory, and the American people needed to be assured that their government leaders would find the underlying cause of it all. So for the next two years, Project Blue Book led the charge and answers appeared imminent. The stalling tactic succeeded as Blue Book floundered and faded into obscurity until its final gasp in 1969—case closed.

The tactics are clearly defined and the pattern is repeated in government affairs to this day for one reason: They have a high level of success. The process, no matter how long the duration, is to first demonstrate a serious intent at looking into a public concern. If the press starts getting impatient, just tell them "you're working on it."

Aside from the public, specifically with any subject that involves national security, our government has to anticipate our enemies. Throughout the entire Air Force investigation of the UFO phenomenon, the Cold War raged. Covert actions become mandatory, and certainly the subject of UFOs traversing our airspace with total impunity outweighed national insecurity. With the recovery at Roswell, the chess match intensified within the intelligence community. In addition, the first thing the generals at the top do is shut down any trickle of truth finding its way to the underlings. None of the three UFO projects was ever directed by anyone higher than the rank of major—the equivalent of middle management in business. The consistent strategy is to keep them intentionally in the dark lest they ever misspeak.

Take the contemporary example of the Air Force's two recent explanations for Roswell. In both cases, the Pentagon selected a mid-level officer, Captain James McAndrew, to research and then write the report. We have absolutely no doubt that McAndrew is not privy to the slightest truth about the 1947 incident. But he undoubtedly knows more about Project Mogul and the Crash Dummy Project than most others in the military do.[2] For that reason, there is no chance that he could say anything out of turn pertaining to the actual event. Everyone at Sign,

Grudge, and Blue Book were kept completely out of the loop—especially their scientific consultant, Dr. J. Allen Hynek. Hynek was their greatest risk. Anytime the military hires a civilian, he or she remains a conduit to the public.

Another example would be a U.S. president's press secretary. Not having a "need to know," they are only briefed on the administration's positions on issues of the day. It is their sworn duty to defend and protect the policies of the president. They represent the official party line of the acting government and have always paid the price should they speak off subject.

Hynek, in many ways, was the "press secretary" for the Air Force on the subject of UFOs. It was Hynek who was often called on not only to temper the media's reaction to a specific report, but also, more times than not, to explain away the cases, which helped present the Air Force in a good light. Publicly, their position remained: Nothing serious is going on, and if there were, the Air Force would say so. To his detriment, Hynek went along with this and became safe in their eyes. Avoiding confrontation, he was not considered a threat to reveal any secrets not intended for public consumption. Desiring to retain access to the limited data that he had, he chose to seldom challenge their authority and remain on the inside—in case something big should happen.

As one might expect, this did not sit well with a number of his colleagues, such as Dr. James McDonald. In 1966, McDonald, professor of atmospheric physics at the University of Arizona and a respected member of the National Academy of Sciences, pounded his fist on Hynek's desk, demanding that he at the least open up to his scientific colleagues about the subject. McDonald took the subject seriously, but all Hynek could do was try to explain that when consulting for the government, you are placed under severe limitations. Hynek, once again, conceded that he was more of a pawn that played by another's set of rules.[3]

In the aftermath of WWII, few politicians would second-guess the military. This was precisely why they left UFOs under uniformed jurisdiction. However, as author Thomas E. Ricks demonstrates in his book *The Generals*, "The U.S. Army is often led by generals who are masterful at combat tactics, at converging battalions on agreed-upon enemy targets, but woefully inept at recognizing changes in the battlefield." The arrival of the UFO phenomenon entirely changed the military mindset. Moreover, Hynek too often was the only adult in the room, but his scientific opinions seldom mattered. Furthermore, he grew more and more frustrated by the diminishing number of legitimate reports that he had access to. True, there were exceptions, such as Socorro and Dexter/Ann Arbor, but as so many times before, the Air Force expected him to diffuse them both. Hynek would remark about Socorro, **"I wish I could, for my own peace of mind, dismiss the Socorro sighting as a hoax or a hallucination, but in all honesty I cannot."** His explanation of "swamp gas" as it applied to one incident in the Michigan sightings, backfired and embarrassed the Air Force, which led to congressional hearings, which quickly led to the Condon Committee.

The good astronomer repeatedly demonstrated the unimpeachable scientific methodology that among military circles were ignored. Most noteworthy is that he understood the old adage about "loose lips sinking ships," as well as they did. He was as good a soldier as most who did wear the uniform. Through it all, Hynek retained the critical awareness of an academic who recognized his myopia in initially dismissing the UFO phenomenon, became an advocate for continuing study, and in his later years wanted to stay in the race.

Hynek had known for years that Blue Book was looking for an out, and that the Air Force's public investigation of the UFO mystery was a sham. As described earlier, his only recourse was to trade on his own reputation and take his case to the public. He planned to have both feet running when the Air Force fired the project—and him. The question remains: Did he know before the inevitable demise of Blue Book that the chase for him would go on—that the government's secret investigation would continue beyond the final project, and that he would become part of it? If we had known about his secret assignment before his passing, certainly, we would have asked him about it—and a hundred questions more.[4]

As it has now been almost 50 years since the U.S. Air Force admitted to any active role in continuing UFO investigations, we would like to suggest our readers conduct a simple test: Please contact any military base and ask about UFO investigations. You will be read a scripted response: **"The Air Force has discontinued the investigation of UFOs with the closing of Blue Book in 1969. If you need to report a sighting, please contact your local law enforcement agency."** *Click.* Members of the press as well as most scientists swallow this story without any awareness of the history behind it. This apathetic behavior from two of the most influential groups in our society is precisely what the Pentagon had worked so hard to accomplish—no more press conferences necessary to explain away sighting reports. No chance of any academic studies looking into the subject; the Condon Committee took care of that. From all accounts, the U.S. government is officially out of the UFO business. The persistent drumbeat of ridicule and derisive propaganda succeeded in making the subject a taboo topic and the domain of conspiracy kooks. Add to the mix the legion of debunkers whose mission is to maintain damage control for a controversy that was laid to rest back in 1969. The obvious question is, *Why wage the war if the British were never coming?*

Now, let us suppose that the government has *not* been telling us the truth about UFOs. Let us suppose that the Air Force did *not* terminate its investigation of UFOs in 1969, and that there may still be a highly classified effort continuing even as you read this book. What if there were other secret, highly classified UFO investigations—covert studies for which we may never know of any resolutions? What if an alien craft did crash in Roswell and set into motion a 22-year period of subterfuge and intelligence efforts not to solve the mystery of UFOs, but to manipulate the public into believing that officialdom was in control of the situation, when, in reality, they were not?

In previous chapters, we have described how outside units such as the 4602nd Air Intelligence Squadron and the 1066th Air Intelligence Service Squadron investigated higher-priority UFO reports during Project Blue Book. Former base commander General Exon described how another project, consisting of all officers, would arrive at Wright-Patterson from Washington to investigate the more sensitive cases, and was not associated with Blue Book. The Blue Book files were declassified in 1977—so where are all these other case files from these independent investigations? Perhaps Brigadier General Carroll H. Bolander, who was Air Force chief of staff of Research and Development at the time Blue Book was shut down, had it right when he said, **"Reports of** unidentified flying objects which could affect national security are made in accordance with JANAP 146 or Air Force Manual 55-11, and are not part of the Blue Book system."[5] While we're at it, let's throw in the hundreds of case files from Air Force Intelligence, the FBI, the CIA, and the NSA of their own independent investigations, ordered released in 1977–78 by federal judges in separate lawsuits. All those organizations claimed for years they never touched the subject. As did the Army and Navy, which also conducted separate investigations. We are finally left to ask, as of the time of this writing, why is JANAP 146 still on the books? It seems that a blackout of the truth about UFOs continues.

Colonel George R. Weinbrenner was stationed at the USAF headquarters in London during the final year of World War II. It was there that he worked on a top-secret project to develop vertical-launch rockets to take out enemy aircraft. In 1950, he was the commanding officer of the 439th Airlift Wing Squadron. Relevant to this chapter, he was the Commander of the Foreign Technology Division at Wright-Patterson from November 1966 through June 1974. He also became Hynek's next boss soon after the Air Force announced to the press that it was officially ending all UFO investigations.[6] Since the end of 1969, the public has been told that such research ended and never resumed. Blue Book unceremoniously passed away on January 31, 1970.

And yet, within the next few months of 1970, in total secrecy, J. Allen Hynek became a consultant on controversial atmospheric phenomena for the FTD.

For the next four years, Hynek would continue to make periodic trips from his home in Evanston, Illinois, down to Wright-Patterson—not to page through a handful of lights-in-the-sky reports, but to clandestinely meet with personnel, including Weinbrenner, at the super-secret FTD. Only those closest to him even knew about these trips.[7] It was only after his passing in 1986 that we discovered, to our complete shock, the documents he had preserved for us to find after he was gone. I suppose one could describe these as the missing years of J. Allen Hynek—the time between Blue Book and the establishment of his own civilian organization, the Center for UFO Studies, in October of 1973.

Many have long speculated about what Hynek really knew and when he knew it. Was he personally running interference for the Air Force because, in his capacity as a civilian scientist, he was more believable to the public?[8] His marriage with the Air Force was rife with mutual distrust, and there remains little in his personal files to suggest that he kept anything secret, except that he continued to make it his life's mission to solve the mystery of UFOs. He suspected that information was being kept from him throughout their 20-year "marriage," so it's not surprising that he would continue to seek to gain their confidence. While Hynek's suspicions remained high, it appears the Air Force chose to keep him on a short leash. We believe they truly feared what Hynek might accomplish without the Air Force's shackles to restrict him— which serves to enlighten us to the greater dynamics involved here. The documentation Hynek left us shows that although he was a willing accomplice at the time, Hynek's greatest legacy may be that he became a true whistleblower to the government deception—the ongoing cover-up that continued after Blue Book.[9] Just as Wright-Patterson itself would go underground, so did their inquiry into controversial atmospheric phenomena.[10]

The last known meeting between General Weinbrenner and Hynek also included Colonel Robert Friend, a former head of Blue Book. The affair took place in early 1974. After a heated exchange, Hynek stormed out of the room, yelling, **"Patsies! Patsies! They're trying to make us patsies all over again!"**[11] His private secretary, Jennie Zeidman, was waiting for him as he entered her car. He was clearly upset, and it was a long, tense drive back to Illinois. Hynek did not say a word.[12]

By preserving the documents and hiding them for us to uncover later, he essentially told us that we should all continue the search. That he was on the right path—that the Air Force knew that he knew, and that it would only be a matter of time before he would prove it—and they wanted to be there when he did.

Shortly after the last "exchange" with Hynek, Weinbrenner was assigned to take command of Brooks AFB in San Antonio, Texas. Nine years before, on November 21, 1963, President Kennedy had dedicated the School for Aerospace Medicine at Brooks to assist NASA in the study of the physical effects of flight crashes.[13] At the time of the dedication, Kennedy met with Major General Theodore C. Bedwell, Jr., who, from

February 1946 through March 1948, was the First Deputy Surgeon and Chief of Industrial Medicine and finally Command Surgeon at Wright-Patterson. Upon Weinbrenner's arrival at Brooks, he also directed the research at the medical laboratory.[14]

Upon retirement from the Air Force, Weinbrenner stayed in San Antonio, and after breaking a hip was moved to the Army Residence Community Center for physical therapy and rehabilitation. He had no children and his wife was totally incapacitated, so he befriended his primary nurse and her husband. His maladies were strictly physical, and according to other family members he was lucid up until the end. Nevertheless, it was not to any family that he made any deathbed remarks. Like so often throughout history, such final confessions are made to someone safe. In this case, it was his nurse. Just days before his passing he made a remark akin to Clark Kent shouting out "I'm Superman!" He told her, "**We have five aliens in Utah.**"[15] That was all he would admit, and he immediately dropped the subject. Finally, Weinbrenner got the question of whether UFOs were extraterrestrial off his chest. His conscience was clearer and he died peacefully on March 7, 2010.

While Weinbrenner was still at Wright-Patterson in 1979, film producer and author Robert Emenegger was contacted by the Department of Defense to do a documentary on UFOs. He was told that they approved of his previous work and that his first military contact to discuss the project was to be in the office of Colonel George Weinbrenner. "**What is the truth about UFOs?**" asked Emenegger. Weinbrenner made some disjointed remarks about the Russians and their aircraft technology as he rose from his chair, stepping over to a bookcase. Sliding a book from one of the shelves, he handed it to the filmographer. "**It's all in there,**" snapped the officer. Glancing through it, Emenegger realized he was quite familiar with the author and his work. The book was *The UFO Experience* by Dr. J. Allen Hynek, and inside, the inscription read, "**To my good friend George.**"[16]

Standard Form 61-B
December 1966
U.S. Civil Service Commission
FPM Chapter 295

DECLARATION OF APPOINTEE
(Data needed for appointment or conversion)

INSTRUCTIONS TO APPOINTEE.—Answer all questions. Your answers will be considered together with other information in your record in determining your present fitness for Federal employment. A false statement or dishonest answer to any question may be grounds for dismissal after appointment or conversion and is punishable by law.

1. NAME (Last—First—Middle)	2. BIRTH DATE	3. PLACE OF BIRTH (City and State or city and foreign country)
Hynek, Joseph Allen	May 1, 1910	Chicago, Illinois

4. PRESENT ADDRESS (Street and number, city, State, and ZIP code)

2623 Ridge Avenue, Evanston, Illinois   60201

5. (A) IN CASE OF EMERGENCY, PLEASE NOTIFY	(B) RELATIONSHIP	(C) STREET AND NUMBER, CITY, STATE, AND ZIP CODE	(D) TELEPHONE NO.
(Mrs.) Mimi Hynek	wife	2623 Ridge Ave, Evanston, Ill 60201	864-1861

6. DOES THE UNITED STATES GOVERNMENT EMPLOY, IN A CIVILIAN CAPACITY, ANY RELATIVE OF YOURS (EITHER BY BLOOD OR MARRIAGE) WITH WHOM YOU LIVE OR HAVE LIVED WITHIN THE PAST 12 MONTHS? ☐ YES ☒ NO
If "Yes," for each such relative fill in the blank below. If additional space is necessary, complete under Item 14.

NAME	PRESENT ADDRESS (Including ZIP code)	RELATIONSHIP	MAR-RIED (Check one)	SIN-GLE	(1) Department or agency in which employed, (2) City and State, ZIP code, (3) Kind of appointment
					1.
					2.
					3.
					1.
					2.
					3.
					1.
					2.
					3.

ANSWER BY PLACING "X" IN PROPER COLUMN — YES / NO

7. ARE YOU A CITIZEN OF THE UNITED STATES OF AMERICA? If "No," give country of which you are a citizen: _____   NO: X

8. ARE YOU AN OFFICIAL OR EMPLOYEE OF ANY STATE, TERRITORY, COUNTY, OR MUNICIPALITY?
If your answer is "Yes," give details in Item 14.   NO: X

9. DO YOU RECEIVE OR HAVE YOU APPLIED FOR AN ANNUITY FROM THE UNITED STATES OR DISTRICT OF COLUMBIA GOVERNMENT UNDER ANY RETIREMENT ACT OR ANY PENSION OR OTHER COMPENSATION FOR MILITARY OR NAVAL SERVICE?
If your answer is "Yes," give details in Item 14.   NO: X

10. SINCE YOU FILED APPLICATION FOR THIS EMPLOYMENT, HAVE YOU:
A. BEEN CONVICTED OF AN OFFENSE AGAINST THE LAW OR FORFEITED COLLATERAL, OR ARE YOU NOW UNDER CHARGES FOR ANY OFFENSE AGAINST THE LAW?
(You may omit: (1) traffic violations for which you paid a fine of $30.00 or less; and (2) any offense committed before your 21st birthday which was finally adjudicated in a juvenile court or under a youth offender law.)   NO: X

B. BEEN CONVICTED BY GENERAL COURT-MARTIAL WHILE IN THE MILITARY SERVICE?
If your answer to A or B is "Yes," give details in Item 14. Show for each offense: (1) date, (2) charge, (3) place, (4) court, and (5) action taken.   NO: X

ANSWER BY PLACING "X" IN PROPER COLUMN — YES / NO

11. SINCE YOU FILED APPLICATION FOR THIS EMPLOYMENT, HAVE YOU
A. BEEN DISCHARGED (FIRED, FROM EMPLOYMENT FOR ANY REASON?   NO: X

B. RESIGNED (QUIT) AFTER BEING INFORMED THAT YOUR EMPLOYER INTENDED TO DISCHARGE (FIRE) YOU FOR ANY REASON?   NO: X

C. BEEN DISCHARGED FROM THE ARMED SERVICES UNDER OTHER THAN HONORABLE CONDITIONS?   NO: X

If your answer to A, B, or C is "Yes," give details in Item 14. Show the name and address (including ZIP code) of employer, approximate date, and reason in each case.

12. SINCE YOU FILED APPLICATION FOR THIS EMPLOYMENT HAVE YOU BEEN BARRED BY THE U.S. CIVIL SERVICE COMMISSION FROM TAKING EXAMINATIONS OR ACCEPTING CIVIL SERVICE APPOINTMENTS?
If your answer is "Yes," give dates and reasons for each debarment in Item 14.   NO: X

13. (A) HAVE YOU EVER FILED A WAIVER OF LIFE INSURANCE COVERAGE UNDER THE FEDERAL EMPLOYEES' GROUP LIFE INSURANCE ACT?   NO: X

(B) IF YOUR ANSWER IS "YES," DID YOU CANCEL THE WAIVER?

14. SPACE FOR DETAILED ANSWERS TO OTHER QUESTIONS (Indicate item numbers to which answers apply) (Continue on reverse if necessary)

ITEM NO. _____   ITEM NO. _____

CERTIFICATION.—I certify that all of the answers to the questions above are true, complete, and correct to the best of my knowledge and belief and are made in good faith.

Signature of appointee _____ J. Allen Hynek _____   Date of signature 6 April 1970

APPOINTING OFFICER.—Enter date of appointment or conversion. 05-05-70
(This form is to be completed before entrance on duty under the appointment or conversion.)

* U.S. GOVERNMENT PRINTING OFFICE: 1967 O—258-319

AFLC-WPAFB-JULY 68   1M

STANDARD FORM 50—Rev. December 1961
U.S. Civil Service Commission
FPM Chap. 295

NOTIFICATION OF PERSONNEL ACTION

(FOR AGENCY USE)

H-84420 PAS: WWHB6KY

1. NAME (CAPS) LAST—FIRST—MIDDLE	MR.—MISS—MRS.	2. (FOR AGENCY USE)	3. BIRTH DATE (Mo., Day, Year)	4. SOCIAL SECURITY NO.
HYNEK, J. ALLEN, MR.			05-01-10	295-34-5228

5. VETERAN PREFERENCE			6. TENURE GROUP	7. SERVICE COMP. DATE
N/A 1—NO 3—10 PT. DISAB. 5—10 PT. OTHER 2—5 PT. 4—10 PT. COMP.			0	0

9. FEGLI 1—COVERED (Regular only—declined Optional)	10. RETIREMENT	11. (FOR CSC USE)
2 2—INELIGIBLE 3—WAIVED 4—COVERED (Req. & Opt.)	2 1—CS 3—FS 5—OTHER 2—FICA 4—NONE	

12. CODE NATURE OF ACTION	13. EFFECTIVE DATE (Mo., Day, Year)	14. CIVIL SERVICE OR OTHER LEGAL AUTHORITY
171 Exc Appt NTE 05-04-71	05-05-70	Sec 15, PL-600, 79th Congress and Current Approp Act

15. FROM: POSITION TITLE AND NUMBER	16. PAY PLAN AND OCCUPATION CODE	17. (a) GRADE OR LEVEL (b) STEP OR RATE	18. SALARY

19. NAME AND LOCATION OF EMPLOYING OFFICE

20. TO: POSITION TITLE AND NUMBER	21. PAY PLAN AND OCCUPATION CODE	22. (a) GRADE OR LEVEL (b) STEP OR RATE	23. SALARY
Consultant AA: TDG	EC		PD $107.00

24. NAME AND LOCATION OF EMPLOYING OFFICE

USAF, AFSC, FTD
Commander, Wright-Patterson AFB, Ohio 45433

25. DUTY STATION (City—county—State)	26. LOCATION CODE
Wright-Patterson AFB, Ohio	34-9165-113

27. APPROPRIATION	FUNCTIONAL CODE	AFSC	28. POSITION OCCUPIED	29. APPORTIONED POSITION			
3DL	1010	02695Z	2 1—COMPETITIVE SERVICE 2—EXCEPTED SERVICE	1—PROVED—I 2—WAIVED-*	FROM	TO	STATE

30. REMARKS A. SUBJECT TO COMPLETION OF 1 ___ YEAR PROBATIONARY (OR TRIAL) PERIOD COMMENCING _____
B. SERVICE COUNTING TOWARD CAREER (OR PERMANENT) TENURE FROM: _____

SEPARATIONS SHOW REASONS BELOW, AS REQUIRED. CHECK IF APPLICABLE: C. DURING PROBATION

POSITION SENSITIVITY	
2 1—NONSENSITIVE 2—SENSITIVE I AW AFR 40-202	Ineligible for Health Benefits.

Subject to conflict of interest laws and regulations as a special Government employee.

"Special Government Employee"

Total work under this appointment is limited to 10 days during period of employment.

31. DATE OF APPOINTMENT AFFIDAVIT (Accessions only)	34. SIGNATURE (Or other authentication) AND TITLE FOR THE APPOINTING OFFICER
04-06-70	
32. OFFICE MAINTAINING PERSONNEL FOLDER (If different from employing office)	Supervisory Personnel Clerk

33. CODE	EMPLOYING DEPARTMENT OR AGENCY	35. DATE	
AF 06	DEPARTMENT OF THE AIR FORCE	Records, Awards & Benefits Branch 05-05-70	2520

6 PART
50-131-21

4. PERSONNEL FOLDER COPY

* U.S. GOVERNMENT PRINTING OFFICE 1969-347-193

STANDARD FORM 50—Rev. December 1961
U.S. Civil Service Commission
FPM Chap. 205

NOTIFICATION OF PERSONNEL ACTION

(EMPLOYEE — See General Information on Reverse)

(FOR AGENCY USE)

B-84420 PAS: UWUB6KY   RS

1. NAME (CAPS) LAST—FIRST—MIDDLE	MR.—MISS—MRS.	2. (FOR AGENCY USE)	3. BIRTH DATE (Mo., Day, Year)	4. SOCIAL SECURITY NO.
NYEEK, J. ALLEN, MR.			**05-01-10**	**295-34-5228**

5. VETERAN PREFERENCE			6. TENURE GROUP	7. SERVICE COMP. DATE
N/A 1—NO 2—5 PT.	3—10 PT. DISAB. 4—10 PT. COMP.	5—10 PT. OTHER	**0**	**0**

9. FEGLI		10. RETIREMENT		11. (FOR CSC USE)
2 1—COVERED (Regular only—declined Optional) 2—INELIGIBLE 3—WAIVED 4—COVERED (Reg. & Opt.)		**2** 1—CS 2—FICA 3—FS 4—NONE 5—OTHER		

12. CODE	NATURE OF ACTION	13. EFFECTIVE DATE (Mo., Day, Year)	14. CIVIL SERVICE OR OTHER LEGAL AUTHORITY
651	**Conv to Exc Appt NTE 05-04-72 INT**	**05-05-71**	**Sec 3109, Title 5, USC**

15. FROM: POSITION TITLE AND NUMBER	16. PAY PLAN AND OCCUPATION CODE	17. (a) GRADE OR LEVEL (b) STEP OR RATE	18. SALARY

19. NAME AND LOCATION OF EMPLOYING OFFICE

20. TO: POSITION TITLE AND NUMBER	21. PAY PLAN AND OCCUPATION CODE	22. (a) GRADE OR LEVEL (b) STEP OR RATE	23. SALARY
Consultant **AA: CC**	**IC**		**pd $107.00**

24. NAME AND LOCATION OF EMPLOYING OFFICE

USAF, AFSC, FTD, Commander
Wright-Patterson AFB, Ohio 45433

25. DUTY STATION (City—county—State)	26. LOCATION CODE
Wright-Patterson AFB, Ohio	**39-9165-113**

27. APPROPRIATION	FUNCTIONAL CODE	AFSC	28. POSITION OCCUPIED	29. APPORTIONED POSITION		
3L	**1010**	**026952**	1—COMPETITIVE SERVICE **2** 2—EXCEPTED SERVICE	FROM: 1—PROVED-I 2—WAIVED-2	TO:	STATE

30. REMARKS: A. SUBJECT TO COMPLETION OF 1   YEAR PROBATIONARY (OR TRIAL) PERIOD COMMENCING ____

B. SERVICE COUNTING TOWARD CAREER (OR PERMANENT) TENURE FROM: ____

SEPARATIONS: SHOW REASONS BELOW, AS REQUIRED. CHECK IF APPLICABLE: C. DURING PROBATION

POSITION SENSITIVITY	**Ineligible for Health Benefits**
2 1—NONSENSITIVE 2—SENSITIVE I AW AFR 40-202	**"Special Government Employee"**

Subject to conflict of interest laws and regulations as a special Government employee.

Employment totaled 4 days from 05-05-70 to 05-04-71.

Intermittent—no prescheduled regular tour of duty.

Total work under this appointment is limited to 20 days during period of employment.

31. DATE OF APPOINTMENT AFFIDAVIT (Accessions only)	34. SIGNATURE (Or other authentication) AND TITLE FOR THE APPOINTING OFFICER
	Margarete E. Letter **Personnel Clerk**
32. OFFICE MAINTAINING PERSONNEL FOLDER (If different from employing office)	**Records, Awards & Benefits Branch** **2520**
33. CODE EMPLOYING DEPARTMENT OR AGENCY	35. DATE
AF 1N DEPARTMENT OF THE AIR FORCE	**05-05-71**

6 PART
50-131-21

4. PERSONNEL FOLDER COPY   ☆ U.S. GOVERNMENT PRINTING OFFICE 1970 431-587/17

STANDARD FORM 50—Rev. December 1961
U.S. Civil Service Commission
FPM Chap. 295

NOTIFICATION OF PERSONNEL ACTION

(FOR AGENCY USE)
B-84420   PAS: mg

1. NAME (CAPS) LAST—FIRST—MIDDLE MR.—MISS—MRS.	2. (FOR AGENCY USE)	3. BIRTH DATE (Mo., Day, Year)	4. SOCIAL SECURITY NO.
HYNEK, J. ALLEN, MR.		05-01-10	295-34-5228

5. VETERAN PREFERENCE	6. TENURE GROUP	7. SERVICE COMP. DATE
N/A 1—NO 2—5 PT. 3—10 PT. DISAB. 4—10 PT. COMP. 5—10 PT. OTHER	0	0

9. FEGLI	10. RETIREMENT	11. (FOR CSC USE)
2 1—COVERED (Regular only—declined Optional) 2—INELIGIBLE 3—WAIVED 4—COVERED (Reg. & Opt.)	2 1—CS 2—FICA 3—FS 4—NONE 5—OTHER	

12. CODE	NATURE OF ACTION	13. EFFECTIVE DATE (Mo., Day, Year)	14. CIVIL SERVICE OR OTHER LEGAL AUTHORITY
651	Conv to Exc Appt NTE 05-04-73 INT	05-05-72	Sec 3109, Title 5, USC

15. FROM: POSITION TITLE AND NUMBER	16. PAY PLAN AND OCCUPATION CODE	17. (a) GRADE OR LEVEL (b) STEP OR RATE	18. SALARY

19. NAME AND LOCATION OF EMPLOYING OFFICE

20. TO: POSITION TITLE AND NUMBER	21. PAY PLAN AND OCCUPATION CODE	22. (a) GRADE OR LEVEL (b) STEP OR RATE	23. SALARY
Consultant AA: 0 CC	EC-1310(031)		pd $107.00

24. NAME AND LOCATION OF EMPLOYING OFFICE
AFSC, FTD, Commander,
Wright-Patterson AFB, Ohio 45433

25. DUTY STATION (City—county—State)	26. LOCATION CODE
Wright-Patterson AFB, Ohio	39-9165-113

27. APPROPRIATION	FUNCTIONAL CODE	AFSC	28. POSITION OCCUPIED 1—COMPETITIVE SERVICE 2—EXCEPTED SERVICE	29. APPORTIONED POSITION FROM: TO: STATE 1—PROVED-1 2—WAIVED-2
30X	1010	2695Z	2	

30. REMARKS   A. SUBJECT TO COMPLETION OF 1 ____ YEAR PROBATIONARY (OR TRIAL) PERIOD COMMENCING ____
B. SERVICE COUNTING TOWARD CAREER (OR PERMANENT) TENURE FROM: ____
SEPARATIONS: SHOW REASONS BELOW, AS REQUIRED. CHECK IF APPLICABLE: C. DURING PROBATION

POSITION SENSITIVITY
1—NONSENSITIVE
2 2—SENSITIVE IAW AFR 40-202

Ineligible for Health Benefits.

"Special Government Employee"

Intermittent-no prescheduled regular tour of duty.

Subject to conflict of interest laws and regulations as a special Government employee.

Employment totaled 6 days in a pay status.

Total work under this appointment is limited to 20 days during period of employment.

31. DATE OF APPOINTMENT AFFIDAVIT (Accessions only)	34. SIGNATURE (Or other authentication) AND TITLE FOR THE APPOINTING OFFICER
32. OFFICE MAINTAINING PERSONNEL FOLDER (If different from employing office)	Personnel Clerk
33. CODE EMPLOYING DEPARTMENT OR AGENCY	Records, Awards & Benefits Branch 2520
AF 1H DEPARTMENT OF THE AIR FORCE	35. DATE 05-05-72

6 PART
50-131-21

4. PERSONNEL FOLDER COPY   * U.S. GOVERNMENT PRINTING OFFICE 1969-391-526

STANDARD FORM 50—Rev. December 1961
U.S. Civil Service Commission
FPM Chap. 296

NOTIFICATION OF PERSONNEL ACTION

(FOR AGENCY USE)

H-84420   PAS: WEHB6KY   gjz

1. NAME (CAPS) LAST—FIRST—MIDDLE MR.—MISS—MRS.	2. (FOR AGENCY USE)	3. BIRTH DATE (Mo., Day, Year)	4. SOCIAL SECURITY NO.
HYNEK, J. ALLEN, MR.		05-01-10	295-34-5228

5. VETERAN PREFERENCE		6. TENURE GROUP	7. SERVICE COMP. DATE
1	1—NO 3—10 PT. DISAB. 5—10 PT. OTHER 2—5 PT. 4—10 PT. COMP.	0	0

9. FEGLI		10. RETIREMENT		11. (FOR CSC USE)
2	1—COVERED (Regular only—declined Optional) 2—INELIGIBLE 3—WAIVED 4—COVERED (Reg. & Opt.)	2	1—CS 3—FS 5—OTHER 2—FICA 4—NONE	

12. CODE	NATURE OF ACTION	13. EFFECTIVE DATE (Mo., Day, Year)	14. CIVIL SERVICE OR OTHER LEGAL AUTHORITY
651	Conv to Exc Appt NTE 05-04-74 - INT	05-05-73	Sec 3109, Title 5, USC

15. FROM: POSITION TITLE AND NUMBER	16. PAY PLAN AND OCCUPATION CODE	17. (a) GRADE OR LEVEL (b) STEP OR RATE	18. SALARY

19. NAME AND LOCATION OF EMPLOYING OFFICE

20. TO: POSITION TITLE AND NUMBER	21. PAY PLAN AND OCCUPATION CODE	22. (a) GRADE OR LEVEL (b) STEP OR RATE	23. SALARY
Consultant AA: CC	EC-1310 (031)		pd $107.00

24. NAME AND LOCATION OF EMPLOYING OFFICE

USAF, AFSC, FTD, Commander,
Wright-Patterson AFB, Ohio 45433

25. DUTY STATION (City—county—State)			26. LOCATION CODE
Wright-Patterson AFB, Ohio			39-9165-113

27. APPROPRIATION	FUNCTIONAL CODE	AFSC	28. POSITION OCCUPIED	29. APPORTIONED POSITION			
3D1	1010	2695Z	1—COMPETITIVE SERVICE 2 2—EXCEPTED SERVICE	FROM:	1—PROVED-1 2—WAIVED-2	TO:	STATE

30. REMARKS   A. SUBJECT TO COMPLETION OF 1   YEAR PROBATIONARY (OR TRIAL) PERIOD COMMENCING ___

B. SERVICE COUNTING TOWARD CAREER (OR PERMANENT) TENURE FROM: ___

SEPARATIONS. SHOW REASONS BELOW, AS REQUIRED   CHECK IF APPLICABLE: ☐ C. DURING PROBATION

POSITION SENSITIVITY	
2	1—NONSENSITIVE 2—SENSITIVE IAW AFR 40-202	Ineligible for Health Benefits. "Special Government Employee". Intermittent — no prescheduled regular tour of duty.

Subject to conflict of interest laws and regulations as a special Government employee.
Total work under this appointment is limited to 20 days during period of employment.
Intermittent employment totaled 3 days in pay status.

31. DATE OF APPOINTMENT AFFIDAVIT (Accessions only)	34. SIGNATURE (Or other authentication) AND TITLE FOR THE APPOINTING OFFICER
32. OFFICE MAINTAINING PERSONNEL FOLDER (If different from employing office)	PERSONNEL CLERK RECORDS AWARDS & BENEFITS BRANCH
33. CODE EMPLOYING DEPARTMENT OR AGENCY AF 1H DEPARTMENT OF THE AIR FORCE	35. DATE 06-07-73 2520

6 PART
50-131-21

4. PERSONNEL FOLDER COPY

* U.S. GOVERNMENT PRINTING OFFICE 1969-391-528

STANDARD FORM 50-Rev. December 1961
U.S. Civil Service Commission
FPM Chap. 295

NOTIFICATION OF PERSONNEL ACTION

(FOR AGENCY USE)

H-84420   CL: 0   WEHB6KY   mes

1. NAME (CAPS) LAST-FIRST-MIDDLE	MR.-MISS-MRS.	2. (FOR AGENCY USE)	3. BIRTH DATE (Mo., Day, Year)	4. SOCIAL SECURITY NO.
HYNEK, J. ALLEN	MR.		05-01-10	295-34-5228

5. VETERAN PREFERENCE	6. TENURE GROUP	7. SERVICE COMP. DATE
1 1-NO 3-10 PT. DISAB. 5-10 PT. OTHER 2-5 PT. 4-10 PT. COMP.	0	0

9. FEGLI
2 1-COVERED (Regular only-declined Optional)
2-INELIGIBLE 3-WAIVED 4-COVERED (Reg. & Opt.)

10. RETIREMENT	11. (FOR CSC USE)
2 1-CS 3-FS 5-OTHER 2-FICA 4-NONE	

12.CODE	NATURE OF ACTION	13. EFFECTIVE DATE (Mo., Day, Year)	14. CIVIL SERVICE OR OTHER LEGAL AUTHORITY
352	Termination - Exp of Appt - I	05-04-74	

15. FROM: POSITION TITLE AND NUMBER	16. PAY PLAN AND OCCUPATION CODE	17. (a) GRADE (b) STEP OR OR LEVEL RATE	18. SALARY
Consultant AA: 0 CC	EC-1310(031)		pd $107.00

19. NAME AND LOCATION OF EMPLOYING OFFICE
USAF, AFSC, FTD, Commander,
Wright-Patterson AFB, Ohio 45433

20. TO: POSITION TITLE AND NUMBER	21. PAY PLAN AND OCCUPATION CODE	22. (a) GRADE (b) STEP OR OR LEVEL RATE	23. SALARY

24. NAME AND LOCATION OF EMPLOYING OFFICE

25. DUTY STATION (City-county-State)	26. LOCATION CODE
Wright-Patterson AFB, Ohio	

27. APPROPRIATION	FUNCTIONAL CODE	AFSC	28. POSITION OCCUPIED	29. APPORTIONED POSITION		STATE
3DL	1010	2695Z	1-COMPETITIVE SERVICE 2 2-EXCEPTED SERVICE	FROM- TO- 1-PROVED-1 2-WAIVED-2		

30. REMARKS:
A. SUBJECT TO COMPLETION OF 1   YEAR PROBATIONARY (OR TRIAL) PERIOD COMMENCING
B. SERVICE COUNTING TOWARD CAREER (OR PERMANENT) TENURE FROM:
C. DURING PROBATION

SEPARATIONS: SHOW REASONS BELOW, AS REQUIRED CHECK IF APPLICABLE

POSITION SENSITIVITY
1-NONSENSITIVE
2-SENSITIVE I AW
AFR 40-202

AD - No other work available.

Intermittent employment totaled 1 day in a pay status.

Mailing Address: 2623 Ridge Ave.
Evanston, Illinois 60201

31. DATE OF APPOINTMENT AFFIDAVIT (Accessions only)	34. SIGNATURE (Or other authentication) AND TITLE FOR THE APPOINTING OFFICER
32. OFFICE MAINTAINING PERSONNEL FOLDER (If different from employing office)	Personnel Clerk
33. CODE EMPLOYING DEPARTMENT OR AGENCY	Records, Awards & Benefits Branch
AF 1H DEPARTMENT OF THE AIR FORCE	35. DATE 05-03-74 2520

6 PART   4. PERSONNEL FOLDER COPY   * U.S. GOVERNMENT PRINTING OFFICE 1971:481-131

STANDARD FORM 61
REVISED DECEMBER 1966
U.S. CIVIL SERVICE COMMISSION
F.P.M. CHAPTER 295
61-105

APPOINTMENT AFFIDAVITS

IMPORTANT.—*Before swearing or affirming to these appointment affidavits, you should read and understand the attached information for appointee*

Consultant   5 May 1970
(Position to which appointed)   (Date of appointment)

USAF, AFSC, Foreign Technology Division, Wright-Patterson AFB, Ohio 45433
(Department or agency)   (Bureau or division)   (Place of employment)

I, Joseph Allen Hynek _____, do solemnly swear (or affirm) that—

A. OATH OF OFFICE

I will support and defend the Constitution of the United States against all enemies, foreign and domestic; that I will bear true faith and allegiance to the same; that I take this obligation freely, without any mental reservation or purpose of evasion; and that I will well and faithfully discharge the duties of the office on which I am about to enter. SO HELP ME GOD.

B. AFFIDAVIT AS TO SUBVERSIVE ACTIVITY AND AFFILIATION

I am not a Communist or Fascist. I do not advocate nor am I knowingly a member of any organization that advocates the overthrow of the constitutional form of the Government of the United States, or which seeks by force or violence to deny other persons their rights under the Constitution of the United States. I do further swear (or affirm) that I will not so advocate, nor will I knowingly become a member of such organization during the period that I am an employee of the Federal Government or any agency thereof.

C. AFFIDAVIT AS TO STRIKING AGAINST THE FEDERAL GOVERNMENT

I am not participating in any strike against the Government of the United States or any agency thereof, and I will not so participate while an employee of the Government of the United States or any agency thereof. I do not and will not assert the right to strike against the Government of the United States or any agency thereof while an employee of the Government of the United States or any agency thereof. I do further swear (or affirm) that I am not knowingly a member of an organization of Government employees that asserts the right to strike against the Government of the United States or any agency thereof and I will not, while an employee of the Government of the United States or any agency thereof, knowingly become a member of such an organization.

D. AFFIDAVIT AS TO PURCHASE AND SALE OF OFFICE

I have not, nor has anyone acting in my behalf, given, transferred, promised or paid any consideration for or in expectation or hope of receiving assistance in securing this appointment.

Joseph A. Hynek
(Signature of appointee)

Subscribed and sworn (or affirmed) before me this 6th day of April _____ A.D. 19 70.,

at Evanston _____   Illinois _____
     (City)   (State)

[SEAL]   *Lillian Hansen*
                                                (Signature of officer)

Commission expires April 7 1971   *Notary Public*
(If by a Notary Public, the date of expiration   (Title)
of his Commission should be shown)

NOTE.—*The oath of office must be administered by a person specified in 5 U.S.C. 2903. The words "SO HELP ME GOD" in the oath and the word "swear" wherever it appears above should be stricken out when the appointee elects to affirm the affidavits; only these words may be stricken and only when the appointee elects to affirm the affidavits.*

U.S. GOVERNMENT PRINTING OFFICE : 1967 O - 257-459

<u>WORK STATEMENT</u>

Dr. Hynek will provide expert advice to the Commander and Chief Scientist in resolving highly complex and controversial problems requiring unusual in-depth technical competence in the physical sciences.

<u>Field of Specialized Knowledge</u>: Specialized knowledge possessed by Dr. Hynek is in the areas of orbital bodies and atmospheric phenomena.

<u>Circumstances Justifying Consultant</u>: There is no one, either civilian or military, with the Foreign Technology Division who possesses the collective qualifications of Dr. Hynek. Therefore, the services and expertise required cannot be obtained through other means, such as detail, promotion, or reassignment. Normal recruitment efforts have not identified any other equally qualified applicant who is willing to accept a short-term appointment. Accordingly, the required expertise can only be obtained by appointing Dr. Hynek as a Consultant.

Hynek, J. Allen
5-5-73

CHAPTER 17

On Assignment at Wright-Patterson

If the crash and retrieval of a flying saucer in New Mexico in 1947 actually occurred, shouldn't there be more reliable testimonies from credible sources? The answer is yes. There should be many good reports from solid citizens, from men and women whose credentials are impeccable, men and women who have nothing to gain by claiming they saw a UFO. And some of those sightings should have been made by highly respected persons.

Brigadier General Vorley "Mike" Rexrold said that he viewed the late Chester W. Lytle Sr., as one of the great unsung heroes of American history—no small compliment from the likes of Rexrold, who received an honorary doctorate in medical humanities, and served in the Office of Special Investigation/Counter Intelligence during WWII.[1]

Lytle was a key player in the Manhattan Project and was with the Motorola Electronics Company in Chicago in 1945, where he was instrumental in their development of the radio transmitter for the detonator of the first atomic bomb. He prepared the United States Air Force Technical Orders in the field of special weapons and research, development, and manufacture of electronic and electromechanical equipment. Among his other accomplishments, he was an active military consultant on nuclear weapons, including warheads and their adaptation to missiles and missile systems. As a civilian scientist, Lytle consulted for the CIA and acquired GS 16 rating, which is the equivalent of a rank of general in the military. Lytle had clearly earned a "need to know" status.

In the years that followed WWII, Lytle served in the government designing and engineering communication systems for the Atomic Energy Commission.[2] It was in that capacity that he became good friends with Major General Kenner F. Hertford, who was then the commander of the U.S. Army Atomic Energy Department. In 1952, Hertford was part of the general staff of the Research and Development Division.[3] Lytle had numerous top-secret projects with R&D, including radar configuration and aircraft and autopilot design. The military called on him frequently for national security projects at major facilities around the world—including Wright-Patterson.[4]

This irreproachable source described to us an afternoon in the late 1950s when he was working with the CIA and on assignment at Wright-Patterson. All at once the base went on full alert as air raid sirens screamed of an intrusion. Lytle and a number of officers were escorted into a special radio room in one of the operations buildings. While there, as military radar and communications personnel professionally operated their posts, Lytle overheard radio communications from the lead pilot of a number of scrambled jet fighters. A lone radarscope also provided a visual for what was about to transpire. Lytle anxiously watched as the

(L-R) Chester Lytle, Don Schmitt, and Nathan Twining Jr.

blips on the screen converged on a lone bogey as it approached the restricted air space over the SAC facility. As the interceptors made visual contact with the UFO, it was then identified as a "smooth, metallic disk" still heading in their direction. The fighters locked all weapons systems on the intruder and prepared to engage when, as though anticipating such maneuvers, the object took evasive action. Lytle thought this had to be a training exercise of some sort, for it all seemed like a page out of some science fiction novel. However, this civilian was also a highly experienced pilot who flew spy missions with the likes of William Lear (inventor of the Lear Jet) and Howard Hughes. There was no doubt this situation was real, and everyone in the room remained calm and collected throughout the ordeal. During the next few minutes, a frustrating game of cat and mouse ensued between the fighters and the UFO; all radio and radar information confirmed the presence of an unknown craft, which easily outmaneuvered our planes. After toying with our fighters, the superior device simply departed the scene, and left the pilots and the observers in the radio room with a sense of awe.

Aside from the excitement of the experience itself, what truly struck Lytle was the manner in which all the trained personnel behaved. Everyone around him acted as though the entire event was routine. Yet this was not a rehearsal. From all accounts and for all of those involved whom Lytle would speak to during and after the alert, this was a regular occurrence. The base commander went so far as to tell Lytle that this type of activity was common over Wright-Patterson.

Throughout the years, Lytle would hear from both military officers and elected officials that, yes, indeed, this was the case. For some "unknown" reason, the UFO phenomenon was paying special attention to Wright-Patterson. This, in itself, was contrary to the observation noted by none other than Edward Ruppelt. He stated,

> **UFOs were habitually reported from areas around "technically interesting" places like our atomic energy installations, harbors, and critical manufacturing areas. Our studies showed that such vital military areas as Strategic Air Command and Air Defense Command bases, some A-bomb storage areas, and large military depots actually produced fewer reports than could be expected from a given area in the United States. Large population centers devoid of any**

major "technically interesting" facilities also produced few reports. According to the laws of normal distribution, if UFOs are not intelligently controlled vehicles, the distribution reports should have been similar to the distribution of population in the United States—it isn't.

It would appear that Wright-Patterson was an exception to that rule.

Chester Lytle was often assigned to government work at Wright-Patterson, and through the years, he became a good friend of General Nathan Twining. On many occasions during dinner parties at the home of the general's son Nathan Jr., Lytle would share with us personal accounts about UFO discussions he had with General Twining. The accounts were always based on the position that the phenomenon was real and that Wright-Patterson was the repository for all the secrets. Lytle would comment how he himself had a general officer rating, and that each and every time he would ask about seeing some of the underground levels and wondered aloud at their connection to the phenomenon, he was always met with a stern "Don't ask."

Aside from his own personal experiences, the one thing that truly sparked his interest in the subject was a serendipitous conversation he had with none other than former Roswell base commander William Blanchard. In February 1953 he and Blanchard, then a general, had been on assignment at Eielson AFB near Fairbanks, Alaska. General Blanchard, as the Eighth Air Force's Deputy Director of Operations, was there to direct the weapons training of B-36 intercontinental bomber flight teams, and Lytle supervised the transporting of atomic weapons from Sandia Laboratory at Kirtland AFB in Albuquerque. Upon completion of their duties, Lytle was anxious to get home to Chicago as his wife, Shirley, was about to give birth to their first son, Chet. Aware of this, Blanchard, a "very close friend," offered personally to fly Lytle in a bomber to the Air Force base nearest his home. During the long flight, the subject of UFOs came up between the two men. The Washington, DC sightings had only occurred the previous July, and there had also been some recent sightings near Elmendorf AFB near Anchorage, Alaska. Suddenly, the general mentioned Roswell. He then told a somewhat startled Lytle that an alien spacecraft with four dead humanoid beings aboard had been recovered there in July 1947.[5]

General William Blanchard.

Lytle later heard from another high-level Air Force source that some of the recovered bodies had gone first to Muroc Field (now Edwards Air Force Base) in California before eventually going to Wright Field in Dayton, Ohio. He also said he heard about autopsies carried out on the remains from firsthand witnesses and that the recovered craft was stored at Wright—in Hangar #5, not in the infamous Hangar #18. "**I had the highest of clearances,**" Lytle regretfully added, "**but I was never allowed into the damn building.**"[6]

To add additional weight to this most incredible source, it was a former chief aid of Mayor Henry Meyer, who served in Milwaukee for 20 years, who first introduced us to Lytle back in February 1989. That man was Richard Budelman, and he was a personal legal advisor to none other than Dr. J. Allen Hynek. Hynek described Lytle as a "close friend" and a "highly reliable source" on the subject of UFOs. They had often worked together at Wright-Patterson through the 1950s.[7]

Chester W. Lytle would go on to become the founder and president of Communications Diversified in Albuquerque, New Mexico, a telecommunications company. Specializing for many years in national defense and satellite projects, he also had the distinction of personally knowing every president of the United States from Franklin Roosevelt through George W. Bush. His stories about John F. Kennedy were priceless, but what will always stand out is how up until the time that he died at the age of 92 in 2004, he was adamant about what he knew to be the truth about not only Roswell, but also the topic of UFOs in general. He also personally knew who was in charge of the cover-up but declined to reveal the name. He would admit that the general officer's secretary was the wife of his Air Force security aide when he worked with the AEC at Wright-Patterson in the early 1950s. It should be pointed out that Lytle spent more and more time at the residence of Nathan Twining, Jr., at his home in Albuquerque, the last five years of his life. Coincidence?[8]

When General Rexrold passed away in 2002, Senator Strom Thurmond made a tribute statement on the floor of Congress paying homage to such a great man. It was Rexrold who had paid tribute to Lytle. We can say no more, and consider his testimony to remain unshakable and undisputed.[9]

Also mentioned earlier in this chapter was Major General Kenner F. Hertford, whom we had the distinct honor of meeting through Chester Lytle in 1992. Hertford would then send us a statement in which he acknowledged, **"I am almost completely convinced that the object that crashed near Roswell was composed of materials not common on Earth. I still do not understand the veil of secrecy maintained for the last 45 years of the arrival on Earth of an object with human-like, living beings."**[10]

And after 66 years, not a single witness to the events of 1947 has stepped forward to provide any evidence to the contrary.

CHAPTER 18

Heart-Attacking the Witnesses

The specific function of the military, as described by the Constitution, is to serve as a specific government body with the sole directive of implementing policies—not *formulating* policies—that require the use of physical force. Military personnel, because of the nature of their jobs, are much more willing to use force to settle disputes with civilians because they are trained strictly in the art of warfare. It was for that very reason that in 1878 the Posse Comitatus Act was created: It prohibits the Army (and later the Air Force) from engaging in domestic law enforcement situations, unless they do so pursuant to lawful authority. That "lawful authority" comes from only one person: the president of the United States.

However, with the implementation of the National Security Act of 1947, much of that authority was transferred back to the military. Under President Truman's signature, it also established the position of the secretary of Defense and created the National Security Council along with the Central Intelligence Agency. The law, as it defines itself, reads: "...to promote the national security by providing for a Secretary of Defense (formerly Secretary of War), for a National Military Establishment... and for the coordination of the activities of the National Military Establishment with other departments and agencies of the Government concerned with the national security."[1] In non-technical language, if an incident is determined to be a threat to our national security, the military is fully authorized by the government to "implement policy." In even plainer words, *use physical force when necessary to ensure the security of the nation.* Unless national security is at stake, forget about it. The question remains: Did the UFO phenomenon fall under such authority, and did the crash at Roswell necessitate such actions on the part of the military?

As we described in an earlier chapter, when it came to the downing of an enemy aircraft, T-2 Intelligence was the best-equipped organization to handle such an incident—including covering up the fact that an incident ever occurred. Yet, there was one specific dilemma always faced by the military in any situation that involved civilians: They cannot be ordered into cooperation. Based on our Constitution, unless the president declares a State of Marshal Law, the United States military has absolutely no authority over any American citizen. Furthermore, both federal and local law enforcement agencies are authorized to have full autonomy over all military personnel, including officers. The uniform does not provide anyone with a "get out of jail free" card—they are subject to the same laws and rights that any other American citizen has. This makes it all the more disturbing for the U.S. military to not only take the law into its own hands, but also to apply its laws to civilians in an attempt to silence them—in a matter that the military claimed did not involve national security! From all accounts, this is precisely what happened in the aftermath of the Roswell incident as the long arm of T-2 extended from Wright Field all the way to New Mexico.[2]

Getting more than a little rough with people was just the style of an Army Air Force officer by the name of Colonel Hunter G. Penn. During WWII, Penn was the bombardier on a bomber in the 303rd Bomb Group known appropriately as "Hell's Angels." After the war, he was "associated" with Wright Field in the summer of 1947, and before his passing he described to his family how he had undertaken a deadly serious assignment that summer. He explained to them that when he was assigned to Wright Field he was ordered to **"visit places around Roswell, New Mexico,"** where a UFO had crashed. Putting it euphemistically, Penn was tasked to **"help manage civilian-military affairs after the crash."** He was to ensure that an "information blackout" regarding the event was put—and kept—in force. Put bluntly, he was to question those who might know something about the crash, and especially about recovered bodies, and "make sure that they did not talk." He was ordered to concentrate on civilians, specifically ranchers, hired hands, and "simple types" residing in the outlying areas who may have seen or heard something contrary to the "official" cover story. Utilizing intimidation and threats if necessary, Penn was not shy in instilling fear to gain compliance from even children and the elderly. The matter was considered so important that, if he could not persuade innocent civilians who were not compliant, Penn was to use physical force, including weaponry, to enforce their silence. He confirmed to his family that the crash near Roswell was extraterrestrial, and that they were concerned at the time about unknown dangers or problems that might be in the offing with the arrival of the unknown visitors. Whether they were facing an invasion or something more benign, special agents like Penn had the responsibility of stalling for time. All the rumors and talk that contradicted anything put out for public consumption needed to be squelched immediately.

It appears that "in the heat of battle" at the time that the Roswell incident was in progress during the first two weeks of July 1947, the military powers-that-be decided to employ "friendlies"—authority figures known to the locals in Roswell and throughout the county—in the personages of the local sheriff and the Roswell Army Air Field base security liaison officer to the City of Roswell to attempt to silence the local citizenry. However, in the weeks and months immediately following the crash, after the initial fervor had died down, the question of how to maintain and enforce the silence of those who knew the truth became a paramount issue. Apparently it was felt that appeals to national security and patriotism would not be enough to achieve the desired result of complete suppression, especially on the part of the outlying ranchers not in the Roswell jurisdiction. In the military mindset at the time, specifically with T-2 at Wright Field, the answer was to "Put the fear of God in them." Enter Hunter Penn. It makes complete sense that Wright Field intelligence sent a stranger such as Penn to New Mexico to do the really dirty work—to intimidate or worse: An officer from the RAAF would not have been proficient in such matters as threatening civilians. Such an officer would still have to coexist in the community, and could be identified and held to account—arrested and criminally charged. An outsider, on the other hand, would be infinitely more preferable: someone who has no compunction about using whatever means necessary to get the job done, someone with no personal ties to the town, someone who had total plausible deniability, someone who could crawl back under the rock of obscurity, someone like Colonel Hunter Penn.

While she was growing up, Penn's foster daughter, Michelle, said she was fearful of her alcoholic father. "He was a brutal person," she said, and she did not need to be told never to say anything about what he had recounted to her about his "secret mission" in New Mexico back in 1947. To this day, she is not sure why he told her, but she feels he was trying to use fear and intimidation to control her behavior—similar to the way she was made to address him as "Sir" as a young girl. According to Michelle, her foster father demonstrated no qualms about being entrusted with the role of Roswell's "Bad Cop." In more dramatic terms, she said, **"He tried to 'heart-attack' people!"** Michelle said that her father would sometimes brandish a military pickaxe (similar to an ice pick). She remembers that he was obsessed with picks and believes he may have used one when visiting the good people of Roswell who simply misidentified a weather balloon.[3] For sure, it worked, because from that moment on, Wright-Patterson explained away most UFO sightings over the next 20 years as—you guessed it—weather balloons.

CHAPTER 19

Leonard Stringfield and the Little Grey Men

Our late colleague and friend Leonard H. Stringfield, who was the first researcher to accept UFO-crash retrievals as legitimate, met with a doctor he described as his "prime medical contact."[1] What was described to him by this individual were the basic physical attributes of the nonhuman victims of such crashes.

On another occasion, Stringfield had the opportunity to converse with another doctor who allegedly participated in an autopsy of an alien specimen at Wright-Patterson. This new source, according to Stringfield, provided a great deal of additional data. **"From him, in time, I was able to envision the body entire,"** Stringfield said. **"I learned of its internal chemistry and some of its organs—or, by human equation, the lack of them."**

Stringfield, working from statements from his medical contacts, was able to draw a number of conclusions. According to Stringfield, the being was humanoid, 3 1/2 to 4 feet tall. It weighed about 40 pounds. The skull was proportionally larger than a human head. The two eyes were large, round, deep-set, and wide apart. The nose was vaguely defined, with only a slight protuberance, and its mouth was a small slit that opened only into a deep cavity. The mouth apparently did not **"function as a means of communication or as an orifice for food ingestion. In addition, there were no teeth. There were no earlobes or protrusive**

Leonard Stringfield.

flesh extending beyond apertures on each side of the head." The head, as well as the rest of the body, was devoid of hair. Its neck was slender, as was its torso. The arms were long and thin, reaching down close to the knees, and the hands had slight webbing between the fingers. "**Skin description is not green,**" Stringfield continued. "**Some claim it was beige, tan, brown, or...pinkish gray, and one said it looked almost 'bluish gray' under deep-freeze lights.... The texture was described as 'scaly' or reptilian' and as 'stretchable, elastic, or mobile over smooth muscle.**" He noted that, "**Under magnification, I was told, the tissue structure appears mesh-like.... This information suggests the texture of the granular-skinned lizards, such as the iguana and chameleon.**"[2]

After more than a year of "negotiations," Stringfield arranged to receive a written statement from a hematologist who claimed to have been involved with a nonhuman autopsy. It also described in nonprofessional terminology the unusual anatomy. The typewritten statement went as follows:

SIZE—The specimen observed was 4 foot 3 and 3/8 in length. I can't remember the weight. It has been so long and my files do not contain the weight. I recall the length well, because we had a disagreement and everyone took their turn at measuring.

HEAD—The head was pear-shaped in appearance and oversized by human standards for the body. The eyes were Mongoloid in appearance. The ends of the eyes furthest from the nasal cavity slanted upward at about a 10-degree angle. The eyes were recessed into the head. There seemed to be no visible eyelids, only what seemed like a fold. The nose consisted of a small fold-like protrusion above the nasal orifices. The mouth seemed to be a wrinkle-like fold. There were no human-type lips as such—just a slit that opened into an oral cavity about two inches deep. A membrane along the rear of the cavity separated it from what would be a digestive tract. The tongue seemed to be atrophied into almost a membrane. No teeth were observed. X-rays revealed a maxilla and mandible as well as cranial bone structure. The outer "ear lobes" didn't exist. The auditory orifices present were similar to our middle and inner ear canals. The head contained no hair follicles. The skin seemed grayish in color and seemed mobile when moved. The above observations are from general anatomical observations. I didn't autopsy or study the head portion in any great detail since this was not my area of specialty.[3]

As originally agreed upon with Stringfield, the statement was unsigned and had no masthead. The name of the doctor remains confidential in his files as per agreement before Stringfield's passing in 1994.

Further confirmation of autopsies has come from another source. Dr. Lejeune Foster, a renowned expert on human spinal-cord structures who had a practice in San Diego in 1947, was called on to perform a special assignment for the military. She did not travel to Wright Field, but went to Washington, DC, where she stayed for approximately one month. During Foster's absence, Dr. Laura Henderson filled in for her at the San Diego clinic.

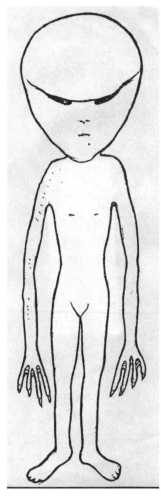

Depiction of one of the Roswell aliens drawn by UFO crash researcher Leonard Stringfield. The drawing is based upon the descriptions given to Stringfield by doctors who were present during the autopsies.

Because Dr. Foster had worked undercover for the FBI during World War II, and because she already had a security clearance, she was flown to Washington to examine the bodies retrieved near Roswell.

She reported that it was possible that one had been recovered alive. Foster would later secretly confide to family members that she examined two of the corpses. Her task was to define their bone structures, which would include the spinal cord. Comparisons would then be drawn to human anatomy. Like the other doctors who saw the bodies, Dr. Foster described the beings as short, with proportionately larger heads than those of humans. She said they had "strange eyes" and that the spinal cords did not resemble our own.

According to her confidants, Foster was very upset upon her return from Washington. As she had been debriefed, she had been told that if she talked about what she had seen, she would lose her license to practice medicine and that she risked being killed. "**Someone in the government is trying to keep me quiet,**" she would often say.[4]

In the mid-1970s a former volunteer at the Wright-Patterson Air Museum had a rather serendipitous encounter that he will not soon forget. Our source of information about this volunteer is Lt. Colonel Richard Hoffman, who presently works on classified projects for the Army Materiel Command in Huntsville, Alabama. Hoffman had a private conversation with this individual, who made reference to the "little fellows" hidden at Wright-Patterson at that time. He would leave Hoffman dumbfounded with the information that would follow.[5]

Our research indicates that this individual was Dr. Leon E. Kazarian, a senior-level scientist with the Air Force Aerospace Medical Research Laboratory at Wright-Patterson in the 1960s and 1970s. He specialized in biomechanics, which is a field of science that studies the structure and function of biological systems such as humans and animals. Kazarian's specialties included spine and backbone anomalies resulting from such factors as atmospheric flight, space flight, microgravity conditions, radiation exposure, and the effects on crashed pilots' bodies and vertebral columns from the physical impact. On a number of occasions, he testified in court as an expert on accident reconstruction and injury causation. He is also the author or coauthor of technical publications such as "Flight Physical Standards of the 1980s," "Spinal Column Considerations," "Bone Mineral Analysis in Space Flight," and "Escape Injury Assessment," among numerous other reports. It should be noted that almost all such research studies were Wright-Patterson publications, and many of them had to be approved for release through the Defense Technology Information Center (DTIC) of the Department of Defense.

Kazarian possessed the highest of clearances given the sensitive nature of his work; he also served as an Air Force witness and consultant in biomechanical-related injuries. As part of his unique resume, he also taught at Wright State University in Dayton.[6]

It was during the private meeting with Hoffman that the medical scientist mentioned, "**He had been to numerous crash sites, examined beings with no backbones, and had to perform autopsies on these.**" According to Hoffman, Kazarian went on to describe his "team's work" in studying the effects of being in a space environment on the human body, and confessed that they had been sharing bone marrow studies with the Soviets on the Cosmonauts who spent extended periods of time in space. He ended the remarks with the position that his team's findings showed conclusively that **if we lived in space for generations, the newborn would have a similar appearance to the "beings reported in UFOs."** Hoffman was left speechless and did not have additional time to ask Kazarian a thousand questions—not even one.[7]

When we called Kazarian, hoping that he would answer our question, he pleaded ignorance of the original incident and expressed his bewilderment that Hoffman would claim such things. Amazingly, what he *would* admit was that he too had heard talk when he was at Aero Med about bodies being brought to Wright-Patterson years before the 1960s.

Likewise, he did not refute the story of a crashed UFO at Roswell and has many times pondered such a possibility. The last corroboration he acknowledged to us was that he was completely aware of "memory-metal experiments" in space by NASA. He added that **such scientific study would be "folded into existing defense research so that no one would realize the extraterrestrial impetus of the technology."**[8]

In 1959, the U.S. government enlisted Dr. Leon B. Visse, a French expert on biological elements connected with cellular tissue (in other words, DNA), for a special assignment at Wright-Patterson. Two years prior, in 1957, one of his colleagues, Dr. Francis Crick, had demonstrated the relationship among DNA, RNA, and proteins. A year later, research began on proving a genetic code, and indeed, 1958 is considered the birth of molecular biology.

At Wright-Patterson, Visse's job was to establish the historic weight of specific cells provided to him for testing. As the analysis proceeded, he noted that the historic weight of his sample was much lower than that of a human being. Each time he repeated the procedure, the same outcome was verified. Astonished by the consistent results, he finally asked to see the contributing specimens. At the time, the biologist did not know if he was dealing with a new virus or genetic organism he had never encountered before. From the lab, Visse was taken into a secret room. There lay the bodies of two humanoids.

Both corpses were badly mangled, as though they had been in some type of crash. **"The forehead high and broad.... The eyes were stretched towards the temples which gave them an Asiatic appearance. The nose and mouth were small. The lips were thin.... The chin was small and slightly pointed.... The hands were human-like but slender."** The French professor was relieved that his genetic hypothesis remained intact, and after being sworn to secrecy, he was very happy to return to Paris and resume more terrestrial studies.

Some 20 years later, when Dr. Jean Gilles of the French Centre for Scientific Research (the CNRS is considered the French equivalent of NASA) tracked down Visse, he denied the story. But, according to Gilles, what he did concede is quite telling. Visse suggested that only a highly qualified biologist and exobiologist could describe the details in such a story, and he noted that the bodies exhibited a far more developed lymphatic system than normal. In contrast, he also suggested that due to prolonged space travel, there would be an atrophied muscular as well as diminished cardiovascular system.[9]

Colonel D'Jack Klinger was a pilot who lost his plane over France during WWII, escaped to England, and wound up assigned to Wright Field after the surrender of Germany. A USAF flight surgeon, Klinger was once given the duty of locating and retrieving a disabled bomber on the U.S./Canadian border armed with nuclear weapons. His mission was successful, and as a result, he was promoted to command a special team that secured downed aircraft, crew or bodies, and/or weapons. This assignment would take him all over the world—including New Mexico.[10]

Klinger retired in 1975 and confided to fellow executive Ronald SeCoy of Ohio the following story: Back in the late 1940s, he witnessed and helped document part of an autopsy performed by pathologists at Wright-Patterson AFB. He observed two humanoids on a table—one, horribly burned, the other appearing uninjured after a crash of some type of ship. Each one was approximately 4 feet in length. Men moved around the body from different angles to film and photograph the entire ordeal. Dr. Klinger described the eyes as having layered membranes, which were more like "optical instruments." The bodies were slender down to the fingers, and there was a lack of discernable genitalia. To him, the skin appeared "fabric-like," and noted that the interior of the torso and apparent skeletal system resembled those of an insect.

Now, 30 years after reliving something so "foreign" to the human psyche, according to SeCoy, the doctor, most visibly upset, made him promise on his word of honor never to repeat what he just described. There was no question that Klinger was still terrified of the government.

He as much as said so. But what haunted his memory and so riveted SeCoy was Klinger's recollection of the badly burned body—specifically the face. He said the expression on its face was "frozen in anguish."[11]

Klinger's story has now come to be included with all the other stories that provide no physical evidence, no proof, just the culmination of circumstantial eyewitness testimony that clearly rises beyond the mundane. Actually, it rather approaches the germane, as surely it does for all of these "storytellers" who have had to live with the fear of government reprisal for speaking out about something that does not exist.

Earlier in 2013, documentary producer James Fox and screenwriter Tracy Torme interviewed one of the former directors of Project Blue Book, Colonel Robert Friend. During the course of the exchange, the subject of Roswell came up. Friend remarked, **"I don't know why they would have taken burned bodies to Wright-Patterson. If they would have had burned bodies they would have gone to Texas. They had the Military Burn Facility there."**[12] Now, neither Fox nor Torme mentioned anything about "burned" bodies during the discussion with the retired officer.[13] And what is more intriguing is that, throughout all of our previous writings about the subject, neither have we.

CHAPTER 20

The Jawbone That Spoke Martian

In July of 2010, an advance copy of an NBC documentary called "Inside Secret Government Warehouses" was presented to a select audience at the International UFO Museum and Research Center at Roswell, New Mexico. Without a doubt, it was the final scenes that generated the greatest buzz during the 90-minute feature: The segment that presented dental anthropologist Dr. Shara Bailey of New York University's Rufus D. Smith Hall Anthropology Department making the statement, **"[I would] bet my career that it is not from a primate,"** drew the most vocal reaction.[1] This was the fourth such scientific validation in an attempt to identify a strange and unidentifiable mold made from an actual piece of bone 30 years earlier—a section of bone that apparently was kept at that time at Wright-Patterson AFB and has only surfaced one time—that we know of.

John Mosgrove, now in his 80s, still works as a dental technician in Dayton, Ohio. Back in October 1979, he worked on the fourth floor of the Brown Veterans Hospital, which is just 30 minutes from the front gate of Wright-Patterson. For more than 60 years he has been contracted by local dentists, and he was honored for developing an effective delivery system to more accurately X-ray patients being fitted for mouth appliances. It is because of Mosgrove that millions of dental patients are now exposed to less radiation in such procedures. John Mosgrove tells an amazing story.

It was a routine day, just after lunch break, as Mosgrove resumed his lab assignments, when the chief of staff of the dental clinic walked in with an urgent request. The doctor unwrapped a thoroughly packed box, and then removed what appeared to be a standard mouth impression of an anterior front portion of a mandible. At first glance, it seemed that it was a cast made for procedural lab purposes—strictly routine. However, Mosgrove was instructed to immediately put aside all other work and attend to the late arrival. The doctor said, "**You are not to make any record of this project. In other words, the events surrounding my visit and those to follow never happened.**"

Mosgrove accepted the confidential work as asked and next went to the sink to rinse off any blood, saliva, or debris normally present on such a relief. Instantly, he noted not only the absence of bodily fluids, but more importantly, upon examining the piece, he realized it was not plaster or any other casting material; it was real bone. Whose bone? *What's* bone? It resembled no human jawbone he had ever seen before.

What also fascinated him was his next thought: "**My God, this is edentulous [without teeth] because there is nothing but bone here.**" He proceeded to cast a mold from the bone using Kwik-Set plaster, and after the relief quickly solidified, it was rinsed and examined for any defects. As he studied it again, he became even more puzzled by it. Mosgrove said, "**I've never seen anything like it before or since. At first, yes, I felt excitement, but as reality set in, fear took over...a fear of something that I wasn't supposed to know about.**" He immediately remembered how the head of the clinic sternly warned him to "forget what you've seen."

Within a day, the same doctor returned to retrieve Mosgrove's work and the original mandible. First, he went to the work table and separated the tray from the model. Pleased with the results, he next took it over to the model trimmer, trimmed off the flash around the edges and then polished it up. Satisfied with the replica from the original, the doctor then took the template, crumbled it in his left hand, and then tossed it in a trash receptacle. He briefly looked around the lab table, and, confident that there remained no evidence, started to exit the room. Mosgrove tried to get an answer. "Doctor, wait a minute. I've got to have the prescription order." He looked back and said, "**John, you never worked on this, you've never seen it, and you never talked about it.**"

Nothing more was said as the doctor departed. Mosgrove was not satisfied and followed from a distance. They reached the first floor, and the doctor walked out through the main door. Mosgrove watched through one of the windows in the reception room as two uniformed officers approached the doctor on the sidewalk. One of the men was a major and the other was a colonel, whom Mosgrove recognized from Wright-Patterson AFB. With few words exchanged, the ranking officer took the original and the reproduction from the doctor. He placed both into a container and then into his briefcase. Snapping it shut, the two officers each shook the doctor's hand and hastily left the area.

As Mosgrove quickly retreated back to his lab he noticed another oddity. "**After they left, I went from the office to see if anything else happened. I walked from the laboratory all the way down to the Chief of Staff's office. Now, along the corridor they have examination and surgical rooms. There was not a soul on the floor. No patients, no doctors, no nurses, no hygienists...nobody was on the floor. That was very unusual.**"

The lab technician kept thinking back to why Air Force officers would enlist the lead dentist at their hospital for such a clandestine mission. Wright-Patterson has its own medical facility and laboratories, which are second to none. Why risk entrusting someone outside of their authority? Unless the risk would have been even greater there, what with all the rumors. This jawbone would certainly have fueled the fire. Mosgrove could not help but wonder, *What if the rumors over at the base were true? What if he had held proof right in his own hands?*

Based on his own experience in his profession, he concluded that the bone had been around for quite a number of years. The mandible was quite pitted and completely dehydrated. The sample showed signs of bone fragmentation, which, to Mosgrove, also suggested a "terrible hit to the face, like slamming into something." But whatever the trauma, it had not broken the mandible. In addition, what could have happened to the teeth? In place of them, someone had originally inserted what appeared to be round pegs or posts into the gum tissue. This may have been done to either prop open the mouth during examination or reinforce the damaged jawbone. What also bothered Mosgrove was that the doctor, almost in a demonstrative way, crushed and then trashed his impression. Although it was broken into pieces, the highly skilled dental technician was able to retrieve the discarded sections. He reassembled them, made a new impression from his original, and finally poured another relief to create his own cast. Mosgrove is confident that it is almost identical to what the Air Force officers salvaged. Although he had been warned to treat the entire incident as though nothing had happened, Mosgrove remained convinced that this was something extraordinary.[2] He just needed some expert opinion on what, if not a human, the jawbone could represent. He recalled a newsman mentioning a top-level UFO meeting held at Wright-Patterson the year before; he seemed like someone who would listen.

(L) "Martian" dental arch (minus ascending ramus) of mandible. (R) "Martian" dental arch compared with a human dental arch (minus ascending ramus). Note the difference.

The late Carl Day was a news anchor and Dayton staple for more than 30 years for both NBC and FOX affiliates. He has the distinction of receiving more awards than any other Ohio broadcaster, including seven Emmys. Day was inducted into the National Broadcaster's Hall of Fame in 1989. Since 1998, he was a member of the Broadcasting Hall of Fame, and in 2009, he was named to the Dayton Walk of Fame. After his passing in 2010, the Associated Press renamed its Outstanding Achievement Award the Carl Day Award for Outstanding Achievement. Clearly, John Mosgrove could not have contacted a more outstanding journalist.

Day used his many connections to enable anthropologists, archaeologists, and forensic dentists to examine the mandible, and they all arrived at the same conclusion. With every new analysis, Day became even more intrigued by the story and would soon associate all the local rumors he had nonchalantly dismissed before. A low drone of suspicion pointed to Wright-Patterson, and if there originally was a jawbone of something that was not human stored there, what had become of the rest of the body? The silence coming from the base ironically presented Day with an opportunity the secret-keepers could not have imagined.

When Carl Day was invited to speak at a luncheon of Air Force officers from the base, he knew that timing was everything; at the appropriate moment, he held up an illustration of a typically described life-size alien face. What happened next was something only someone like Day would do. While still displaying the drawing, like a magician, he took Mosgrove's mandible from his jacket and held it in front of the mouth area. It lined up perfectly. Not only were the brass in the room muttering among themselves, but later they would express how displeased they were with the ambush. Anticipating such a reaction, Day had covered himself; his bosses back at the TV station knew what he was about to do. Instead of laughter, Day was met with controlled anger from the officers.[3] What other public reaction could they make in front of an elite member of the press?

Someone had to be watching Mosgrove or had a file on him. After all, it isn't every day that a couple of officers slip a mandible bone, kept for God knows what reason, out of Wright-Patterson to have a copy made by an outside dental lab. Maybe they were using them as paperweights. We don't mean to belittle the situation with Mosgrove, who would soon receive an anonymous call from a man who sternly informed him that if he proceeded to talk about "certain things" his well-being and that of his family would be in jeopardy. The caller went on to say that they could also ruin his reputation.

Because of the seriousness of what was clearly a death threat, the replica of the mandible given to Carl Day was locked away in a bank security box for the next 30 years—that is, until we were contacted by NBC with the request of getting a film crew into Wright-Patterson. (Details of that project are in the final chapter.) We later suggested including Day for an on-camera interview, as we were quite familiar with his Wright-Patterson research and he was an admired personal friend of ours for almost 20 years. Much to our surprise, we had no idea what he had preserved in that bank box. As expected, NBC was thrilled that he was willing to provide the mandible impression for renewed scientific examination with the hope of finally identifying it. The mandible was about to make its television début.[4]

NBC arranged for six more experts in an attempt to match the impression with any known species on this planet. The position statements remained unanimous: They all agreed with Dr. Bailey from New York University, which has one of the largest collections in the United States, including more than 2,000 primate casts in its anthropology department. To date, all who have been consulted agree that:

1. The mandible was definitely cast from an actual skeleton.

2. It definitely displays gum tissue.

3. No comparison can be made to any existing humans or primates.

Dr. Bailey added, "**The mandible is not from any creature that comes from Earth. That's for sure.**"[5] We believe those two officers at Wright-Patterson felt the same way.

CHAPTER 21

In the Shadows of Ghosts

More than a million visitors a year tour the world-famous Aviation Museum at Wright-Patterson to get a glimpse of rare aircraft, prototypes, and even a captured Soviet MiG fighter. In the spotlight is the history of manned flight and our amazing journey to escape Earth's gravity and put a man on the moon. The past hundred years have demonstrated a remarkable and courageous effort by many individuals to experience the magic of flight. The museum serves as a proud testament to what human ingenuity is capable of in just a short span of existence on this planet.

Unfortunately, the same can hardly be said about the 23 years that Wright-Patterson was the headquarters of government-sponsored UFO investigations. True, there is a UFO exhibit at the museum, in the form of a single glass case, displaying fake UFO photos, hoaxed artifacts, a blob of melted plastic, a large block of cinder, and a metal ball contraption with radio tubes and wires—clearly painting the picture that the subject has been reduced to sideshow status. As an extra attraction, there is a massive collection of Blue Book summary papers, a copy of the Condon Report, and the National Academy of Sciences' support of Condon's controversial mangling of the topic. Also on display is a chronological listing of notated status reports—replete with all the original negative and dismissive remarks. There is also an engineering attempt to demonstrate just how aerodynamically unfeasible is the very shape of a UFO and how unlikely it would be for it to maneuver in atmospheric flight. The hallmark of this jaded exhibit is the assertion that the Air Force never found any reliable evidence or witnesses to support the theory that UFOs represented any technology beyond our own.

Is this rudimentary exhibition really the end result of 23 years of tax-funded investigation? The words, "The Air Force isn't hiding anything" ring false next to such a churlish attempt to relegate the subject of UFOs to the realm of absurdity. The Wright-Patterson fact sheet states, "**There are not now nor ever have been any extraterrestrial visitors or equipment on WPAFB.**" Based on their shameful UFO display, it seems such extraterrestrials would have had a difficult time even crossing the street.[1]

Let's advance 40 years after Blue Book gasped its last sighting explanation. In January of 2010, NBC News and Peacock Productions contacted us about consulting on a news documentary about underground government facilities. We were asked to secure permission for a film crew to enter Wright-Patterson base proper and interview on camera a base representative discussing the base's history and the importance of a number of facilities. Specific buildings were named, including Foreign Technology Division, Buildings 620, 45, and 18, and Hangar 23. The producers, who included Larry Landsman and Kimberly Ferdinando, were aware that we had been to the base with film crews in the past. It was believed that we should have no problem—especially for NBC. It all should have been routine.[2]

For years, we had heard about a vast portion of the base being underground—all the underground bunkers and tunnels large enough for the passage of trucks, the manmade hills in Area B, large hangars with no windows. (Those that once had them were painted over). On the numerous occasions we had been on the base, we observed clusters of ventilation pipes coming out of the ground with no buildings around them. We noted large open areas with what obviously were heavy metal doors going into the side of a hill. There were "Road Closed" signs all over and we were told that the Propulsion Research and Development building had a walkway/ramp that led to an underground door. We had also heard about the underground refrigerated rooms for the storage of old acetate film, we guess it becomes combustible when heat builds up when it is stored normally. Along with Stan Friedman, we even listened to the son of the German engineer who described his design for a vault under the base's nuclear reactor. As did his father, we all thought it was a bi-zarre place for such a chamber.[3] For decades, Carl Day, Len Stringfield, Stanton Friedman, and numerous others have taken the testimony of witnesses to such things. Navy photo analyst Dr. Bruce Macabbee informed us about a military photographer who was assigned to Wright-Patterson in 1971–72 after his return from Vietnam. He described, "**On one occasion we did some filming underneath one of the flight lines where there were acres of storage areas, all underground. We saw two C-124s down there, but never figured out how they got them down there. There was a huge museum storage area and it would be very easy to hide just about anything in there. None of this was visible from the surface save for some ventilation and an auxiliary power generating system.**"[4]

So all the talk and all the rumors had finally caught the attention of NBC. For the record, Wright-Patterson denies that any such underground levels even exist—neither today nor ever before. With nothing to hide, they should not have an issue with us coming back with the media. Besides, our current information is that if there had indeed been any UFO physical evidence at Wright-Patterson, it had all been cleared out by the mid-1980s.

When we contacted Daryl Mayer, the base public affairs liaison, with NBC's request, we were surprised that on this occasion we were referred to Russell Maheras of Air Force Entertainment out in Hollywood. After providing our proposal and jumping through an exorbitant number of legal hoops, it was requested that we shorten the scope of our production. Trimmed down to a single camera operator with NBC news commentator Lester Holt, we were still rejected.[5] Maheras informed us that "[i]f a unit declines to support a documentary request, **Air Force Entertainment doesn't approve.**"[6] To say we were dumbfounded would be an understatement. The March 2010 filming date was looming, and after six denials, we made one last attempt.

Retired Air Force Colonel Jeffrey Thau is a former deputy commander of Wright Patterson, a graduate of the War College, and currently a consultant for the DOD in major weapon system acquisition and development. He has an office not only at the Pentagon but also at his former base in Dayton. Serving more than 30 years in the military, he is now the president and head CEO at American Aerospace. "Colonel Jeffrey," as he is called, is also a good friend to coauthor Donald Schmitt. "Jeff, they're not letting me on the base," Don told him. "Can you see what you can do ASAP?"[7] Again, we assured the network's executive producer, Gretchen Eisele, that we would make the deadline, as she, too, was petitioning the base for the green light.[7] Col. Thau's initial efforts were a repeat of the same protocol we had already followed to no avail. He too was rejected, and attributed the problem to "entrenched bureaucracy." Even the offer to provide them with final review and editing approval was turned down. The days were running out.

We had one final idea: The colonel would personally ask the base commander, Colonel Richard Stacy, for special permission. We went to the very top, hoping that he would waive all the red tape and, out of professional courtesy, open the door for a fellow officer. The remaining days to deadline passed, and at last the call came from Col. Thau with the ultimate decision. After explaining to Don Schmitt that everyone in the base commander's office "knew who you were," he recounted Col. Stacy's final determination: **"Jeff, I don't care if you have four stars... Don Schmitt is not getting on this base."**[8] As he apologized for having failed Schmitt's request, Schmitt couldn't help but smile to himself as he thought Dr. Hynek was somewhere doing the same.

NOTES

Chapter 1

1. Anderson, *Inventing Flight*.
2. Walker and Wickam, *From Hoffman Prairie to the Moon*.
3. "Wright-Patterson Air Force Base: Introduction Information," 1994, 1997, 2009.
4. "Wright-Patterson Air Force Base." U.S. Air Force Fact Sheet. Dayton, Ohio: History Office, Aeronautical Systems Center WPAFB, posted December 2, 2008.
5. National Museum of the US Air Force: *www.nationalmuseum.af.mil*.
6. Lasby, *Project Paperclip*.

Chapter 2

1. Correll, "USAF and the UFOs."
2. E-mail from Janis Yoder to the *International UFO Museum & Research Center* in Roswell, N.M.; September 30, 1997.
3. E-mail from Lance Winkler to Donald Schmitt, June 11, 2007.
4. Ibid.

5. E-mail from Allen P. Kovacs, PhD, to Thomas Carey, February 25, 2010.

6. Ibid.

7. Ibid.

8. Ibid.

9. "RAAF Captures Flying Saucer in Roswell Region."

10. "General Ramey Empties Roswell Saucer."

11. Ibid.

12. Patricia Rice, telephone interview, June 3, 2000; quoted in the *Dallas Morning News*, July 6, 1997.

13. Berlitz and Moore, *The Roswell Incident*.

14. Carey and Schmitt, *Witness to Roswell*.

15. A few interviewees mentioned that some of the wreckage and a body or two might have gone to Los Alamos, White Sands, and/or Kirtland Field (all in New Mexico); Berlitz and Moore suggested that Muroc Field (now Edwards AFB) in California might have been a destination for the bodies, but the overall destination consensus of most was Wright Field.

16. An FBI memo drafted the same day as General Ramey's press conference, July 8, 1947, has survived to us today. Sent from an agent in the Dallas FBI field office to the Cincinnati field office with a copy to FBI Director J. Edgar Hoover, it confirmed that the shipment of the Roswell crash debris to Wright Field was indeed taking place.

17. At the time of the Roswell incident, the engineering function was referred to as "T-3," and the intelligence function as "T-2." In 1951, "T-2" was changed to the "Air Technical Intelligence Center." In 1961, it became the "Foreign Technology Division," and in 1992 it became the present-day "National Air & Space Intelligence Center." For the sake of convenience, we will use the term "Foreign Technology Division" for all time periods.

18. E-mail from James Conway to Anthony Bragaglia, March 3, 2013.

19. Scully, *Behind the Flying Saucers.*

20. Stringfield, "Item B-6."

21. Correll, "USAF and the UFOs."

22. Ibid.

23. This was almost certainly the inspiration for a later "nurse story" told by a Roswell mortician by the name of Glenn Dennis, who claimed that he had a nurse friend who was present during an attempted autopsy of one of the alien bodies at the Roswell base, but he refused to name her; we searched for several years but never found a military nurse by that name. He later admitted that he had provided us a fictitious name for her.

24. Carr, "Son of Originator of 'Alien Autopsy' Story Casts Doubt on Father's Credibility."

25. Ibid.

26. Collins, with Doty, "The Vaults at Wright-Patterson AFB."

27. Robert Marshall, signed and notarized Affidavit, July 8, 1996.

28. Ibid.

29. Ibid. NOTE: The reader is asked to recall Corona rancher Mack Brazel's response to a question from Roswell radio announcer Frank Joyce regarding "Little Green Men." In a calm, matter-of-fact voice, Brazel casually replied, "They weren't green."

30. Ibid.

31. Ben Hansen, telephone interviews with Tom Carey, 2010 and 2013; exchange of e-mails with Carey in 2010, 2011, 2012, and 2013; in-person interview with Don Schmitt in 2011.

32. Dr. M. David Hansen, telephone interview, December 2010.

33. Ibid.

34. Ibid.

35. Ibid.

36. "Statement of Dr. M. David Hansen, 22 February 2011," attached to an e-mail from Ben Hansen to Tom Carey, March 2, 2011.

37. Ben Hansen, e-mail to Tom Carey, March 5, 2011.

38. "Wright-Patterson Air Force Base, Area B, Building 18, Power Plant Complex."

39. Ibid.

40. Collins with Doty, "The Vaults at Wright-Patterson AFB."

41. Newton, "Corps Restores Historical Gem at Wright-Patterson Air Force Base."

42. Ibid.

43. Collins with Doty, "The Vaults at Wright-Patterson AFB."

44. Ben Hansen, e-mail to Tom Carey, March 5, 2011.

45. George Quigley, telephone interviews with Tom Carey, 2010, 2013. Quigley knew Stringfield well as the publisher of two of Stringfield's books, *Inside Saucer Post 3-0 Blue* (1957) and *Situation Red: The UFO Siege* (1977).

46. Bragalia, "Is This Where Alien Bodies Are Stored?"

47. Collins, with Doty, "The Vaults at Wright-Patterson AFB."

48. Ronald SeCoy, e-mail to Tom Carey, September 9, 2004.

Chapter 3

1. Sagan, *Cosmos*.

2. Gross, *UFOs: A History*.

3. Randle and Schmitt, *UFO Crash at Roswell*.

4. Keyhoe, *The Flying Saucers Are Real*.

5. *www.FBI.gov*.

6. See Carey and Schmitt, *Witness to Roswell*, for full details of Mack Brazel's find.

7. Schmitt, *UFO Crash at Roswell II*.

8. Ibid.

9. Swords, *The Summer of 1947*.

10. Maccabee, *The Government UFO Connection*.

11. Swords and Powel, *UFOs and the Government*.

12. Kantor, *Mission With Lemay*.

13. "Flying Disks" memorandum from E.G. Fitch to D.M. Ladd, July 10, 1947.

14. Air Intelligence Requirement Division (AIRD), "Draft of Collection Memorandum," October 28, 1947. Reprinted in Maccabee, *Documents and Supporting Information*.

15. Ibid.

16. Ibid.

17. Swords, *The Summer of 1947*.

18. Ruppelt, *The Report on Unidentified Flying Objects*.

19. Dolan, *UFOs and the National Security State*.

20. Ruppelt, *The Report on Unidentified Flying Objects*.

21. Ibid.

Chapter 4

1. Richelson, *The U.S. Intelligence Community*. See also *www.gwu .edu/~nsarchv/nsa/publications/ic/intelligence_com.html*.

2. Carey and Schmitt, *Witness to Roswell*.

3. In 1989, Robert Lazar claimed to have been a technician who had worked on alien technology inside of hangars located in Section "S-4" of Area 51 near Groom Lake. When a background investigation of Lazar's claimed work history and academic degrees did not check out, his Area 51 tale lost credibility and has been dismissed by most researchers. Lazar's statements, however, served to link Area 51 with UFOs, government cover-ups, and the secret re-engineering of alien technology.

4. Strickland, "How Area 51 Works."

5. Broad, "Senator Regrets Role in Book on Aliens."

6. Anthony Bragalia, telephone discussion with Tom Carey, March 14, 2013.

7. Bragalia, "Roswell Debris Confirmed as Extraterrestrial."

8. As recounted in *The Roswell Incident*, according to family members Corona sheep rancher Mack Brazel described the strange symbols as reminding him of the "petroglyphs" inscribed on rocks by Native Americans.

9. Bragalia, "Roswell Debris Confirmed."

10. Bragalia, Anthony, "My Conversation w/ Elroy Center's Confidante!" e-mail to Tom Carey, February 23, 2012.

11. Bragalia, Anthony, "Elroy Center's Daughter Reveals," e-mail to Tom Carey, February 23, 2010.

12. Bragalia, "Scientist Admits to Study of Roswell Crash Debris!"

13. Bragalia, "Roswell, Battelle & Memory Metal."

14. Bragalia, "Roswell's Memory Metal."

15. Ibid.

16. Ibid.

17. Nathan Twining Jr., personal interviews, 1998 through 2008.

18. Sydney Johnston, telephone interviews, 2009, 2010.

19. Johnston daughter, telephone interview, 2011.

20. Ibid.

21. John P. Stapp, personal biography, The Stapp Association, 2004. Society of Automobile Institute of Engineering, Inc., Warrendale, Penn., 1966–2004.

22. Johnston daughter, telephone interview, 2011.

23. Research and Development Personnel Directory, 1947.

24. Johnston daughter, telephone interview, 2011.

25. Robert Sarbacher, personal correspondence, William Steinman, November 29, 1983. Telephone interviews with Stanton Friedman and Bruce Maccabee, 1983.

26. Sarbacher, personal biography.

27. Carey and Schmitt, *Witness to Roswell.*

Chapter 5

1. "Major General Barry M. Goldwater."

2. "Arizona Wing of the Commemorative Air Force."

3. Letter from Sen. Goldwater to Mr. Schlomo Arnon, dated March 28, 1975. From Goldwater, "The 'UFO Letters' of Senator Barry Goldwater" (originally archived from *www.rense.com/ufo2/goldwater2.htm*, March 20, 2003).

4. Letter from retired Sen. Goldwater to Kent Jeffrey dated July 26, 1994. From Goldwater, "The 'UFO Letters' of Senator Barry Goldwater."

5. Senator Goldwater letter to Mr. Schlomo Arnon on March 28, 1975; in this letter, Goldwater stated that it was "about 10 or 12 years ago" that he tried to gain entrance into the "Blue Room" at Wright-Patterson, only to be turned down by Gen. LeMay.

6. Stringfield, "Case A-3."

7. Berlitz and Moore, *The Roswell Incident*.

8. Letter from Sen. Goldwater to Mr. Lee Graham dated October 19, 1981. From Goldwater, "The 'UFO Letters' of Senator Barry Goldwater."

9. Letter from Senator Goldwater to Mr. Sclomo Arnon.

10. Letter from Sen. Goldwater to UFO researcher William Steinman, dated June 20, 1983. From Goldwater, "The 'UFO Letters' of Senator Barry Goldwater.

11. Stringfield, "Abstract Number Three."

12. Stringfield, "Case A-3."

13. Berlitz and Moore, *The Roswell Incident*.

14. Letter from Sen. Goldwater to Mr. Lee Graham dated October 19, 1981. Copy of original supplied to authors by Mr. Graham.

15. Burnstein, "AUH20."

16. Cameron, Presidential UFO.

17. Wilbert Smith stated in 1950 after a visit with officials in Washington, D.C., that the subject of UFOs was "classified higher than the H-bomb."

18. Cameron, Presidential UFO.

19. Ibid.

20. Ibid.

21. Copy of letter from Freedom of Information Manager, FTD, Wright-Patterson AFB, to William Moore, dated January 7, 1981. From Bragalia, "Opening the Door to the Blue Room."

22. Copy of letter from the Chief, Documentation Branch, FTD, Wright-Patterson AFB, dated November 5, 1982, provided to authors by Lee Graham.

23. Copy of archived film record provided to the authors by Grant Cameron.

24. Copy of letter from the Director of Information Management, Scott AFB, IL dated October 9, 1991 provided to the authors by Brian Parks.

25. Transcription of letter from the WPAFB FOIA Analyst to Anthony Bragalia, dated May 14, 2012, in Bragalia, "Opening the Door to the Blue Room."

26. Bragalia, "Opening the Door to the Blue Room."

27. Stringfield, "The Blue Room."

28. Ibid.

29. Ibid.

30. "Statement by Barry Goldwater Concerning UFOs," *Larry King Radio Show*, October 13, 1988.

Chapter 6

1. "General Ramey Empties Roswell Saucer."

2. FBI telex dated July 8, 1947, from the Dallas Field Office to the Cincinnati Field Office and to FBI Director J. Edgar Hoover, stating that the wreckage was being flown to Wright Field in Dayton, Ohio for examination, and that the weather balloon explanation of General Ramey was not borne out.

3. Sappho Henderson, videotaped interview in *Recollections of Roswell Part II*.

4. Ibid. In this interview and in subsequent interviews, Mrs. Henderson maintained that her husband did not mention "bodies" to her; however, a dentist "friend of the family," Dr. John Kromschroeder, confirmed in the same video the fact that "Pappy" Henderson told him about transporting bodies to Wright Field in addition to physical wreckage.

5. Mrs. David Ackroyd, telephone interview, 2004.

6. All living crew members from Henderson's WWII bomber crew, including Vere McCarty, who could be found, were interviewed by telephone in the 1990s, and all confirmed hearing the story. When each was asked if they thought Henderson was joking, each responded that Henderson was definitely serious—and not joking—about it.

7. Vere McCarty, letter of July 12, 1989.

8. Sappho Henderson, telephone interview, 2010.

9. Joseph Toth, telephone interviews, 2008, 2012.

10. Arthur Exon, telephone interviews, 1990, 1991, and 1994; in-person interview, 2000.

11. Stanton Friedman, e-mail to Don Schmitt, January 2013. Original statement told to Friedman by Raymond Madson in Albuquerque, N.M., in 1997.

12. Randle and Donald R. Schmitt, *UFO Crash at Roswell.*

13. Ibid.

14. Stringfield, *The UFO Crash/Retrieval Syndrome.*

15. Ibid.

16. Ibid.

17. Ibid.

18. Ibid. It was a Roswell mortician by the name of Glenn Dennis who first introduced the notion that some of the alien bodies smelled badly. According to Dennis, on July 8, 1947, he paid a chance visit to the Roswell base hospital apparently at the very time that a preliminary autopsy was being attempted on the second set of alien bodies recovered from the crashed flying

saucer. He then encountered a nurse friend who had emerged from the autopsy room holding a towel over her face, after which he was unceremoniously removed from the hospital by armed MPs. The next day, Dennis learned from the nurse that she had been called in to assist in an attempted autopsy of an "alien creature," but the smell from them was so foul that it made everyone in the room sick, and the autopsy was terminated. The next day, July 9, 1947, these "smelly bodies" were flown to Fort Worth, Texas, in a large wooden crate in the bomb bay of a B-29 dubbed the *Straight Flush*. The final leg of the journey to Wright Field was accomplished by John Tiffany's flight with the smelly bodies hermetically sealed inside a large cylindrical container.

19. Randle and Schmitt, *UFO Crash at Roswell*.

20. Ibid. A similar warning had been administered to the B-29 crew that had flown the bodies from Roswell to Fort Worth on the first leg of their journey to Wright-Patterson.

21. Ibid.

22. John Kromschroeder, personal interview, 1990.

23. Ibid.

24. Ibid.

25. Ibid.

26. Randle and Schmitt, *UFO Crash at Roswell*.

27. Peter Robbins, telephone interviews, 2009, 2010, and 2011; in-person interview in 2011.

28. Heather MacRae, telephone interview, 2010.

29. Son (name on file) of the military photographer who worked at WPAFB and was ordered to photograph two alien "creatures" in glass cases; he told his son about his encounter in 1957, and the son recounted the story to us in a 2010 in-person interview.

30. Carl Day, telephone interview followed up with e-mail, April 2010.

31. Thomas Blann, in-person interview, 1992.

32. Daughter (name on file) of Yanic Ritger, in-person interview, 2011; see also "Case B-1" in *UFO Crash Retrievals: Amassing the Evidence, Status Report III* by Leonard H. Stringfield.

33. Ibid.

34. Ibid.

35. Ibid.

36. Ibid.

37. General Exon stated that one of the original Roswell bodies went to a mortuary in Denver; and we have other witnesses who saw one or more bodies under examination at two different AeroMedical Facilities in Texas in 1964. Marion "Black Mac" Magruder told his sons that the bodies later went to a base in Florida, and there have been suggestions that they also went to Area 51 in Nevada and Dugway in Utah.

38. The names are known to us but are being withheld pending completion of our investigation.

Chapter 7

1. Randle and Schmitt, *The Truth About the UFO Crash At Roswell.*

2. Ibid.

3. Ibid.

4. Clarkson, *Tell My Story.*

5. Ibid.

6. James Clarkson, telephone interview with Tom Carey, January 2013.

7. Clarkson, *Tell My Story.*

8. McAndrew, *The Roswell Report: Case Closed.* The first explanation for the Roswell crash by the Air Force was that it was a "flying saucer" (July 8, 1947); the second explanation was that it was a "weather balloon" (July 9, 1947); the third was that the wreckage was multiple rubber balloons and tinfoil radar targets from a top-secret project, "Project Mogul" (1994); and the fourth was that

the little bodies reportedly found among the wreckage were just anthropomorphic, dime-store mannequins used in high-altitude parachute test-drops—in the 1950s (1997).

9. Clarkson, *Tell My Story*.

10. Clarkson, telephone interview, 2013. See also Clarkson, *Tell My Story*.

11. Kevin Randle, telephone conversation with Tom Carey, January 2013; dates of June Crain's employment also verified by James Clarkson in a separate e-mail to Tom Carey, January 2013. These were: (1) June 19, 1942–July 17, 1943; (2) May 13, 1948–July 21, 1948; and (3) March 8, 1951–May 2, 1952.

12. Clarkson, *Tell My Story*.

13. Ibid.

14. Ibid.

15. Ibid.

16. Smith, "Memorandum to the Controller of Telecommunications [Top Secret]." In Good, *Need to Know*. See also Dolan, *UFOs and the National Security State*.

17. Clarkson, *Tell My Story*.

18. Mazza, Wheeler, et al., "High Altitude Bailouts."

19. Clarkson, *Tell My Story*.

20. Clarkson, telephone interview, 2013.

21. Good, *Need to Know*.

22. Carey and Schmitt, *Witness to Roswell*.

23. Dolan, *UFOs and the National Security State*.

24. Clarkson, *Tell My Story*.

25. Ibid.

26. Ibid.

27. Ibid.

28. Ibid.

Chapter 8

1. Magruder, *Nightfighter*.
2. Randle, "Mac Magruder and the Air War College."
3. Magruder, *Nightfighter*.
4. The 1947/48 AWC class that Col. Magruder was a part of spent five days (April 5–9, 1948) at Wright-Patterson Air Force Base. Magruder's official Marine Corps historical document confirms this. A review of the subject/teaching schedule for the entire class year shows that classes were to have been in session for seven hours each day, five days a week. In each one-hour block for each day of the week there was indicated the subject matter to be discussed and the name of the instructor. For the week that Magruder's class was at Wright, however, there were no such indications of what was to be discussed—just the notation, "FIELD TRIP TO WRIGHT FIELD," typed in each of the 35 hourly blocks for the week. That was all. No indications of what to expect.
5. Birnes, "Squiggly."
6. Mark Magruder, telephone interviews with Tom Carey, 2002, 2008, 2010, 2011.
7. The Roswell crash was only a one- or two-day story at most in the national news media after the balloon explanation, and internally, the Air Force quickly quashed talk about it on the threat of lengthy prison time for anyone who did.
8. Magruder, Mark. Videotaped interview with Roger Leir, Derrel Simms, and Jesse Marcel, Jr; May 5, 1998.
9. Birnes, "Squiggly."
10. Magruder, telephone interviews with Tom Carey.
11. Ibid. See also Birnes, "Squiggly" for the "They weren't green" comment.
12. Birnes, "Squiggly."
13. Magruder, telephone interviews with Tom Carey.
14. Ibid.

15. Birnes, "Squiggly."

16. Magruder, telephone interviews with Tom Carey. See also Birnes, "Squiggly."

17. Carey and Schmitt, *Witness to Roswell.*

18. Birnes, "Squiggly."

19. John Kromshroeder, videotaped interview in *Recollections of Roswell II.*

20. Herschel Grice, telephone interview with Tom Carey, 2003.

21. Birnes, "Squiggly."

22. Magruder, *Nightfighter.*

23. Ibid.

24. Magruder, telephone interviews with Tom Carey.

25. Ibid.

26. Birnes, "Squiggly."

27. Magruder, videotaped interview.

28. Randle, "Mac Magruder and the Air War College."

Chapter 9

1. "The Twining Memo." (General Nathan Twining Sr., letter to General George F. Schulgen.)

2. Hall and Connors, *Alfred Loedding and the Great Flying Saucer Wave of 1947.*

3. Wendy Connors, telephone interviews with Anthony Bragalia, 2012.

4. Earl L. Zimmerman, sworn affidavit, November 2, 1993; also telephone interview, 1995.

5. Journalist Billy Cox in the *Sarasota Herald Tribune* first reported Benjamin Games's story; Cox subsequently contacted our investigation and our investigative colleague Anthony Bragalia, who resides near Games; each then conducted separate interviews of Games in 2008, ours by telephone and Bragalia's in person.

6. Michael Hall and Wendy Connors, personal interview with Victor H. Bilek, October 29–30, 1999.

7. Hall and Connors, *Alfred Loedding and the Great Flying Saucer Wave of 1947*.

8. Swords, "Project Sign and the Estimate of the Situation."

9. Ruppelt, *The Report on Unidentified Flying Objects*.

10. Ibid.

11. U.S. Air Force Technical Intelligence Division, Air Material Command Memorandum, August 6, 1948.

12. Hall and Connors, *Alfred Loedding and the Great Flying Saucer Wave of 1947*.

13. Ruppelt, *The Report on Unidentified Flying Objects*.

14. Swords, "Project Sign."

15. Ruppelt, *The Report on Unidentified Flying Objects*.

16. Ibid.

17. Swords and Powell, *UFOs and Government*.

18. U.S. Air Force Technical Intelligence Division, Air Material Command, "Unidentified Aerial Objects: Project Sign" (Dayton, Ohio: Wright Patterson Air Force Base, February 1949). Technical Report n. F-TR-2274-1A.

19. Hall and Connors, *Alfred Loedding and the Great Flying Saucer Wave of 1947*.

Chapter 10

1. Schopenhauer, *The Art of Being Right*.

2. Ruppelt, *The Report on Unidentified Flying Objects*.

3. Ibid.

4. Ibid.

5. Swords and Powell, *UFOs and the Government*.

6. Project Grudge Report. Grudge file collection, Research Department, International UFO Museum and Research Center, Roswell, N.M.

7. Ginna and Darrach Jr., "Have We Visitors From Space?"

8. Ruppelt, *The Report on Unidentified Flying Saucers*. Also Cabell, *Charles P. Cabell: A Man of Intelligence*.

9. Ibid.

10. Tolstoy, Leo. *The Most Difficult Subjects can Be Explained* (Russia, 1894)

11. Ruppelt, *The Report on Unidentified Flying Objects*.

Chapter 11

1. Project Stork Report, Preliminary Introduction, Research Department, International UFO Museum and Research Center.

2. Project Stork Status Report No. 1.

3. Hynek, *The UFO Experience*. In 1952, Hynek conducted a survey with 44 astronomers. Five of his colleagues admitted to having observed UFOs. In a personal letter he sent to the Air Force he stated that this internal polling demonstrated "a higher percentage than among the public at large."

4. Personal research, Department of Meteoritrics, University of New Mexico at Albuquerque, 1989, 1998.

5. Project Stork files collection, Research Department, International UFO Museum and Research Center.

6. Hynek, personal interviews, 1978, 1979.

7. Paul M. Fitts, Project Blue Book files, January 27, 1956, letter to Commander Air Material Command, Wright-Patterson Air Force Base, Captain C.A. Hardin AFOIN.

8. Hynek, Project Stork Report, IUFOMRC.

9. Project Stork No. 9974 Summary Outline.

10. Jennie Zeidman, personal interview, 1992.

11. Stork Special Report 14: Analysis of Reports of Unidentified Aerial Objects. October 25, 1955.

12. Zeidman, "I Remember Blue Book."

Chapter 12

1. Bennett, *An American Demonology*.

2. McDonald, *Science in Default*.

3. Ruppelt, *The Report on Unidentified Flying Objects*.

4. Randle and Cornett, "How the Air Force Hid UFO Evidence From the Public."

5. Memorandum for the Deputy Director, Intelligence, from Ralph Clark: "Recent sightings of unexplained objects." July 29, 1952.

6. J. Allen Hynek, personal interview, 1980.

7. Durant, Report of Meetings of Scientific Advisory Panel.

8. Huneeus, "Revisiting the 1953 CIA's Robertson Panel."

9. Bernstein, "The CIA and the Media." The Church Committee was chaired in 1975 by Senator Frank Church to investigate the CIA, FBI, and National Security Agency (NSA) for illegal intelligence-gathering practices.

10. Air Force regulation no. 200-2 in reference to JANAP-146.

11. Blue Book files collection, Research Department, International UFO Museum and Research Center.

12. United States Air Force History, Squadron 4602nd.

13. Air Force Regulation 200-2.

14. 4602nd Air Intelligence Service Squadron, Air Force Regulation 24-4, January 3, 1953.

15. Webb, "Allen Hynek As I Knew Him."

16. 4602nd Air Intelligence Service Squadron, A Summary of the Third Commanders' Conference, January 13–16, 1954, Headquarters Captain Joseph A.Cybulski.

17. Blue Book files collection, Research Department, International UFO Museum and Research Center.

18. Jacobs, *The UFO Controversy in America*.

19. Blue Book files collection, Research Department, International UFO Museum and Research Center.

20. Ibid.

21. Webb, "Inside Building 263."

22. Jacobs, *The UFO Controversy*.

23. Randle and Cornett, "How the Air Force Hid UFO Evidence."

24. Ibid.

25. Ibid.

26. Hynek, *The UFO Experience*.

27. Project Blue Book case no. 8766.

28. Hynek, "Are Flying Saucers Real?"

29. Smith, *The UFO Enigma*.

30. Hippler, "Scientific Panel to Investigate Reported Sightings."

31. Senator Barry Goldwater, letter to *Bradenton Herald*. Bradenton, Fla., 1967.

Chapter 13

1. Sappho Henderson, telephone interviews 1990, 2010; videotaped interview, in *Recollections of Roswell Part II*.

2. Thomas J. DuBose, personal interview, 1991; videotaped interview, in *Recollections of Roswell Part II*.

3. Teletyped message authored by Percy Wyly of the Dallas, Texas, FBI office to the FBI office in Cincinnati, Ohio, and to the FBI directo; July 8, 1947.

4. John Kromschoeder, *Recollections of Roswell II*.

5. John Tiffany, personal interview, 1989.

6. "Brigadier General Arthur Ernest Exon."

7. Ibid.

8. Ibid.

9. Strieber, "The Goldwater UFO Files and the Mystery of the Cover-Up."

10. Ibid.

11. Arthur Exon, telephone interviews, 1990, 1991, 1994; personal interview conducted with Gen. Exon at his retirement village in Irvine, California, 2000.

12. Ibid.

13. Strieber, "The Goldwater UFO Files and the Mystery of the Cover-Up."

14. Randle and Schmitt, *UFO Crash at Roswell*.

15. Ibid. NOTE: Exon obviously was unaware of a third site, the so-called "Dee Proctor Body Site," located 2 1/2 miles from the Debris Field Site, where we believe one or two additional alien crew members fell to earth and met their fate when their craft exploded; we first learned of this site in 1994.

16. Ibid. NOTE: The private flight that Exon was on was not specifically sent to investigate the Roswell crash sites; it was returning from another mission that had taken it to the West Coast when Exon convinced the pilot to divert it from its original flight plan and fly over southeastern New Mexico "to see where the flying saucer crashed."

17. Ibid.

18. Randle and Schmitt, *UFO Crash at Roswell*.

19. Exon interviews.

20. Some recent publications have postulated that the UFO artifacts thought to have been stored at Wright-Patterson since 1947 have been moved to another location, such as Area 51 in Nevada, Dugway in Utah, or an airbase in Florida.

21. Randle and Schmitt, *UFO Crash at Roswell*.

22. Carey and Schmitt, *Witness to Roswell*.

23. Ibid.

24. Randle and Schmitt, *UFO Crash at Roswell*.

25. Randle and Schmitt, *The Truth About the UFO Crash at Roswell*.

26. See Carey and Schmitt, *Witness to Roswell*, for Haut's full statement.

27. The Air Force's chief of staff, General Carl "Tooey" Spaatz, of World War II fame, was away on a fishing trip in Oregon at the time of the Roswell crash; the handling of it, therefore, fell to next senior officer in line, General Hoyt S.Vandenberg, who would replace Spaatz as Air Force chief of staff the following year.

28. Randle and Schmitt, *UFO Crash at Roswell*. NOTE: The control group has been referred to as "Majestic-12" or "Majic-12" elsewhere; we agree that there was a control group established as described by Gen. Exon, but disagree that it was ever identified as endnoted here; we also believe that the so-called "Majestic-12 documents" used to support the identity of this group are fraudulent.

29. Ibid. NOTE: At some point in time, we believe that all or just certain presidents were also excluded from participation and access.

30. Randle and Schmitt, *The Truth About the UFO Crash at Roswell*.

31. Randle and Schmitt, *UFO Crash at Roswell*.

32. Ibid. NOTE: In 1953, Blue Book was stripped of its investigative function, and the 4602nd Air Intelligence Service Squadron was created at Ent AFB, Colorado, as part of the Air Defense Command. Under Air Force Regulation 200-2 dated August 26, 1953, the 4602nd was tasked with the official investigation of UFOs, with the added requirement that all UFO reports be transmitted to the 4602nd *before* they were sent on to Project Blue Book.

33. Randle and Schmitt, *The Truth About the UFO Crash at Roswell*.

34. Ibid.

35. Ibid.

36. Carey and Schmitt, *Witness to Roswell*.

37. Ibid.

Chapter 14

1. Richard Hall, personal interviews, 1981, 1985, 1990.

2. Randle and Cornett, *How the Air Force Hid UFO Evidence from the Public*.

3. Project Blue Book files collection, Research Department, International UFO Museum and Research Center.

4. Ibid.

5. Randle and Cornett, *How the Air Force Hid UFO Evidence*.

6. Craig, *An Insider's View of the official Quest for Evidence.*
7. Saunders and Harkins. *UFOs? Yes!*
8. McDonald, *UFOs and the Condon Report.*
9. Fuller, "Flying Saucer Fiasco."
10. Robert Low memorandum to Edward U. Condon, August 9, 1966.
11. Condon Report reviews: Saunders, McDonald, Hynek, and Sturrock.
12. Randle and Cornett, *How the Air Force Hid UFO Evidence.*
13. "History of the CIA," CIA Official Website.
14. Daniel Inouye, Chairman, Iran-Contra Senate Hearings, 1987–1989.
15. Condon, *Scientific Study of Unidentified Flying Objects.*
16. Annotated bibliography for Edward Condon; see also Digital Library for Nuclear Resources.
17. Mimi Hynek, personal interviews, 1978 through 1994.

Chapter 15

1. J. Allen Hynek, personal interviews, 1978 through 1984.
2. J. Allen Hynek, personal interview, 1981.
3. Hynek, personal interviews, 1978 through 1984.
4. Ibid.
5. Davis, "Did the USAF Ask Walt Disney to Make a Movie Revealing That UFOs Are Real?"
6. Hynek, personal interviews.
7. Hynek, personal correspondence.
8. The next time SETI scientists dismiss UFOs and then defend the relevance of their own jobs, they had better take a course in national security and then heed the dire words of one of their colleagues. When noted space scientist and mathematician Dr. Albert Hibbs of Cal Tech's Jet Propulsion Laboratory was asked how we should reply to the first message from another planet,

he sternly answered, **"Hang up! Look what happened to the Indians."** (See Keyhoe, *The Flying Saucers Are Real*, for this quotation.)

9. Allan Hendry, telephone interviews, 1986, and personal interview, 1987. Hendry was the chief investigator for Hynek at the Center for UFO Studies. From there, he became a technical writer for Hughes Aircraft in Tucson, Arizona.

10. Mimi Hynek, telephone conversation, March 1986.

11. Hynek, telephone conversation, March 1986.

12. Jennie Zeidman, personal interview, 1986.

Chapter 16

1. Weaver and McAndrew, *The Roswell Report: Fact Versus Fiction in the New Mexican Desert.*

2. McAndrew, *The Roswell Report: Case Closed.*

3. J. Allen Hynek, personal interview, 1978.

4. Hynek, personal interviews, 1978 through 1984.

5. Freedom of Information Act request by Robert Todd. The "Bolander memorandum" was released October 20, 1969. According to researcher Brad Sparks, there were 16 attachments listed for the memo, but some of them were not released to Todd, in violation of FOIA law. For those that were disclosed, it took years for the Air Force to acknowledge them, also in violation of FOIA law and regulation.

6. Jacque Vallee, personal interviews, 1994, 2005.

7. Colonel Robert Friend, personal interviews, 1994, 2013.

8. Colonel George R. Weinbrenner, personal interview with Dr. Mark Rodeghier, 1994. Rodeghier is the scientific director of the J. Allen Hynek Center for UFO Studies in Chicago, Illinois, who was assigned by Hynek before his death in 1986.

9. Personnel Action, Re: J. Allen Hynek, USAF, Foreign Technology Division, Wright Patterson Air Force Base, Dayton, Ohio.

10. Ibid.

11. Ibid.

12. Jennie Zeidman, personal interviews, 1989 through 1994.

13. Weinbrenner, USAF History, Personnel Biography.

14. Major General Theodore C. Bedwell Jr., USAF History, Personnel Biography.

15. Weinbrenner, personal interview, nurse (anonymity requested) by Angelia Jonier and Grant Cameron, 2010.

16. Robert Emenegger, correspondence, 2010.

Chapter 17

1. General Michael Rexrold, telephone interviews, 1989, 1990, 1991, 1997.

2. Chester A. Lytle, personal interviews, 1989 through 2003.

3. General Kenner F. Hertford, personal interview, 1992.

4. *History of New Mexico*.

5. Lytle, personal interviews with Robert Hastings, 1998.

6. Lytle, personal interviews.

7. Richard Budeman, personal interviews, 1988, 1989.

8. Nathan Twining Jr., personal interviews, 2000 through 2003.

9. "In Remembrance of Brigadier General Vorley (Mike) Rexrold," *Capitalwords* Vol. 148, No. 145.

10. Personal letter from Major General Kenner F. Hertford, 1992.

Chapter 18

1. *Posse Comitatus Law*, U.S. Department of Justice; Act 20, Statute L., 145, Chapter 263.

2. Bert Schulz, personal interview, Nevada, February 2008. Schulz, who was assigned to the Roswell Army Air Field in December, 1947, stated that there was still a "buzz" about what had all transpired at the "big hangar" (P-3) that previous July. He would note that what specifically "soured" him on making the military a career was numerous encounters he had with military police on the base. According to Schulz, "They were bragging

and laughing about how rough they got with ranchers north of Roswell," during the UFO crash-retrieval event.

3. Michelle Penn, telephone interviews with Anthony Bragalia, 2008.

Chapter 19

1. Stringfield, *The UFO Crash/Retrieval Syndrome*.

2. Leonard Stringfield, personal interviews, 1990, 1991, 1992.

3. Stringfield, *UFO Crash/Retrievals: The Inner Sanctum*.

4. Son (anonymity requested) of Dr. Foster's housekeeper (anonymity requested), telephone interviews, 1992.

5. Lt. Colonel Richard Hoffman, personal interviews, July 2012.

6. Dr. Leon E. Kazarian, personal biography.

7. Hoffman, personal interview, telephone interviews, and correspondence, 2012.

8. Dr. Leon E. Kazarian, telephone interviews with Anthony Bragalia, November 2012.

9. Fumoux, *Preuves Scientifique*.

10. Aaron Clark, telephone interviews, 2007.

11. Ronald SeCoy, e-mail correspondence, 2010, 2011, 2012.

12. Tracy Torme, telephone interview, February 2013.

13. James Fox, telephone interview, February 2013.

Chapter 20

1. Holt, "Inside Secret Government Warehouses."

2. John Mosgrove, telephone interviews, March 2010–March 2013.

3. Carl Day, personal interviews, 1994, 2010. E-mail correspondence 2005, 2008, 2009, and 2010.

4. Larry Landsman, telephone interview, January 2013.

5. Larry Landsman, telephone conversation, March 2010.

Chapter 21

1. Personal tour, National USAF Museum, Dayton Ohio, 1994, 1997.

2. Larry Landsman (producer, NBC/Peacock Productions, New York), telephone conversations, January, February, March, and April 2010.

3. Larry Landsman and producer Kimberly Ferdinando, personal meeting, Dayton, Ohio, March 2010.

4. John G. Tiffany interview with Stanton Friedman and Donald Schmitt, Louisville, Ky., August 1991.

5. Daryl Mayer, telephone conversations, January, February, March 2010.

6. Russell Maheras, telephone conversations, February, March 2010. We were concerned that, unlike previous occasions, we were referred to Air Force Entertainment in Hollywood, California. However, in each conversation with Mr. Maheras, he insisted that officials at Wright Patterson would make the final decision. It was Air Force Entertainment's function simply to draw up an actual filming schedule. This was contrary to public relations people at Wright-Patterson, who always stated the decision rested with Maheras.

7. Gretchen Eisele (executive producer, NBC/Peacock Productions, New York), telephone interview, February, 2010

8. Colonel Jeffrey Thau, telephone conversations, March and April 2010; personal interview, June 2011. When Colonel Thau called to give me the bad news, he started out by saying, "Don, I have a new quote for you."

BIBLIOGRAPHY

Anderson, John. *Inventing Flight: The Wright Brothers and Their Predecessors.* Baltimore, Md.: Johns Hopkins University Press, 2004.

"Arizona Wing of the Commemorative Air Force: Major General Barry Goldwater (USAFR)." *www.azcaf.org/pages/woh_inductees .html#barry_goldwater.*

Bennett, Colin. *An American Demonology: Flying Saucers Over the White House—Captain Edward J. Ruppelt and the Official UFO Investigation of the United States Air Force.* Manchester, England: Headpress/Critical Vision, 2005.

Berlitz, Charles, and William L. Moore. *The Roswell Incident.* New York: Grosset & Dunlap, 1980.

Bernstein, Carl. "The CIA and the Media: How America's Most Powerful News Media Worked Hand in Glove With the Central Intelligence Agency and Why the Church Committee Covered it Up." *Rolling Stone*, October 29, 1977.

Birnes, William J. "Squiggly." *UFO Magazine* 21.4, June 2004.

Bloecher, Ted. *Report on the UFO Wave of 1947.* Washington, D.C.: NICAP, 1967.

Bragalia, Anthony. "Is This Where Alien Bodies Are Stored? The Secrets of a Place Called Dugway." *The UFO Iconoclast(s)*. February 7, 2011. *http://ufocon.blogspot.com/2011/02/is-this-where-alien-bodies-are-stored.html*.

———. "Opening the Door to the Blue Room." *The Bragalia Files*. June 11, 2012. *http://bragalia.homestead.com/blueroom.html*.

———. "Roswell, Battelle & Memory Metal: The New Revelations." *The UFO Iconoclast(s)*. August 8, 2010. *http://ufocon.blogspot.com/2010/08/roswell-battelle-memory-metal-new.html*.

———. "Roswell Debris Confirmed as Extraterrestrial: Lab Located, Scientists Named." *The UFO Iconoclast(s)*. May 26, 2009. *http://ufocon.blogspot.com/2009/05/roswell-debris-confirmed-as.html*.

———. "Roswell's Memory Metal: The Air Force Comments; NASA Gets Involved & New Clues Are Found." *The Bragalia Files*. July 31, 2011. *http://bragalia.blogspot.com/2011/07/roswells-memory-metal-air-force.html*.

———. "Science Reports Show Roswell Crash was ET." In *Witness to Roswell: Unmasking the Government's Biggest Cover-Up* by Thomas J. Carey and Donald R. Schmitt. Franklin Lakes, N.J.: New Page Books, 2009.

———. "Scientist Admits to Study of Roswell Crash Debris! (Confirmed by FOIA Document)." *The UFO Iconoclast(s)*. August 16, 2009. *http://ufocon.blogspot.com/2009/08/scientist-admits-to-study-of-roswell.html*.

"Brigadier General Arthur Ernest Exon." Official Biography, United States Air Force. *www.af.mil/information/bios/bio.asp?bioID=5381*.

Broad, William J. "Senator Regrets Role in Book on Aliens." *New York Times*, June 5, 1997.

Brokaw, Tom. *The Greatest Generation*. New York: Random House, 1998.

Burnstein, Burton. "AUH20." *The New Yorker*, April 25, 1988. *www.newyorker.com/archive/1988/04/25/1988_04_25_043_TNY_CARDS_000350367*.

Cabell, Charles P. *Charles P. Cabell: A Man of Intelligence—Memoirs of War, Peace, and the CIA.* Colorado Springs, Colo.: Impavide Publications, 1997.

Cameron, Grant. *Presidential UFO* (Website). *www.presidentialufo .com/barry-goldwater-ufo/cat_view/105-goldwater-ufo-documents.*

Carey, Thomas J., and Donald R. Schmitt. *Witness to Roswell: Unmasking the 60-Year Cover-Up.* Franklin Lakes, N.J.: Career Press/New Page Books, 2007.

———. *Witness to Roswell: Unmasking the Government's Biggest Cover-Up.* Franklin Lakes, N.J.: Career Press/New Page Books, 2009.

Carr, Timothy Spencer. "Son of Originator of 'Alien Autopsy' Story Casts Doubt on Father's Credibility." *Skeptical Inquirer,* July/August, 1997.

Carre, John le. *The Spy Who Came in from the Cold.* London: Victor Gollancz & Pan, 1963.

Clark, Jerome. *The UFO Encyclopedia, 2nd Edition.* Detroit, Mich.: Omnigraphics, 1998.

Clarkson, James E. *Tell My Story: June Crain, the Air Force & UFOs.* Olympia, Wash.: Black Triangle Press, 2010.

Collins, Robert M., with Richard C. Doty. "The Vaults at Wright-Patterson AFB." *Exempt From Disclosure: The Black World of UFOs.* Vandalia, Ohio: Peregrine Communications, 2010.

Condon, Edward. *Scientific Study of Unidentified Flying Objects.* New York: Bantam Books, 1969.

Correll, John T. "USAF and the UFOs." *Air Force Magazine: Journal of the Air Force Association,* June 2011.

Corso, Col. Philip J., with William J. Birnes. *The Day After Roswell.* New York: Pocket Books, 1997.

Craig, Roy. *An Insider's View of the Official Quest for Evidence: Review of the University of Colorado Report on Unidentified Flying Objects by a Panel of the National Academy of Science, 1969.* Denton, Texas: University of North Texas Press, 1995.

Davis, Erik. "Did the USAF Ask Walt Disney to Make a Movie Revealing that UFOs Are Real?" Movies.com, February 12, 2013. *www.movies .com/movie-news/did-u-s-air-force-ask-walt-disney-to-make-movie-revealing-that-ufos-are-real/11238.*

"The Day After Roswell." Wikipedia. August 1, 2008. *http://en.wikipedia. org/wiki/The_Day_After_Roswell.*

Dolan, Richard. *UFOs and the National Security State 1941–1973.* Rochester, N.Y.: Keyhole Publishing, 2000.

Dolan, Richard M. *UFOs and the National Security State: Chronology of a Cover-Up 1941–1973, Revised Edition.* Charlottesville, Va.: Hampton Roads Publishing Company, Inc., 2002.

Dulles, Allen. *The Craft of Intelligence.* New York: Harper & Row, 1963.

Durant, F.C. Report of Meetings of Scientific Advisory Panel on Unidentified Flying Objects Convened by Office of Scientific Intelligence, CIA. January 14–18, 1953.

Emenegger, Robert. *UFOs, Past, Present, and Future.* New York: Ballantine, 1974.

Fuller, John G. "Flying Saucer Fiasco." *Look Magazine,* May 14, 1968.

Fumoux, Jean Charles. *Preuves Scientifique.* Monaco, France: OVNI, 1981.

"General Ramey Empties Roswell Saucer." *Roswell Daily Record,* July 9, 1947.

Ginna, Robert, and H.B. Darrach Jr. "Have We Visitors From Space?" *LIFE Magazine,* April 7, 1952.

Goldwater, Barry. "The 'UFO Letters' of Senator Barry Goldwater." *www.stealthskater.com/Documents/Goldwater_1.doc.*

Good, Timothy. *Above Top Secret: The Worldwide UFO Cover-Up.* London, England: Sidgwick & Jackson, 1987.

———. *Need to Know: UFOs, the Military and Intelligence.* New York: Pegasus Books LLC, 2007.

Gross, Loren. *UFOs: A History, Vol. 1: 1947.* Stone Mountain, Ga.: Arcturas Book Service, 1990.

Hall, Michael, and Wendy Connors. *Alfred Loedding and the Great Flying Saucer Wave of 1947.* Albuquerque, N.M.: Rose Press, 1998.

Hall, Richard. *The UFO Evidence*. Washington, D.C.: NICAP, 1964.

Hippler, Robert. "Scientific Panel to Investigate Reported Sightings of Unidentified Flying Objects." Blue Book files, April 1966.

History of New Mexico Family and Personal History Vol. III. New York: Lewis Historical Publishing Company, Inc., 1961.

Holt, Lester, host. "Inside Secret Government Warehouses: Shocking Revelations." Documentary. NBC/SyFy/Peacock Productions, July 2010.

Huneeus, Antonio. "Revisiting the 1953 CIA's Robertson Panel: A Milestone in UFO Policies." *Open Minds* 18 (2013).

Hynek, J. Allen. "Are Flying Saucers Real? A Surprising Report from the Top Scientific Authority." *Saturday Evening Post*, December 17, 1966.

―――. *The UFO Experience: A Scientific Inquiry*. Chicago, Ill.: Henry Regnery Company, 1972.

Jacobs, David. *The UFO Controversy in America*. Bloomington, IN.: University of Indiana Press, 1975.

Jennings, Peter. "The UFO Phenomenon: Seeing Is Believing." *ABC News Special Report*, February 2005.

Kantor, MacKinlay. *Mission With LeMay: My Story*. New York: Doubleday & Company, 1965.

Keyhoe, Donald. *Aliens from Space*. Garden City, N.Y.: Doubleday & Company, 1973.

―――. *The Flying Saucers Are Real*. New York: Fawcett Publishing Inc., 1950.

Lasby, Clarence. *Project Paperclip: German Scientists and the Cold War*. New York: Atheneum, 1971.

Maccabee, Bruce. *Documents and Supporting Information Related to Crashed Flying Saucers and Operation Majestic Twelve*. Mt. Rainier, Md.: Fund for UFO Research, 1987.

―――. *The Government UFO Connection: A Collection of UFO Documents From the Governments of the USA and Canada*. Mt. Rainier, Md.: Fund for UFO Research, 1981–1985.

Magruder, Mark A. *Nightfighter: Radar Intercept Killer.* Gretna, La.: Pelican, 2012.

———. Videotaped interview with Roger Leir, Derrel Simms, and Jesse Marcel, Jr., May 5, 1998.

"Major General Barry M. Goldwater." Official biography, United States Air Force. *www.af.mil/information/bios/bio.asp?bioID=5574.*

Mazza, Vincent, Richard V. Wheeler, et al. "High Altitude Bailouts." *Memorandum Report.* AMC/Wright-Patterson AFB, OH/Engineering Division. 18 SEP 50.

McAndrew, Captain James. *The Roswell Report: Case Closed.* Washington, D.C.: Headquarters United States Air Force/U.S. Government Printing Office, 1997.

McDonald, James. *Science in Default: Twenty-Two Years of Inadequate UFO Investigation.* Ithaca, N.Y.: Cornell University Press, 1972.

———. *UFOs and the Condon Report.* Phoenix, Ariz.: University of Arizona Colloquium, 1969.

Menzel, Donald. *Flying Saucers.* Cambridge, Mass.: Harvard University Press, 1953.

Newton, Katie. "Corps Restores Historical Gem at Wright-Patterson Air Force Base." U.S. Army Corps of Engineers Website. June 12, 2012. *www.lrl.usace.army.mil/Media/NewsStories/tabid/10554/ Article/7684/corps-restores-historical-gem-at-wright-patterson-air- force-base.aspx.*

"RAAF Captures Flying Saucer in Roswell Region." *Roswell Daily Record*, July 8, 1947.

Randle, Kevin D. "Mac Magruder and the Air War College." *A Different Perspective* (blog). *http://kevinrandle.blogspot.com/2008/08/mac- magruder-and-air-war-college.html.* August 10, 2008.

Randle, Kevin D., and Robert C. Cornett. "How the Air Force Hid UFO Evidence From the Public." *The UFO Report* 2.5 (Fall 1975).

Randle, Kevin D., and Donald R. Schmitt. *The Truth About the UFO Crash at Roswell.* New York: Avon Books, 1994.

———. *UFO Crash at Roswell.* New York: Avon Books, 1991.

Recollections of Roswell, Part II. DVD. Mount Rainier, Md.: Fund for UFO Research, 1992.

Richelson, Jeffrey. *The U.S. Intelligence Community: Organization, Operations and Management, 1947–1989, 3rd Edition*. Boulder Colo.: Westview Press, 1995. See also *www.gwu.edu/~nsarchiv/nsa/publications/ic/intelligence_com.html*.

Ricks, Thomas. *The Generals: American Military Commanders from World War II to Today*. New York: Penguin Press, 2012.

Ruppelt, Edward. *The Report on Unidentified Flying Objects*. New York: Doubleday & Company, 1956.

Sagan, Carl. *Cosmos*. New York: Ballantine Books, 1980.

Saunders, David, and Roger Harkins. *UFOs? Yes! Where the Condon Committee Went Wrong: The Inside Story by an Ex-Member of the Official Study Group*. New York: World Publishing, 1968.

Schmitt, Donald. *UFO Crash at Roswell II: The Chronological Pictorial*. Louisville, Ky.: Moonset Productions, 2001.

Schopenhauer, Arthur. *The Art of Being Right*. Translated by Thomas Bailey Saunders. Gloucester, UK: Dodo Press, 2008.

Scully, Frank. *Behind the Flying Saucers*. New York: Henry Holt, 1950.

Smith, Marcia. *The UFO Enigma*. Washington, D.C.: House Armed Services Committee, 1966. Report No. 83-205S PR. 1983.

Smith, W.B. "Memorandum to the Controller of Telecommunications [Top Secret]." Department of Transport. Ottawa, Ontario, Canada. November 21, 1950.

Strickland, Jonathan. "How Area 51 Works: Reverse Engineering at Area 51." *http://science.howstuffworks.com/space/aliens-ufos/area-517.htm*.

Strieber, Whitley. *Breakthrough: The Next Step*. New York: HarperPaperbacks, 1996.

———. "The Goldwater UFO Files and the Mystery of the Cover-Up." *Whitley's Journal* (blog). March 5, 2012. *www.unknowncountry.com/journal/goldwater-ufo-files-and-mystery-cover*.

Stringfield, Leonard. "Abstract Number Three." *Retrievals of the Third Kind: A Case Study of Alleged UFOs and Occupants in Military Custody.* Presented as a speaker at the Ninth Annual MUFON Symposium in Dayton, Ohio, July 1978.

———. "The Blue Room." *UFO Crash/Retrievals: The Inner Sanctum /Status Report VI.* Cincinnati, Ohio: Leonard H. Stringfield, July 1991.

———. "Case A-3." *The UFO Crash/Retrieval Syndrome, Status Report II: New Sources, New Data.* Seguin, Tx.: Mutual UFO Network, January 1980.

———. "Item B-6." In *The UFO Crash/Retrieval Syndrome, Status Report II: New Sources, New Data.* Seguin, Texas: Mutual UFO Network, January 1980.

———. *Situation Red: The UFO Siege.* New York: Fawcett Crest Books, 1977.

———. *The UFO Crash/Retrieval Syndrome, Status Report II: New Sources, New Data.* Seguin, Tx.: Mutual UFO Network, January 1980.

———. *UFO Crash/Retrievals: The Inner Sanctum.* Cincinnati, Ohio: Leonard Stringfield, 1991.

Sturrock, Peter. *The UFO Enigma.* New York: Warner Books, 2000.

Swords, Michael. *The Summer of 1947 and the U.S. Government at the Beginning.* Chicago, Ill.: Center for UFO Studies, 1991.

Swords, Michael D. "Project Sign and the Estimate of the Situation." Kalamazoo, Mich.: Environmental Institute, Western Michigan University. Undated. *www.bibliotecapleyades.net/sociopolitica/sign/sign.htm.*

Swords, Michael, and Robert Powel. *UFOs and the Government.* San Antonio, Tx.: Anomalist Books, 2012.

Trench, Brinsley Le Poer. *The Flying Saucer Story.* New York: Ace Books Inc., 1966.

"The Twining Memo." *www.roswellfiles.com/FOIA/twining.htm.*

Vallee, Jacques. *Anatomy of a Phenomenon.* Chicago, Ill.: Regnery, 1965.

Walker, Lois, and Shelby Wickam. *From Hoffman Prairie to the Moon: A History of Wright-Patterson Air Base.* Dayton, Ohio: WPAFB, 1986.

Weaver, Richard, and James McAndrew. *The Roswell Report: Fact Versus Fiction in the New Mexican Desert.* Washington, D.C.: Headquarters, ASAF, 1994.

Webb, Walter N. "Allen Hynek as I Knew Him." *International UFO Reporter* 18.1, January/February 1993.

————. "Inside Building 263: A Visit to Blue Book, 1956." *International UFO Reporter* 17.5, September/October 1992.

"Wright-Patterson Air Force Base, Area B, Building 18, Power Plant Complex." *Report No. HAER OH-79-AN.* Historic American Engineering Record. Washington, D.C.: Department of the Interior, 1991–1993.

Wyly, Percy. Teletyped message from the Dallas, Texas FBI office to the Cincinnati, Ohio FBI office and to the FBI Director in Washington, D.C., July 8, 1947.

Zeidman, Jennie. "I Remember Blue Book." *International UFO Reporter* 16.2, March/April 1991.

INDEX

ABOUT THE AUTHORS

Donald R. Schmitt is the former co-director of the J. Allen Hynek Center for UFO Studies (CUFOS) in Chicago, where he served as the director of special investigations for 10 years. He is a cofounder of the International UFO Museum and Research Center, where he serves as an advisor to the board of directors. A four-time best-selling author, his first book, coauthored with Kevin D. Randle, *UFO Crash at Roswell*, was made into the Golden Globe–nominated made-for-TV movie *Roswell*.

His last book, *Witness to Roswell*, coauthored with Thomas Carey, was the number-one selling UFO book in the world for 2007 and 2008. The book has been optioned for feature film production by Stellar Productions under the title "Majic Men."

prolific writer and international public speaker, he has appeared *Oprah, CBS 48 Hours, Larry King Live, Paul Harvey News, The Today Show, Good Morning America*, and hundreds more programs. A graduate of Concordia University, "Cum Laude," he lives with his wife, Marie, at Holy Hill, Wisconsin.

Thomas J. Carey, a native Philadelphian, holds degrees from Temple University and California State University, Sacramento, and attended the University of Toronto's PhD Programme in Anthropology. An Air Force veteran who held a Top Secret/Crypto clearance, Tom is now retired. He has been a Mutual UFO Network (MUFON) State Section Director for Southeastern Pennsylvania, a Special Investigator for the J. Allen Hynek Center for UFO Studies, and a member of its board of directors. Tom began investigating aspects of the "Roswell incident" in 1991 for the Roswell investigative team of Kevin Randle and Don Schmitt, and since 1998 has teamed exclusively with Don Schmitt to continue a proactive investigation of the case. Tom has authored or coauthored more than 40 published articles about the Roswell events of 1947. He has appeared as a guest on many radio and TV shows, including *Coast to Coast AM*, *The Jeff Rense Show*, *Fox and Friends*, and *Larry King Live!*, and he has also appeared in a number of Roswell-related documentaries such as the highly acclaimed two-hour SyFy Channel documentary, "The Roswell Crash: Startling New Evidence," and the "UFO Hunters," as well as documentaries for The History Channel, The Discovery Channel, The Travel Channel, and The National Geographic Channel. His 2007 book with Don Schmitt, *Witness to Roswell* *Cover-Up*, was the #1 best-selling UFO book in the 8. It and its second edition, which appeared the best books ever written about the "Roswell inci ture and a miniseries both based on *Witness to Roswell* are in the stages of development. Tom and his wife of 45 years, Do grown children and reside in Huntingdon Valley, Pennsylvania.

For more supporting governm please visit the authors' Website, Ros